Four-Play to Business as *UNusual*

THE UN-GAME

To Judy
Un-game player
extraordinaire
who helped inspire
this book. To empowerment!
Enjoy!
Ingrid Martine

TreeHouse
books

1430 W. Susquehanna Ave
Philadelphia, PA 19121
215-236-1760 | treehousebooks.org

INGRID MARTINE

The *Un*-Game:
Four-Play to Business as *Un*usual
By Ingrid Martine
Your Leaders' Edge Press

Published by Your Leaders' Edge Press, Waco, Texas

Editors: Kim Pearson, www.primary-sources.com and Rachel Crawford
Cover and Interior design: Cathy Davis and Jack Davis,
www.daviscreative.com

Library of Congress Control Number: 2011924774
ISBN: 978-0-9834454-0-1
Subjects:
    personal growth, empowerment, coaching, executive ability,
    executive-attitudes, learning organization, management, leadership,
    organizational effectiveness, teams

The *Un*-Game

Four-Play to Business as *Un*usual

By Ingrid Martine

"The *Un*-Game" is for leaders and for their coaches. Ingrid Martine's four-step process delivers both principles and tools for a clear path to performance excellence and more powerful leadership. Her book invites brilliant insights while providing essential skills for those dedicated to moving an organization to the next level. I'm a better coach for having read "The *Un*-Game."

Susan Ann Koenig, JD, PCC
Executive Coach

By focusing on perceptual issues and paradigm shifts rather than the broader notion of change, this engaging and readable book gives managers a better way to influence and grow team members. Those who grasp and use the four-step process described here have a road map for achieving their goals.

George Kilishek, Fmr SVP
World Operations
Allergan Optical

I loved this book! As an international trainer on leadership, I found it a brilliant tool for unleashing human potential, whether in the corporate managers that Ingrid Martine focuses on, or in anybody (in fact, I'm taking her book with me to help train citizen activists in Sierra Leone!). Martine's extended case study approach is a creative and convincing guide for building conscious, courageous, and compassionate leaders—people who are catalysts and not controllers, and who can tap the innate power of freedom and innovation instead of getting stuck in "the rules."

John Graham, Director
Giraffe Heroes International

"The *Un*-Game" goes a lot deeper and broader than most books on management. It focuses on managers within the sometimes chaotic environment of their workplace. No one-size-fits-all approach to leadership is offered in this fine book—and that is a relief. The notion of a collective immune system may cause many readers to see their organization in a very different and revealing light. I recommend this book.

Rick Maurer, Author
"Beyond the Wall of Resistance"

What I love about Ingrid Martine's book, "The *Un*-Game," is how she engages readers in the story woven around a simple, four-step coaching process that illuminates how we make meaning of our lives. Although Ingrid speaks to managers, her book gives all of us a powerful new possibility to observe what can obscure our vision and block access to a transformed mind-set. Writing with humor, compassion and creativity, Ingrid leaves us hopeful that it may be easier than we think to awaken to our self-imposed limitations. From there, she clarifies how to shift our focus to what's far more important—making our unique contribution to a world that is eager to receive it and be transformed by it.

Lynne Twist, Author,
"The Soul of Money"
President, The Soul of Money Institute;
Co-Founder, The Pachamama Alliance

For Jason,
who taught me the importance
of playing the *un*-game well

Table of Contents

Preface

Why are there so few great workplaces when we know what creates them? After all, no one goes to work saying, "I think I'll produce ordinary results and annoy people today."

The gap between the principles and the practices of an ordinary workplace and one people can't wait to get to each morning has always intrigued me, especially how leaders and managers could shrink the distance between them. "The *Un*-Game: Four-Play to Business as *Un*usual" offers to narrow the gap.

Only in my life's rear-view mirror do I see that I began to write "The *Un*-Game" long ago. As a cross-culturally naïve eleven-year-old, my world was rocked upon my arrival in New York City with my immigrant family. The assault on my German mind-set felt like an earthquake snatching away all my precious, *un*questioned certainty.

Butter was supposed to be *un*salted, bread squish-resistant, and a sandwich open. Every American was supposed to be fiercely passionate about being an Olympic gold medalist. Those were the rules.

Cognitive dissonance. Conflict. Broken rules. My palate, used to sweet butter and hearty German rye bread, was offended by Wonder Bread. Ditto for piles of cold cuts, mayonnaise, lettuce and tomato hugged by those two slices of limp white bread. And insult of insults: the American girls whose raison d'être was supposed to be sports—after all, Americans dominated the Olympic Games— why, they were more interested in football players, hot cars, and bras I was sure they didn't need! The latter was anathema for a very certain and highly critical eleven year old German girl dubbed "tomboy" by her equally critical American counterparts who told her, "America, love it or leave it!"

This then was my earliest training as an observer, a necessary skill for playing what I came to call the *un*-game, the subject of this book. Americans saw their way as the only way—just as I assumed the German way was the only way until my parents put an ocean between my experience and me. I then saw myself with new eyes and Americans as others might see them. I was the Other only for a short while, but I have never lost my appreciation for the power bestowed upon the observer. It's no surprise to me that I used "The *Un*-Game" as an opportunity to flesh out the process for becoming a highly skilled observer of self and others.

In hindsight, the moment I first became a conscious observer was a moment of grace. It was an *un*asked-for gift I didn't know I wanted. All of a sudden I had a much needed beginner's mind. I was curious, alert, and attentive. Having to start over almost from scratch to make sense out my new environment, I needed a beginner's mind. Nothing was as expected. What had happened to all the givens? Cosmopolitan New York was not my provincial village in northern Germany.

If not with a hopeful heart, then at least with a quest for control over my own destiny, I used my newly acquired beginner's mind to try to figure out American rules, then master them—knowing that breaking or bending the rules would be an option in the future. After all, I saw rules being broken all around me—rules that my young mind had previously believed to be incontrovertible. Butter wasn't sweet anymore. And none of the American girls I came to know was passionate about becoming an Olympic champion.

I am my father's daughter, and he intuitively understood my preoccupation with control and power over my own life. Coming to the new world, both of us had lost some. He told me, "If you want to lead, you first have to follow." I listened, and so I dutifully followed the American rules.

In my early twenties I had a crisis of confidence, however. I became aware of an assertion that wouldn't let me go. The assertion was "There's got to be more to life than this." In other words, I knew there had to be more to life than the successful one—by conventional standards—I had created. I was educated, had good work, a sweet family, a nice house with a two-car garage and a riding lawn-mower.

This assertion was really a profound question: "What does a life lived with a purpose I consider to be a mighty one look and feel like?" A life beyond the boundaries of my narrow self-interest? One which is able to make a contribution to a greater good?

The question was not to be answered swiftly. It begged for ongoing reflection. And so, through the fruits born of observation, I reinvented how I played the game that was my own life. It is that which eventually got me on the path that has led me to the writing of this book.

In "The *Un*-Game" I say "yes," no longer shaking my head in profound vexation, to the assertion I made as a very young woman. Yes, there *is* more to life—be it at work, at home, at play, in the community. I *did* have the power to reinvent how I played the game called life. Everyone does. We can change the rules, take nothing as a given; it's all up for grabs. It's the *un*-game. Heady stuff!

I wanted to share what I had learned on my path—we need tools to play the *un*-game—but how could I share something so intensely personal…yet universal…through an ordinary medium of sharing information? Already people are burdened with information overload. No. I needed a medium that is Velcro to the memory.

*Un*like a carefully crafted but dry textbook, a story attaches effortlessly to the mind. "The *Un*-Game" is that story. I hope it will attach to your memory.

It is a second hope that in this book, you will learn to play the *un*-game along with the protagonist, a talented young manager named Sam Adler who would not have been successful in management models of by-gone eras. He needed a contemporary model suitable for the dawn of the 21st century, a new era full of new demands and promises. Lastly I hope that you will enrich your own repertoire of management practices, a repertoire born of challenging your current thinking, and that you will find yourself able to apply some of what Sam learns with satisfying results to challenges you care about. I'm certain that you too can play this game called management…with clear vision, purposeful focus, and—imagine this—even with ease. Would that be OK with you?

Introduction

With all the powerful information available for becoming an effective manager, do we really need more? If you've said "No, we don't," I agree. What we *do* need is to connect the information to the manager's ability to convert it into effective action—and to do that with greater ease. That's the intent and the promise of "The *Un*-Game."

There are many good ways to play the *un*-game. In this book I develop only one in great detail.* I develop only this one because the distinctions and the skill-sets you can learn from this unique way to play the *un*-game will be useful for any other version of the *un*-game you might decide to play. I made the decision based on knowledge about how and why adults learn. The skill-set featured in the book is also useful for life challenges outside the corporation. After all, everyone is the manager of his or her own life.

Why is the capacity to observe—a valuable skill worth honing—encouraged again and again in "The *Un*-Game?" It's because I consider the *un*aware life to be incompatible with success in any domain of human concern, least of all in relationships, the cornerstone of good management practices.

Like the individual, business needs to harness the power of observation. Observation is different than analysis, a distinction we sometimes don't make. As leaders, managers, and team members, we would do well to bolster our capacity by cultivating a beginner's mind in regard to self-observation. There are so many *un*questioned givens. So many conventions to be challenged. So much real power to wrest from the recesses of our mind. We need to take stock and claim observation as our ally. An ally for what? For achieving clarity, which is the source of our power to act on behalf of our concerns.

*Inspired by the outstanding coach training program of the Academy for Coaching Excellence. See resources section.

So where are we not clear? Where do we operate in the dark or on auto-pilot? Of course we aren't in the dark in areas of our expertise—our technical training. CFOs know a lot about accounting. A Director of Marketing knows proven marketing principles and strategies. But despite the available knowledge, we're largely in the dark about ourselves and each other.

Take personal learning, for example. How does it occur? Is it really true that people can't change much after reaching adulthood? That is an *un*examined assumption which has been masquerading as truth for a long time—with hidden effects on corporate training programs.

A greater capacity for learning is now demanded of all of us, not just of our top management teams. "The *Un*-Game" recognizes this. The light we seek is a new capacity of mind with which to "up" our game. The mind-set we've inherited, fine for yesterday's demands, is *un*able to meet today's. Rapid change means a faster, flatter, more inter-connected world. The shift we're experiencing is even more dramatic than our shift in previous eras from physical work to mind work. It demands we "up" our game in our human interactions. You don't bring a knife to a gun fight.

"Upping" our game, then, means developing our capacity for thinking at a more complex level. Albert Einstein rightly submitted that we can't solve our problems with the level of thinking that created them in the first place. So we need to move beyond the mind-set we've inherited from our culture—the socialized mind-set—to a higher level of thinking.

Since higher levels of thinking help make a complex world more manageable, we need a technology for personal learning—as "The *Un*-Game" asserts—that helps us achieve those higher levels of thinking. At a minimum this technology must help us answer two questions:

1. How have I been captivated such that I can't deliver on my aspirations? For example, I want to delegate. I need to delegate. What am I not seeing about my thinking that has me *not* delegate?

2. What faulty assumptions are we making that we're *un*aware of and which keep an *un*desirable status quo firmly in place? For example, we want to hire more minority executives, but it's not happening.

Do you notice that the questions assume there may be a problem in our thinking?

"The *Un*-Game" responds to those questions. Sam Adler, the young protagonist, is a newly-minted manager in a fictitious company dedicated to reinventing the business of doing business. He reluctantly chooses a development opportunity in which he meets a coach and four great manager mentors who help him *un*cover his meaning-making system.

In a supportive yet challenging environment, the coach and the managers offer Sam a technology for examining his meaning-making. In what might be called "mind-zengineering "—it is after all a step-by-step, organized process that cools the agitated mind down—he voluntarily *un*covers thoughts, opinions, and conclusions he firmly believes to be true. He says "yes" to having his world view assaulted time and again in return for the promise that he will be able to *un*leash his power to produce extraordinary results in his failing department. Not the hero of the old "command and control" model of management, he suits up for the coming world.

Observation is the means by which he extends the limits of his meaning-making system. It moves him toward the light at the far end of the tunnel. He inches his way toward becoming a competent observer who will be rewarded with the capacity to produce *un*common results.

Competent observers have experienced the power of observation in producing extraordinary results. The promise of having greater power makes the assault on their world view acceptable, if not desirable. Competent observers know they are just feathers in the wind when they stay inside their experience. So they'll do whatever it takes to get outside it.

Without the grand escape from their experience, people are subjected to it—acted upon, or tossed about. Their brain overheats. Decisions they make while inside their experience are not to be trusted. Do they make them to escape discomfort? Are the decisions irrational or erratic, determined by impulse, not cool deliberation? People *in* their experience are *out* of their minds. Rather than having the experience, the experience has them! They are the feather. Something else is the wind.

Competent observers say "No thank you" to being the feather. They know the secret of becoming the wind. "The *Un*-Game" assures the serious reader that he or she will become a more competent observer.

Competent observers can act on the data they generate from the questions "How have I been captivated such that I can't deliver on my aspirations?" and "What faulty assumptions are we making that we're *un*aware of and which keep an *un*desirable status quo firmly in place?" But they know they can't rest on their laurels. They must do it again and again in an endless cycle of awareness-*un*awareness-awareness-*un*awareness-awareness. After all, to be human is to be alternately asleep and awake.

People might say, "But if I'm always observing, is there time for action?" The answer is a resounding "yes." Think of it as learning to drive. Once you know how, it becomes automatic. Similarly, once you acquire some tools for observation, you can use them at will. Drive, don't walk to work. Will you make time now to save time later?

There are many tools that enhance a person's ability to become a good observer of self and others. The good tools take into account an immutable but little talked-about fact. People, even successful people, constantly deal with fear; anxiety is perhaps the most important and least understood private emotion that we're *not* dealing with in public life. We have compartmentalized it as belonging in the realm of counseling, and business is not that. We are businessmen and women, not social workers.

But wait a minute! Are you willing to challenge the assumption that business shouldn't deal with emotions—with the thoughts and feelings that usually don't appear at the office? If so, the exercise might expand your meaning-making system. Expanding your meaning-making system can create potent results and is available to you in "The *Un*-Game."

Does that interest you?

It has been said that we can't get where we want to go without acknowledging where we are, that is, without acknowledging what is so. And what's so is that we experience a constant, low-level anxiety which has become like the screensaver we no longer notice. Nevertheless, like the screensaver, it is there. We build an elaborate immunity to change which constrains action, causes blind spots, and prevents new learning. We are *not* giddy with a just-recognized advantage that assures us we can score big. In fact, we have an enormous amount of energy tied up in assuring nothing bad happens to us. *What* advantage? We're too distracted to see it.

What if we could re-channel this tied-up energy and apply it to accelerate the goal of delegating effectively or being better organized? And what if we could do it predictably rather than by chance? Well, we *can* when we outplay our opponent—the chatter of our self-limiting internal talk that is the bedrock of our immunity to change. "The *Un*-Game" readers begin to recognize that talk in themselves—a valuable ability for the manager who wants to improve his or her game.

The characters in "The *Un*-Game" desensitize themselves to the mischief of their immunity to change—revealed through their conversation—by demystifying its perceived danger. They recognize it for the role it plays in human affairs—for its value and for its limitations. It is not the enemy. Rather, it's our loyal opponent. Within that distinction lies a rich world in which repudiation of the status quo becomes possible. Its welcome by-product is a higher level of thinking.

A new conversation can occur once we see our immunity to change with open eyes. Business, having become so powerful, must be the container in which these new, powerful, mind-expanding conversations can occur—conversations that challenge a perceived reality, tackle the tough stuff, provoke learning, and ultimately enrich the relationships of the people who have them. They are conversations that no longer put forward, explicitly or implicitly, "We can't talk about that here."

Far from limiting, these new conversations develop a robust, organization-wide capacity for self-observation and self-reflection which results in the organization's dramatically enhanced capacity to deliver on its aspirations. They are authentic conversations not for the faint of heart. But neither are the 21st century challenges they can transform into *un*precedented opportunities.

The four-step process Sam Adler learns in "The *Un*-Game" reveals his immunity to change. It teaches him who he really is right here, right now; what really matters right here, right now; and how to recognize his voice of wisdom right here, right now. The four-step process—"four-play to business as *un*usual"—is learnable and leads to effective action—right here, right now. Its immediacy is appealing. But more than that, it has the capacity to transform what is most in need of transformation—Sam's capacity to think from a new place. It moves him from darkness into the light.

What can be generalized from Sam's experience is that thinking from a new place involves both the head and the heart. It's messy in that it thrives in the midst of a particular kind of internal upheaval or conflict. Something puzzles us in an area of our deep concern. We're frustrated about something—some quandary or problem we've mulled over and over but can't get an answer to. We've come to the limits of our current thinking. The hope that we can find the answers on our own has been lost. This is the moment of opportunity, but only if we are neither overwhelmed by our dilemma nor able to direct attention away from it.

Supreme Court Justice Oliver Wendell Holmes stated famously, "I don't give a fig for simplicity this side of complexity, but I would give my life for the simplicity on the other side of complexity." Certain of our world view, we feel that life is simple. It follows accustomed rules. Except that life is guaranteed to be messy. It doesn't arrange itself forever according to our simplistic expectations. And that is very, very good. To be all that we can be, we have no choice but to get to the other side of complexity. Whether we *un*cover Holmes's coveted simplicity there depends on the opportunities we recognize, say "yes" to, and learn from, and whose lessons we apply in committed action. "The *Un*-Game" provides some opportunities to do just that, among them the "Dear Reader" section at the end of each chapter.

The "Dear Reader" section is an invitation for you to engage in personal reflection. It may be a learning opportunity. You are the expert in how you learn best. Perhaps you'll start a discussion group and reflect on all the questions. Perhaps you'll write answers only to questions that interest you. Perhaps you'll limit your discussions to a trusted friend or colleague. And perhaps you'll just read or skip the questions and leave it at that. After all, an invitation can be accepted or declined.

Sam Adler's adventurous journey begins "In the Fog" and ends with "Business as *Un*usual." However you choose to engage with the story that *un*folds here, I wish you a fruitful journey.

Ingrid Martine

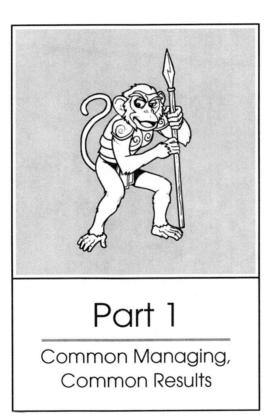

Part 1

Common Managing,
Common Results

Chapter 1

IN THE FOG

A s Sam Adler was dropping his boss off at JFK Airport to catch a plane to Sydney, the last words he heard were: "Sam, when I come back I want to see a different department. You've had adequate time to analyze what's what. It's time for some visible results. Don't disappoint me." His boss had patted Sam on the shoulder in a gesture meant to be friendly, but the only thing Sam recalled later were those ominous words.

What to do? Sam returned to his office in a foul mood. He was an achiever and had done well in school and previous positions. But he was a realist too. In spite of his past strong performance, Sam knew he might not have been among the top picks of most corporations still governed by 20th century standards of management practices. He was different. Achievement-oriented—yes. Driven in the standard and customary sense—no. But L-4 was different too. Apparently they'd seen something in him, something that would make him a successful 21st century manager. Sam didn't want to let his company down.

He scanned his emails as if they contained an answer to his dilemma, but he didn't really expect one. There were a couple of recent ones from his boss, one of which made him sit up straight. "Damn, why this?" Sam thought, "I don't need any help." But he picked up the phone to make the appointment.

🕇🕇🕇🕇🕇

Sam was at least a head taller than the woman motioning him to have a seat in her office. And she was *old*. At least in her fifties, maybe even her sixties. Sam couldn't imagine her among the guys who flew in the corporate jet.

Sam knew that at twenty-five he was young for a department manager. Still, he'd expected someone a little closer to his age. But oh well. His boss had recommended he work with L-4's legendary management coach. So what choice did he have? Right?

He scanned Coach Zabar's office hoping for clues to why she was so famous at L-4. He saw nothing extraordinary, just an easel with the kind of old-fashioned, over-sized pad of paper he thought had gone extinct with the advent of PowerPoint. He read the heading "The *Un*-Game," followed by a list of words, each beginning with an italicized "*un*."

"Weird," he thought. He knew from conversations with other managers that Coach Sophia Zabar had worked with L-4's greatest managers—and L-4 was known throughout the software industry for its outstanding management team. But he'd also heard that some managers had left the company or transferred into another job after coaching with Coach Zabar. He wasn't sure what to expect.

Sam looked at the coach sitting across from him. She didn't look tough, but he'd heard she was. She was a certified Master Coach, meaning she'd coached at least twenty-five hundred hours and passed rigorous exams. Other junior managers said she talked about management being a game, but in a different sense than the game theory Sam had learned about in grad school. And this four-step process that she claimed turned out great managers, he'd never heard of that either. Still, resentment notwithstanding, Sam was oddly intrigued. "I'm tough too," he thought, squaring his shoulders.

"After you leave here, what would cause you to say that your time was well spent?" asked Coach Zabar, after they had greeted one another—she in a friendly, business-like manner, Sam merely with reserve.

"Here goes," Sam said to himself, searching for a non-committal answer. "Well," he said to the coach, "I manage the customer support department, and something is missing. My boss is *un*happy. I'm not satisfied either. People just don't look glad to be there. We have customer complaints that take too long to resolve. One guy keeps showing up late a lot. There's other stuff." To Sam's surprise, his account was frank, even if it didn't exactly answer the coach's question. He reminded himself that he really didn't want to be there.

"This is really big for you, isn't it?" she said. It was an invitation more than a question.

"Yeah, I want to do a great job, but..." Sam's voice trailed off.

"So what concerns you most about what you're telling me?"

"We're on a downhill slide. And profits, productivity, customer satisfaction, and retention are all there at the bottom to greet me," Sam sighed, remembering how his boss had studied the productivity stats, looking glum. It was a look that Sam hadn't been prepared for. He'd done well at Wharton—he knew a lot of management theory. He'd even done well in his various jobs, from waiting tables to editing books. He was proud to have inherited his mother's language skills. And up until recently Sam had been certain that his mother's people skills had been gifted to him as well. She came from Berlin, wanted desperately to study linguistics, and cultivated friends who, *un*like her, could attend college.

He had expected challenges, but a failing team that could get him fired wasn't one of them. His team was supposed to be the secret envy of all the other departments. Sam expected to be noticed and promoted into managing the quality control department in two to three years. Eventually he envisioned himself in L-4's overseas division impressing the nationals with the *un*usual sight of an American manager with real language skills. He sometimes daydreamed about their surprise and admiration.

Instead there was his boss's warning at the airport and—what about Bob? Bob Harley spent more time at the water cooler than on the phone with customers. And the customer complaints— overhearing Joe, Amanda and even Russell helping customers didn't exactly inspire. It was hard to put his finger on it. He knew their performance wouldn't be memorable to the customer.

Sam cared about his people. He wished they were more successful. Like him, they'd be happier coming to work. Surely they had hopes and dreams for their future.

He sighed again. He was tired of listening to his mind flit back and forth between doubt and worry about what he should be doing that he wasn't.

Coach Zabar's next question broke into his thoughts. "If it were different than you describe, what would it look like?" she asked.

"I'd know how to fix it."

"Maybe nothing is broken," suggested the coach.

"What do you mean? Everything's going in the toilet, and I'm just sitting here like a bump on a pickle." Sam sometimes used language that amused people. He was also known to be hard on himself. His boss's glumness was a mere shadow of his own.

"Is it possible that nothing is broken *and* you're just being a bump on a pickle?"

"I suppose so," said Sam less reluctantly. "There may be something I'm not seeing, and it feels like something's wrong."

"Good," said Coach Zabar, with not a trace of sarcasm. So what you're saying is that you're not seeing something, which if you saw it, would allow you to take effective action. Is that right?"

"Well at least that's a possibility," offered Sam.

"So what is it that you're *un*clear about in regard to your job?"

"Well, as a manager I'm supposed to make sure everybody does what they're supposed to do and fix what's broken."

"In other words, you see your job as controlling and correcting," said the coach, adding, "What if that's not your job?"

"That would be nice, because I'm not good at it," said Sam, wondering if he had successfully hidden his frustration.

"So if things were the best they could be, what would you be seeing?"

"My team being energetic, focused, clear, motivated and empowered to assist customers speedily without loss of customer smiles." Sam leaned forward, his voice suddenly sure and steady.

"How are you experiencing your energy right now?" the coach asked.

"Great. High. I'm pumped. That's what I want to see."

"Yes. All great managers want to see that. And I'm clear you want to be a great manager." She paused. "So that's your job."

Sam was pleased. "At least she sees I *want* to be a great manager," he thought. The chance to put his knowledge and skills to work at a company with world-wide presence that aligned with some of his most closely held values thrilled him. L-4, unlike many companies, took the conversation about corporate responsibility for environmental sustainability and social justice seriously.

Aloud he asked, "Yeah, I want to be a great manager, but how do I do that?"

"Whoa, Nellie!" laughed Coach Zabar. "Notice how much you want to jump into action. Very American. How well do you think that would work while you're still in the fog?"

Not waiting for an answer, the coach continued. "Think of yourself in the wrong lane of a four-lane highway, and there's an eighteen-wheeler about a mile away. Without the fog lifting you can't see him. What's going to happen?"

"I'll be road kill," asserted Sam.

"Not if the fog lifts." The coach pressed on. "What will you do?"

"Get in the right lane, of course," said Sam, thinking "Isn't that obvious?"

"Good. You see, you have all your own answers once the fog lifts. So let's get you into the sunshine and into your lane." Coach Zabar arranged her hands in kind of tent and leaned back in her chair.

"Breathe, Sam," she commanded. "It'll bring oxygen to your brain." She paused. "It could be said that your job is to be a catalyst. Now tell me—what does a catalyst do?"

Sam thought for a moment. "Well, a catalyst speeds up the reaction between two substances and winds up creating a particular desired product," he said.

"Aha! And what are you seeing about how that applies to your performance and the performance of your team?"

"I guess the desired product is reaching a company goal, or even filling a need. For example, if there's a particular customer who responds well to a direct communicator, I'd do well to let Russell talk to him or her, because he's decent at it, whereas Bob..." He stopped. He was decidedly not ready to talk about Bob.

"So you're seeing that one of the substances the catalyst works with is the goal or the need. You seem to have alluded to the other substance. Do you see it? You're doing great." The coach looked intently at Sam.

"Hmm. I'm not sure, but the other substance is my people. So it seems I could speed up reaching our goals if I had people doing the work they're good at." Sam paused and thought about what he'd just said.

"What's coming up for you right now?"

"Well, I'm seeing that up until now I've just been making the best of what I've got."

"Are you certain of that?" The coach prodded, but gently.

Sam sat in silence. "No," he said suddenly. "I guess rather than making the best of what I got, I've been making *do* with what I've got! That would be a more accurate description."

"So making the best of what you've got may still be ahead of you then?" The coach smiled.

"Yes."

"OK, so summarize for me what you're getting from what we're saying here?"

After a deep breath the young manager—his voice firm—said, "I'm getting that I've been trying to do the wrong things right. I've limited my options for acting because up until now being a catalyst was more a concept than a reality. Fact is I haven't thought of myself as a catalyst. It's exciting and disconcerting at the same time. Exciting that it's my thinking that has constricted what I see as possible. Disconcerting because what if I can't figure out how to be a good catalyst?"

"Maybe there's nothing to figure out. Maybe for now it's enough to know that great managers excel at this 'catalyst' role. Are you *willing* to be a great manager?"

"What the hell. Wasn't she listening? I already told her that," thought Sam. Aloud he said, "Yes, I really want to be a great manager."

"But that wasn't my question," said Coach Zabar in a neutral tone of voice. "I asked you if you were *willing* to be a great manager. That's not the same thing as *wanting* to be a great manager. It may be worth your while to reflect on the difference.

> Being willing to be a great manager is not the same thing as wanting to be a great manager. It may be worth your while to reflect on the difference.

"We only have a few more minutes. So tell me, out of what you've learned here today, is there an action you're willing to take?"

Sam blinked, paused, and struggled to keep his outward composure as he tried to see the difference between wanting and being willing. "Yes, I'm willing," he answered. "I hadn't seen myself as a catalyst before, and that's huge."

"It *is* huge. So how will you translate that *un*covery into action?"

"*Uncovery?* What does she mean?" wondered Sam. To the coach he said, "I'm going to be alert, wander around my department, and think about what it means for me to be a catalyst. I'll take a few notes, and then I'm going to look for some opportunities to practice *being* one."

"That would be good, wouldn't it? And by when will you do that?"

"Oh, I'll do the wandering and other stuff no later than tomorrow. And I'll practice when I see an opening. One way or another, I'll create at least one opportunity."

Getting her 5'3" frame up out of the chair, the coach responded with a friendly nod. "You did some good work here today. What would you like to be acknowledged for?"

"Weird," Sam thought. "Maybe for just showing up?" His mocking tone betrayed his assessment.

> You might wind up breaking some of the rules you've learned about management. Are you up for that?

"Yes, that took more courage than you think," said the coach, taking his comment at face value. She smiled. "One more thing. If you could meet some great managers, would that interest you?"

Sam hesitated then surprised himself for the second time. "Definitely," he said.

"There's something you ought to know." The coach looked at him as if to size him up. "You might wind up breaking some of the rules you've learned about management. Are you up for that?" Her eyes held his for a moment. Sam wasn't really quite sure, but a "yes" slipped out of his mouth almost before he knew it.

"Very well then. Please close the door when you go out, and I'll see you next time."

As Sam left the office he glanced at the easel. He saw the word "*un*cover" among the partially italicized "*un*" words. *Un*cover. Rules to break. "What surprising rules about management am I going to *un*cover?" he wondered. This was all rather *un*settling. He made a mental note to find out what those "*un*" words on Coach Zabar's old-fashioned easel had to do with management.

Dear Reader

1. Can you recall some conventional wisdom that you've challenged in your life? What was that like, and what difference has it made in your life?
2. Sam has some hopes and dreams for his team that had been obscured by the fog. What goals or dreams of yours, if any, have slipped into the fog?
3. Would it be all right to recover any of your goals and dreams that may have slipped into the fog?

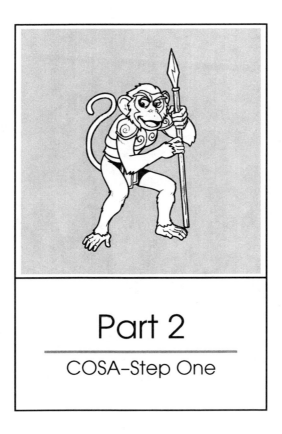

Part 2

COSA–Step One

Chapter 2

THE VISIT

S am returned to his office. With each step he heard *catalyst,*
catalyst, catalyst. Wandering around he scanned the large
office area divided into twenty cubicles facing an open area.
Without being intrusive he could easily overhear the conversations
his team members were having with customers. Amanda was really
eager to help. She seemed to like her job. Customers liked her.
How to specifically determine what makes her good? Then there
was Bob, off to the water cooler where others were gathered.
Bob is never that animated with customers. "What are Bob's
strengths?" Sam wondered, noticing the absence of his customary,
intensely critical reaction to Bob. His energy felt higher than
usual.

Seeing Joe dampened Sam's spirits. Joe just seemed aimless
much of the time. He decided to have a meeting with Joe later. His
thoughts veered to the offer Coach Zabar had made. Have him
talk to some great managers. Truth be told, he was up for that. He
had some questions. "Clearly I have some answers too…present
challenge notwithstanding," he muttered.

Back in his office Sam scanned his emails and saw one from
Coach Zabar's assistant. It contained the names of four managers.
Sam picked up the phone. He would start by meeting Peter Black,

who managed the quality control department. To Sam's satisfaction, he readily agreed to meet him the next day.

"Thanks for seeing me, Mr. Black. I'm Sam Adler. I manage customer support," said Sam as he walked into the quality control manager's office.

"Call me Peter," replied the short, middle-aged man, his face filled with laugh wrinkles. Sam felt instantly comfortable.

Losing no time Sam said, "I'm told you've been coached by Coach Zabar. Game theory aside, is it true she teaches you that 'management is a game,' as in 'fun?'" He emphasized "fun" as if he were examining a slightly suspect laboratory specimen. "It doesn't seem like much of a game to me."

"Part of what you say is true," said the older manager. "Management at L-4 is a great game. We call it the *un*-game around here. But Coach Zabar doesn't teach it to you."

"What do you mean she doesn't teach it to you? Isn't that what she coaches on?"

"Yes, but coaching and teaching aren't the same."

Sam sighed inwardly. "Come on, man," he thought. Aloud he asked, "Please tell me more about the *un*-game and management, if you would. I suppose that list of words beginning with "*un*" in Coach Zabar's office is related to the *un*-game."

"Yes it is."

Sam waited for more detail. When he saw it wasn't forthcoming, he asked, "Why is the "*un*" italicized and the rest of the word isn't?" Given that he didn't even know what the *un*-game was, it seemed like a trivial question.

"For starters, the *un*-game is about *un*covering rules by which you live and work that may or may not be useful to you," said Peter. "Once you *un*cover a rule, you will probably examine and maybe deconstruct it. Coach Zabar just wants to remind us that this is a process of mental '*un*doing' which is probably '*un*settling' and '*un*comfortable.' But it's the price of entry."

"What do you mean 'It's the price of entry'?"

"If you want to be a great manager, you must be able to challenge existing conventional wisdom. If something *un*conventional works better than what you've got, fabulous! At L-4 we're encouraged to seek the *un*conventional. Taking the triple bottom line of 'people, planet, profit' seriously is certainly an example. Business on a large scale doesn't have the blueprint for doing that successfully yet. Neither do we. But it's the coming world. So we're quite interested in good *un*-game players—people who are at home with challenging existing rules and structures and creating better ones."

That fascinated Sam. One of his summer jobs had been with a successful small business that made all its decisions based on the triple bottom line. It had been an eye-opener to him.

"There are a lot of managers, some good, some bad, and a few great ones," continued Peter. "The great ones don't follow many of the sacrosanct rules that other managers follow. Coach Zabar just helps you *un*cover what you don't know you don't

> You could be a catalyst rather than a controller and corrector.

know that could be affecting your performance excellence." Peter paused briefly. "So you've been in to see her?"

Still grappling for an understanding of "She helps you *un*cover what you don't know you don't know," the young manager said, "Yes. I've seen her once."

"And do you know something now that you didn't know when you walked in?"

"Actually, yes!" Sam said, his voice betraying excitement. "I discovered that I thought managers should control and correct, and what I saw was that I could be a catalyst rather than a controller and corrector. That had been completely invisible to me."

"Great. So you *un*covered a rule by which you were managing. You then examined it, and now you're considering replacing it with a new possibility?"

"Yes. That's exactly what happened."

"And did she teach you?" asked the older manager. After a pause, Sam said, "No, I guess not. She just asked a lot of questions."

"Did you notice what kinds of questions she asked?"

"Well, they made me think."

"Are you sure?"

After what seemed like a long silence, Sam slowly answered. "It's more like her questions made me look into my experience rather than think. I could say I didn't discover anything. I *un*covered it because it was already in my experience."

> Great managers are able to make distinctions and create effective actions based on those distinctions.

He turned for affirmation to the older manager, proud of this realization. "There really is a difference between discovering and *un*covering," he said, although he didn't see what difference this would make for his management concerns. It was interesting, however, for someone good at language to make that distinction. Not everyone could do that, he decided.

"Very good," said Peter. "It's important to see the difference between thinking and observing. Great managers are able to make distinctions and create effective actions based on those distinctions. So you're now seeing that *un*covering and discovering aren't the same thing, and that her questions didn't make you think. They were a trigger for you to open yourself up to your experience and take a look around. Thinking and observing are apples and oranges. Not at all the same thing."

"Seems like splitting hairs," Sam thought, trying hard to keep his exasperation to himself. Peter asked, "Has she talked to you about the COSA process yet?"

"No, what's that?"

Peter smiled at the younger man's shift from exasperation to eagerness. "It's the four-step process that moves the performance of talented managers from good to great. It gives you the skill-set that lets you be a better *un*-game player." He paused, his smile growing wider. "Has she asked you yet if you're willing to be a great manager?"

Sam was taken aback. "Yeah, she did." He continued with a hint of indignation. "And then when I answered with 'of course I want to be a great manager,' she split hairs about some difference between wanting and being willing, and that she'd asked me a different question than the one I was answering. It was all pretty weird."

"Well, Sam, let me suggest that she wasn't splitting hairs. Rather she was making something distinct that was foggy for you. And it's really the key to the first step in the COSA process. The 'C' stands for CHOOSE. Great managers are aware of choices they have in any given moment. So let's say the manager is you. The results that you'll produce hinge on the choices you make. If you choose the road less traveled, you'll produce extraordinary results. If you choose the well-trodden path, you'll get mediocre results. Which do you find more interesting?"

"The road to extraordinary results, naturally. That's an easy one. But that's just a metaphor. It isn't clear to me what I'm choosing when I have my staff meeting, or when my boss looks at the customer complaint log." Sam shot Peter an expectant look. "Could you give me an example of what you mean by that first key, CHOOSE? And what would I be doing?"

"Those are great questions," said Peter. "You ought to bring them up with Coach Zabar the next time you talk to her. But I can tell you this much. The 'C' part has everything to do with the distinction of 'wanting' versus 'being willing' to be a great manager, which I suspect you consider 'hairsplitting.' Allow me a question before you go, Sam. What are you aware of right now in regard to the questions you just asked me?"

"I'm disappointed you didn't give me an example," was the immediate and honest reply.

"Exactly. You wanted an answer here and now. What else are you noticing?"

A flash of recognition spread briefly across Sam's face. "I wanted an answer to my question right away, but I'm going to make another appointment with Coach Zabar. Therefore, I'm willing to wait even though I don't want to." Pleased with himself, he added, "So I see the difference. I may not want to wait. Nevertheless, I'm willing."

"You got it," responded the older manager, a satisfied look on his face.

Sam was happy about getting the difference between 'wanting' and 'being willing,' but clueless as to why that was important in the first place.

Thanking the older manager for his time, he left the office thinking maybe he should visit one other great manager. This coaching stuff disturbed his peace of mind.

Dear Reader

1. Both the coach and the older manager are precise with the young manager. What value, if any, do you see in being precise?
2. Peter Black insists that coaching and teaching aren't the same. What's your picture of coaching, and, from the little you've witnessed, does Coach Zabar fit your picture? Why or why not?

 # THE KEY CHOICE

The second name on Sam's list was Marguerite Chan, manager of the Programming Division. Her division was the reason L-4 USA had been able to bring the Northwest region into the fold, leaving no room for competitors to make inroads for at least three years. Marguerite Chan was a great manager.

She had said "yes" to seeing Sam Adler. Seated in the outer office, he heard a friendly voice inviting him into her inner sanctum. An attractive, self-assured woman in her mid-forties belonged to the friendly voice. Marguerite's office was neat, comfortable, and minimalist. A photo of a black Labrador Retriever sat on a corner of her desk. "An animal lover," Sam surmised, "no wonder she's friendly."

"What can I do for you, Sam?" she asked after introductions and brief pleasantries had been exchanged.

"I've come here to learn more about this COSA process, and more specifically about the first step, CHOOSE. I understand you've been through it. It's supposed to make good managers great, and I'm willing to be a great manager. But it isn't that good, is it? I never heard of it at Wharton," Sam said.

"Oh yes, it *is* that good, but just one correction," replied

Marguerite. "It doesn't and can't make good managers great. But it can make talented managers great. You see, as a great manager you not only bring skills and knowledge to the job. You also bring talent. Skills and knowledge can be taught, but talent can't."

"So what makes someone a talented manager?" Sam was hoping he would qualify.

"You may not even be aware of your talent. But you think about people a lot, even outside of work, and about managing them to be their best." Marguerite chuckled. "In the shower, for example, and before you go to sleep. You're curious and always wanting to learn. And besides finding ways to talk about what you've learned, you also look for how you can productively apply it. Talent respects rules but isn't afraid to challenge them. Talent can take risks and see possibilities where others don't. You can see why talent can't be taught." It was clear Marguerite Chan loved to talk about talent.

"That's provocative," responded Sam thoughtfully. "I always heard that anybody could do anything if they just applied themselves. In other words, get enough skills and knowledge, put some consistent elbow grease toward your goal, and you should reach it."

"Yes," agreed Marguerite. "That's one of the *un*examined assumptions great managers are aware of, and they challenge it. Better said, most managers apply that assumption and make it a rule while great managers do no such thing. That rule assumes everyone has *un*limited potential. Take that thinking to its logical conclusion, and you get that everyone's the same. Which we're not, thank goodness.

"That's why you see the perennial development plans after the yearly performance review. Or people sent to workshops to fix what their managers think needs fixing. It's a waste of time, energy, and talent. Managers would do better to find the talents that their people *do* have and put that talent to work on behalf of a company goal or need. Sometimes the company doesn't make that easy, but that's a different conversation."

"You're not saying development plans and workshops are a waste of time, are you?" said Sam with suspicion.

"No, not when they're appropriately used to develop skills and increase knowledge. But more often they're used to be remedial. That's a problem. Trying to teach people what they have no talent for *is* a waste of time. Great managers facilitate the use of their people's talents and offer them support for their shortcomings."

"What you're saying is what I've learned," said Sam with mounting enthusiasm. "The great manager is a catalyst. He or she speeds up the reaction between an employee's talent and the accomplishment of a company goal. He'd be a corrector, not a catalyst, if he focused on remediation.

"That's a great example of the concept. And now I understand why you said the four-step COSA process doesn't make good managers great. But good managers who are talented can get to be great, right?" Sam smiled, pleased with his growing understanding.

> Great managers facilitate the use of their people's talents and offer them support for their shortcomings.

"That's right," answered Marguerite. "But you came to hear about the 'C' in the four-step COSA process. What do you want to know?"

"I'm paraphrasing Peter Black from Quality Control," began Sam. "Great managers make distinctions that others don't. And they make conscious choices moment by moment. But that isn't anything new to me. Of course they don't just fly by the seat of their pants! They base their decisions on good management practices they've learned. I need more clarity about what to do. What am I supposed to be making a choice about?"

"You feel compelled to act, don't you?" Marguerite said almost as an after-thought. That's the second time Sam had heard that. Well, of course he wanted to act. What the hell else was he supposed to do? "These people are weird," he thought.

"Here's what I'd advise you," Marguerite proposed. "Don't just do something. Sit there." She stifled a laugh.

"Don't get me wrong, Sam," she said, recovering her serious, professional voice. "The ultimate purpose is action. The ultimate purpose is to score the goals you've set for your department and to produce extraordinary results. But the rush to action is often a mistake. You know, something can be urgent without being important. And you can easily get sidetracked. Or disconnected from what's really important and driving the goal. Let me make this real.

"Why are you seeing Coach Zabar?"

"For starters, because my department is crummy, and I want customers to be raving fans, absenteeism to drop, and people to be happy doing great work," was Sam's immediate answer. He didn't notice that he no longer experienced the coaching he was getting as his boss's idea.

> Don't just
> do something.
> Sit there.

"And if that were so, what would that be a demonstration of?"

He hesitated, fearing that he'd be seen as arrogant, but he decided to risk it. "I want to be, and I'm willing to be a great manager," he said quietly. "And I think it would be a demonstration of my intention to be a great manager, because I would have to be the catalyst to produce that change. It isn't going to happen by itself or just because I wish it."

"That's wonderful," said Marguerite. "You've convinced me that you're aware of your role as catalyst and that you both want to and are

willing to be a great manager. That's what drives you. You're restless
and dissatisfied when the outside facts don't match your inside vision."

Sam wondered how she knew that.

"Now listen carefully, Sam. Chances are your 'I want to' isn't going
to get you all the way to your goal. It can quickly turn into 'I don't
want to.' There are lots of challenges to meet, and you could get tired
and give up. But your 'I'm willing' can get you all the way to your goal
because it has the capacity to deal with obstacles. 'I'm willing' doesn't
give up. It uses obstacles to get more resilient, creative, alert, attentive,
and courageous, among other things. Great managers don't just want
to be great managers. Wanting helps, but more importantly, they're
willing to be great managers." She
paused, studying Sam's face.

"One of the most powerful
choices you can make, Sam, is to
say 'I am willing.' It's not the only
choice in the 'C' of the COSA
process, but it's the key to all the
others." Marguerite leaned back
and let out a deep breath.

> One of the most
> powerful choices you
> can make is to say,
> "I am willing."

"Does that help?"

"Yes," said Sam, nodding
slowly, thinking briefly that the
juxtaposition of "powerful choice"
and "I am willing" was *un*usual but strangely fitting.

"Can you tell me how it helps?"

"I've been dissatisfied for at least two months and looking at what
I could do differently. My energy has been low. I've been critical of
myself and my people. My actions have been like moths buzzing
around a light very busy but devoid of a purpose that makes sense to
me. And of course the results aren't very good. But what I'm getting
from this conversation are several things," he said forcefully. "One
is that in moving toward a goal, it's vitally important that the goal be
an expression of a value that's important to me. Like 'being a great

manager' is the value that's very important to me. Not for the glory. Not for the promotion. Not for the money. Those are all nice, but being a great manager sings to me. I want it. I can taste it. And I'm willing to do what it takes to bring that about. It's not for any reason. It just is."

"Aha. Fire in the belly," Marguerite thought to herself. To Sam she said, "Great! Anything else?"

"Yes. The second thing I see now is that I have a choice when I come up against the inevitable obstacles. I can observe the 'I don't wanna' fit that'll probably be there." Sam knew himself pretty well. He laughed and added, "And then I can say, 'I may not want to, but I'm nevertheless willing.' I don't know how well I can put that into practice, but..." His voice trailed off.

"That's why you have a coach and a network of support," said Marguerite. "Everything is easier with support. Would it be all right with you if there were less to your challenges than meets the eye?" Her smile betrayed amusement.

"Yeah, that would definitely be all right," Sam sighed.

"Good. When's your next session with Coach Zabar?"

"She told me to come back when I knew I was in a fog. I feel clear right now, but with this coaching stuff, if the past predicts the future, she'll find something that I don't know I'm in a fog about." Sam harrumphed.

"Hey, I know," he cried out a moment later. "I'm in the fog about how I could put into practice 'I'm willing' when the you-know-what hits the fan!"

Thanking Marguerite for her help, Sam got up to leave. In parting Marguerite said, "Yes, getting out there on life's playing field is not for the faint at heart. You definitely need some tools to play the game well—especially the *un*-game. COSA is going to support you in what you're up to. And it's clear that you're up to something big."

Sam stepped outside her door. He felt strangely warm around his heart region. And open.

Maybe he and L-4 weren't such a bad fit after all.

Dear Reader

1. Can you recall a time when you didn't want to do something, but you were nevertheless willing and did it anyway? What did you notice about that choice? Can you think of a similar experience in your role as manager?

2. What talents do you think you have? To find them, look at what occupies you, and what you love to do. Do you have recurrent thoughts, feelings, and behaviors that could be applied toward creating or supporting something useful?

3. If you concluded that performance reviews are a waste of time, energy, and talent, how would you measure performance? How would you and your employee interact about this?

Chapter 4

THE WOLF YOU FEED

G ood morning, Sam." Coach Zabar's voice was warm and welcoming. "Have you been having any fun lately?"

Sam thought this an extraordinary question in a corporate environment. But then he remembered that Coach Zabar thought of management as a game, and you're supposed to have fun at a game.

"To be honest, no, not really. But I've given a lot of thought to what I've learned."

"Excellent. And you've been to see some of our great managers? Would you like to share something that you've learned?"

"OK." Choosing his words carefully, Sam continued. "I've learned some distinctions. Like I'm now clearer [he didn't want to risk saying he was clear] about the difference between 'wanting' and 'being willing' and how that might relate to choice. And I've also learned some of the rules great managers ignore that other managers follow. For example, great managers don't assume that anyone could do anything if they just applied themselves and worked hard enough. There's more. It's all very provocative."

"It sounds like you've had a good education this last week. So what specifically would you like coaching on today? How can I best support you?"

"Well," Sam hesitated—slightly jarred that the decision was entirely his—and searched for his next words. "I want to learn the four-step process for being a great manager. I hope I have what it takes. And Peter Black and Marguerite Chan told me what the 'C' in COSA stands for, but so far it still feels like a concept to me. It's not real. I'd like to understand it better."

What he was leaving out was that his current understanding hadn't led to effective action. And he really didn't know at all what to do with manager Chan's advice, "Don't just do something. Sit there."

"Ah, yes. We so want to understand things," said the coach. "Would it be OK with you if you discovered that understanding is the booby prize? And that there's something much better?"

> Understanding is the booby prize. There's something much better.

"I suppose so," said Sam, not sure at all.

"Good. So tell me more about you and your understanding of the 'C' in the COSA process."

Sam took a deep breath and said, "Well, all the great managers in their role as catalyst make things happen. They speed things up. And the achievement of corporate goals, or the filling of a need, depends on action. Marguerite Chan cautioned me that the rush to action can be a mistake, and I can agree with that. And she talked about connecting actions to what's really important. I can relate that to company values. I can even see that being willing can be a useful choice to override my feelings when I don't want to do something, like for example fire an employee."

Having obsessed about what he *couldn't* fit into his present mental model, Sam felt relief saying "The thing that eludes me is why everybody is making such a big deal out of this choosing thing in COSA."

"Do you have a sense of possibility or spaciousness in what you've just said?" the coach asked. Sam blinked—what did she mean? It sounded like a non sequitur. He mumbled, "No. I get frustrated when I don't understand."

"And so right now, as you're frustrated, how are you showing up?"

"Do you mean, how am I acting?"

"Yes. What do you see?"

"Well, I see that I'm trying to fit this into a frame of reference I can relate to," said Sam, feeling a bit lost.

"And if you *could* put it into a frame of reference that you already have, then everything would be all right?"

"Yes. Then I could make use of it."

"I suggest that rather than making use of it, you would dismiss it." There was no hint of judgment in Coach Zabar's voice.

"What do you mean?" Sam sounded indignant.

"Our brains are wired in such a way that new information is not always welcome. It's especially not welcome when it goes against what we already know. We work hard to make it fit, and if it doesn't, we tend to dismiss it. It's threatening to our peace of mind because it challenges our mental models of how things ought to work." The coach paused, giving Sam space to consider her assertions.

"So, Sam—if you weren't focused on trying to fit this into something you understand, something you already know, what would you be doing?" she said finally.

"I don't know. Just be *un*comfortable, I think."

"Don't think. Just look. Are you *un*comfortable now?"

"Yes." Sam gave himself time to reflect before venturing forth with, "And at the same time I'm curious. I'd say I'm receptive and open to what I can learn."

"Are you seeing that, or is this something that you think you ought to be?"

Nothing in the coach's tone had changed. "She's not out to get me," Sam decided.

"I'm seeing that's so for me right now," he said, studying the coach's face.

"Very good. So look and see what's coming up for you right now."

Nodding slightly, Sam said, "That being open and receptive without an agenda would be a great way to learn about the 'C' in the COSA process."

"What you say is true, Sam. But perhaps more important is what you've just experienced. You saw how natural it is for you to want to put something into categories you already know. We all do that. Why? Because we want to reestablish our equilibrium. We want to be comfortable once again. Nevertheless our discomfort may offer us valuable information. It pays to be interested in it. Well done, young man."

> Our discomfort may offer us valuable information. It pays to be interested in it.

Sam felt as if he had done a lot of work. He was tired yet energized, and aware of a sense of clarity. At the same time he was experiencing a vague loss he couldn't name. Whatever the loss, he didn't mourn it.

The coach could have told him that the loss he was experiencing was the loss of the assumption "Everything can be categorized to fit into something I already know." *Un*beknownst to Sam, he was already playing the *un*-game.

"Let me tell you a story," said the coach, relaxing into her chair. "You may know it. It has many versions." She folded her hands and her eyes acquired a far-away look. For a moment Sam recalled his grandmother telling him one of Grimm's fairy tales when he was a little boy. A little embarrassed, he took a deep breath and listened.

"Once upon a time there was a Cherokee Elder, who was a fine storyteller. On one particular storytelling evening, the flames of the fire throwing dancing shadows on the faces of the gathered crowd of men, women, and children, he told the familiar story of two wolves. "'A fight is going on inside me,' said the storyteller. 'It is a terrible fight between two wolves.'

"The crowd listened intently even though they knew the story.

"'One wolf is angry, envious, greedy, and acts with false pride, coarseness, and arrogance. He spreads lies, deceit, fear, hatred, and divisiveness.' The storyteller paused. When he spoke again he said, 'The other wolf is friendly, joyous, loving, kind, just, generous, truthful, compassionate, grateful, and brave. He creates peace and community.'

"The people hung on his every word. The elder continued, his voice deep and clear. 'This same fight is going on inside you and inside all other human beings as well.'"

Coach Zabar asked, "What do you suppose, Sam, was the question on everybody's mind?"

"Which wolf will win the fight would be on my mind," replied Sam after only a moment's hesitation.

"Indeed. And what do you suppose the answer was?"

After what seemed like a long silence, Sam replied. "Since the wolves are inside him, I think the elder would say, 'The one I pay attention to.' Or he'd say, 'The one I feed.'"

Both Coach Zabar and Sam sat very still.

"So what are you getting from this story, Sam?"

He cleared his throat, but said nothing. The coach seemed in no hurry.

"The quality of what we do depends on choices we make before we do the doing, if that makes any sense," he said at last. "Those choices result in action, but they're choices that seem to have more to do with guiding people's actions than the actions themselves. They don't seem to come from the mind."

"Very good. Would you say that they're choices not about *doing*, but choices about who you are willing to *be*?"

"Yes, that's a good way of putting it. Like in the story of the two wolves. You could choose to be the good one or the bad one. The one you choose is the one you feed, so to speak. My doing is always dependent on who I choose to be. And that's true for everybody else. That's a powerful principle!"

Sam didn't move.

"What's coming up for you right now?" Coach Zabar asked, leaning forward.

"I'm seeing the possibility—it doesn't feel quite real yet—that I can choose who I'm willing to be moment by moment by moment. That would be really huge. I always thought I couldn't help my feelings, and I would just have to suck it up and go forward in spite of my feelings. It felt oppressive, like I was denying my feelings. But this seems different." His voice became firm as he added, "I don't know why, but what comes up for me is the word *freedom*."

> You can have your feelings. Feelings provide you with good information. But they don't "have *you*" when you're aware there's more to you than your emotional self.

"It *is* different. It could be said that it comes from a different self. If you come again you'll probably find out much more about what you're beginning to see. You can have your feelings. I recommend you not ignore them. Feelings provide you with good information. But they don't 'have *you*' when you're aware there's more to you than your emotional self. In addition to your psychological self which harbors your emotions, you have an ontological self. The ontological self harbors the you who is able to choose who you're willing to be. Ontology is the study of being. It has much to teach us."

The coach gave Sam time to take in what she had just said before asking, "Is there anything else you saw in the story?"

"I sure did. The positive qualities the elder mentions have to result in positive outcomes. It's just natural."

"Would it be fair to say that the qualities or attributes in and of themselves are a contribution?" offered the coach.

Sam thought about that. "Yes it would be. Unless you're corrupted by self-deception, it's always a contribution to be compassionate—outcome produced or not."

The coach nodded and continued. "You mentioned earlier that if you were here without an agenda and without trying to fit this into an 'I already know' box, that you would be open and receptive. In what ways might those qualities show up as a contribution?"

Sam didn't have to think about his answer. "It seems to me if I were open and receptive, it would be hard to get into a defensive interchange, and that would be an example of them being a contribution."

"Great. Actually it's impossible to be defensive and at the same time open and receptive. Try it some time. On another note, were your visits with Peter Black and Marguerite Chan valuable to you? And if so, can you tell me a little about what attributes or qualities they demonstrated that were contributions to you?"

"My meetings with them were definitely valuable," said Sam. "Both wanted to be helpful. They weren't arrogant know-it-alls, even though they're more experienced than I am. They were friendly, even eager and enthusiastic, come to think of it. Yeah, they were very supportive."

"What else?"

"Well, empowering too. I walked away with new distinctions that I can apply to my world."

"What else?"

"Generous. They didn't hoard their knowledge."

"Anything else?"

"Yes, they were gentle and kind but very clear and direct. Did I say compassionate?"

"No, but I bet they were."

"Yes, they were. And they didn't let me off the hook."

"Say more about that."

"Well, for example, they didn't just let my misunderstanding of 'discovering' and '*un*covering' and 'being willing' remain *un*examined. They were alert, and they focused on robbing me of some of my *un*examined assumptions." Sam smiled and relaxed. He was actually enjoying himself.

"So they were focused and alert?"

"Yeah. And pressing me like they did, that took some guts."

"So you admired that they were being courageous and truthful."

"Yes, I did. And I do. And they were very attentive. Also appreciative that I wanted to learn something." Sam was on a roll. It occurred to him that he had been pretty observant.

"Attentive and appreciative too. Hmm. You, young man, observed a lot. Congratulations. So the qualities you observed were..." She ticked them off on her fingers as she recited.

"Did I miss any?" she asked, a smile on her face. Sam was aware he really liked the coach.

"How did you remember all those qualities?" he asked, pleased with his observation but *un*aware of how her skillful questions had helped him see.

Ignoring his question, the coach said, "What are you seeing about all these qualities?"

"Well, they all make a contribution. There's no doubt about that."

"There isn't, is there?"

"No, there's no doubt that those attributes make a contribution, and they seem to come from a different place. I can't quite put my finger on it."

Coach Zabar put her hands over her heart and feigned a Mona Lisa smile. Sam looked at her and burst out, "Those are qualities of the heart. They're our best qualities."

"Yes they are. Have you heard of Joseph Campbell?" Coach Zabar asked.

"Oh yes. He wrote *The Hero with a Thousand Faces* and *Myths to Live By*. What surprised me was what his research indicated. Imagine, all cultures everywhere have similar stories about our human condition and our place in the cosmos. I like and admire him. He broke a lot of rules in how he went about things… like great managers." Sam always liked to bring things back to management.

Coach Zabar said, "I'm glad you like Joseph Campbell. Then you've read about his hero archetype, yes?"

Somehow it seemed incongruent in a corporate setting to be talking about stories and hero archetypes, but Sam was enjoying it. "I sure have," he nodded.

"It could be said," the coach continued, "that we're all on a hero's journey, and that being here on this corporate playing field or on any playing field of life, is not for the faint of heart. It's like entering a forest. Each of us has a special path. In order to find your special path you can't go where anyone else has gone. If it's already there, it's not your path.

> Each of us has a special path. In order to find your special path you can't go where anyone else has gone. If it's already there, it's not your path.

"So for you to be well-equipped for this hero's journey, you'll need special tools. Then you can be free to meet the challenges and obstacles." She paused briefly. "And so you've come for your first and most important of all the tools. Without this one you cannot use the rest."

She paused again. Her voice assumed a more solemn quality

as she said, "You've come for the 'C' in COSA. The 'C' is about choosing who you are willing to be, moment by moment by moment as you move through life. Like now. And now. And this evening at home when it becomes the now."

There was a long, pregnant-with-possibilities silence which neither the coach nor Sam needed to break. Finally the coach asked, "What's coming up for you as you hear me say this to you?"

"That you've given me a very powerful guide for my actions. It can guide me as I'm going about the business of being a catalyst."

"Allow me to tweak what you said just a little," the coach said kindly. "I didn't give you the guide. You *un*covered what you've always known…that you're free to choose."

Sam was delighted. "Hmm," he murmured. It was true. What he was learning had been there all along. He just hadn't had access to it. "This is way cool," he thought.

"But tell me, Sam," the coach asked, returning to Sam's comment about being a catalyst. "Just what do you see yourself doing in a catalyst role once you've chosen who you're willing to be? For example, you might choose to be clear and focused, but how would you exercise that choice? Can you give me an actual example of you as a catalyst with one or more of your direct reports?"

Sam wished he had a ready answer, but he didn't. "You're an idiot! You got all puffed up about how cool it is to choose qualities to demonstrate, and now you can't even come up with a real example of how you'd apply it." He glanced at the coach. His face felt hot.

He looked longingly toward the door. "With all your focus on trying to understand the 'C' in this COSA thing, you forgot about Bob and Joe and any practical applications. What happened to the importance of catalyst? You're so damn enamored with the theory, you forget about what's really important. That's what she meant when she talked about understanding being the booby prize."

The catalyst conversation had slipped back—without Sam's permission—into the recesses of his mind, taking up space as a concept rather than as a guiding principle.

"When you're up to your ass in alligators, it's easy to forget your objective was to drain the swamp," he thought. But that aphorism gave him no solace. People were often impressed by the fact that Sam learned something the first time around. "Second chances are for others, not for me. I should get it on the first try," he always said privately.

He wasn't cut out to be a great manager. At this moment he was dead sure about that. Sam thought that his self-doubts were abnormal. He hadn't learned yet that even the most successful people have them.

"Sam," he heard the coach say. "I know you know what your job is."

Sam straightened up. "Yeah," he said. "My role could be defined as selecting people for the job. I didn't get to do that with two of the people I'm concerned about. Bob and Joe were in my department before I got the job. But setting expectations, motivating, and developing them—the other three tasks of a catalyst—I have the power to influence. Tell you the truth, I'd pretty much forgotten that," he muttered, slumping once more.

"Good. And what are you making that mean?"

"That I'm pretty stupid," Sam blurted out. "And that good grades in grad school don't mean crap."

"What's the most stupid thing you're noticing about yourself as you reflect on this?"

"Well, I should've thought about the practical applications of being a catalyst. I didn't think about them at all. I was much more focused on the 'C' in COSA."

"Sam, is being hard on yourself familiar to you?"

"If you mean do I have high standards for myself, then the answer would be 'yes.'"

"But that wasn't my question. I wondered whether being hard on yourself is familiar to you?"

"I've never thought about it."

"Don't think about it. Just look and see."

"Yes. It's familiar," Sam replied, keeping eye contact with the coach. There was a mixture of curiosity and irritation in his voice.

"Can you share an example?"

"Well, like right now. I'd learned about the catalyst deal in my session with you as well as with Peter Black and Marguerite Chan. I even thought how important it was to stop thinking of myself as having to fix something or someone. And how much more fun and challenging the catalyst role is, and then I forgot about it and focused on trying to figure out the 'C' in COSA. Being a catalyst just disappeared into the background for me despite the fact that two of my guys need me to play that role as we speak."

"So when you learn something new, your expectation is what?"

"To apply it. Not forget about it."

"I see. When you compare expectations you have of yourself with those you have for your employees in a similar situation, what do you notice?"

Sam hesitated then said, "I give them more of a break than I give myself."

"Hmm."

"Yeah, they should have the benefit of some practice to guarantee improvement." Sam's voice trailed off.

"But you shouldn't?"

"Well now that you mention it, that makes no sense at all." After a brief pause he said, "After all, I'm no different from them."

"So what you're saying is that there's a quality of being that you're choosing to apply to your employees that you could choose to apply to yourself. Is that right?"

"Yes, that's right. Except that I haven't chosen it consciously. I could choose to be more generous with myself. I just never saw that. I thought as a manager I should be hard on myself."

"What you've thought up until now is that being hard on yourself and having high expectations of yourself are the same thing, and they're not. Can you see that choosing high standards and being generous could actually peacefully co-exist and support each other?"

Sam sat up straight. "Yeah, if I'm really committed to continuous improvement rather than perfection. I just need some practice in applying what I learn instead of expecting to be perfect from the start. That's a new way of being for me. I'll forget from time to time, won't I?"

"If you're like the rest of us mortals, yes you will."

"But then when I notice it I can choose to be generous about my forgetting, can't I?" Sam grinned.

"You're a quick study, Sam."

"I don't think so, but with lots of practice I can get to be darn good."

"Yes, you will. Would it be all right with you to learn that you aren't special?"

The smile on Sam's face froze, but he quickly regained his equilibrium. "Yeah, it's a relief to realize I can have the same learning curve as everybody else. That gives me a lot of breathing room. It might make it easier to be as terrific as I want to be."

"Great. So if you reflect on what just happened, can you articulate what's most important to you about what you just learned?" The coach smiled as she met Sam's gaze.

"I was worried you'd think I was stupid. After all, *I* thought I was. But I doubt that thought even crossed your mind. All you saw was that I was willing to learn and shift my focus. In terms of the 'C' in COSA, you saw who I was willing to be." Sam experienced a sense of peace and gratitude. He returned Coach Zabar's smile.

"So who are you willing to be with your team now, and how will you show up, for example, in your next team meeting?"

"I'm willing to be clear, focused, and generous with Bob, or Joe—no, with my whole team—in Tuesday's team meeting. I'll keep my eye on the ball we're playing with at the time. We'll need to take a look at our practices. Our service is just hovering around average. I sense no excitement. There's no sizzle. I'm up for finding out what's going on. If I notice they're *un*clear as to expectations,

then I go there. For examples of under-performance, I investigate
to see what's missing that would restore motivation. We'd discover
that in conversation, provided I can create an atmosphere in which
they can be like I can be here with you."

"And how can you be here?"

"It may sound strange, but I feel free to learn when I talk to you."

The coach nodded. "That's a plus. And you create that
atmosphere how?" Her direct gaze never left Sam's face.

"By choosing and demonstrating, for example, the qualities of
being from the list we generated," replied Sam, equally focused.

"A brilliant start. Let me suggest that you'll *un*cover in
conversation what's missing in your people's performance or
motivation. Why do you suppose I say '*un*cover' rather than
'discover?'"

This time Sam didn't hesitate. "Because the answers are already
there, and it's my job to *un*cover them."

"Well done, Sam."

"Thank you, Coach." Sam sat up a little straighter. "May I ask
you a question before I go?"

"Shoot."

"How can I remember all those qualities? And how do I choose?"

"You can make a list of the qualities to choose from. And each
day you can choose five that you're willing to be. Or even just two.
You could choose them any way you like. Maybe you decide you're
likely to need 'courageous' and 'truthful' today, because you may
call in an employee who's under-performing. So those qualities
would be among the five you choose. But it's up to you. You might
even review at intervals during the day how you applied those
qualities. Or notice if you forgot to apply them. That's all good
information for you. What possibilities do you see out of those
suggestions?"

The coach's practical answer pleased Sam. He tended to be
enamored with theory, and it was useful to be reminded of the
application. "All the theory in the world is useless if you can't apply

it in action," he thought.

Sam considered the coach's question. "The most immediate thing I see about such focused observation is that I'll be clearer, and therefore I'll focus better on the four basic roles I play: selecting, setting expectations, motivating, and developing my people. It'll also be a chance to observe myself and see if I'm walking my talk. That's real important to me, and I see this as supporting me. But why choose only five or two of those qualities? I want to be all of them." He leaned forward.

"If you were to answer that question, what would you say?"

After a short hesitation Sam said, "It's easier to keep up with five than with all of those."

"And would it be all right with you, Sam, if life were easier?" teased the coach.

"Yes, it would be very all right with me." Sam let out a breath. "Phew."

"Good. Then save your questions for another time. As my mother used to say when I was sure I needed that on-sale sweater, 'There's always another sale, Sophia.' So there's always another coaching session, if you decide you want one."

Sam was elated. "She's willing to work with me," he thought. "That must mean she thinks I could be a great manager."

"Before we end today, is there an action you're willing to design with me that would be a reflection of what you learned here today?" asked the coach.

"That's easy. I'm going to choose five qualities every day, and I'm going to notice how I demonstrate them. I'll keep a log of what happened, or better yet, of what I'm learning. I'm going to feed the right wolf," he declared with a smile. "And I'm going to have a conversation with Joe, one of my employees, to make sure he's clear about his job expectations. He seems aimless much of the time."

"Super. By when will you have that conversation?"

"By tomorrow, Coach," was Sam's prompt reply. "Thank you very much," he said, as they walked toward the door, "for giving me this time."

"It's good to be able to support you. One of the things I appreciate about you, Sam, is how alert and attentive you are. You've made some fine observations. That's going to serve you well as a manager and in learning the COSA process. See you soon." She nodded and closed the door.

Walking out of the coach's office, Sam noticed that the building appeared different—brighter, more colorful. The light streaming through the large skylights in the giant lobby seemed to caress the plants in the center. The railing of the staircase felt smooth and cool to his touch. He experienced a sense of…he didn't quite know how to describe it…a sense of well-being. "Yes," he decided. "It's good. It's all good."

Dear Reader

1. What do you make of the coach's statement that we tend to
    dismiss information that doesn't fit our mental models? Can
    you recall dismissing information that didn't fit your pre-
    existing opinion? You probably can't—why not?
2. What's your experience as you reflect on the metaphors of the
    two wolves and the hero's journey? Can you see how they may
    apply in many areas of life?
3. As you reflect on the four roles of a manager, is there one that
    you're paying more attention to than another? Which one, if
    any, needs more of your attention right now? Less?

Chapter 5

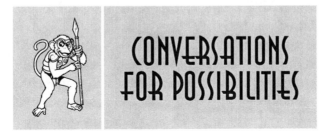

CONVERSATIONS FOR POSSIBILITIES

S am entered his department softly humming the theme song from *Chariots of Fire,* an old movie he loved. He thought about the purpose of the customer support department. "When all is said and done," he mused, "our real purpose is to turn customers into clients who keep coming back to L-4." And he was the catalyst for taking that assertion from vision to action.

He looked at the schedule. Sam held team meetings in two shifts so the promise to return support calls within an hour could be met. He spent ten minutes writing some notes on a yellow pad, then sent out the email setting up the meetings.

Three hours later half his team filed silently into the meeting room. The donuts Sam had brought raised a few eyebrows. "I want us to use this meeting to talk about what our job is," he announced. That seemed to surprise everyone at the table. There was a moment of silence.

"Well, that's easy," Russell said. "We should be out of here in no time. We're the support department, so our job is to support the customer. We do that by answering their questions and by getting them up and running again when they're down."

"Thanks, Russell," said Sam. "Let's hear from everybody." Everyone dutifully gave a similar version of Russell's statement, minus the sarcasm Sam had noted but let pass.

"Hmm, that's interesting," he said. "If we were known for excellent performance, would we be defining our job in the same way as we just did? It seems as if we're defining our job by listing activities we engage in."

There was another silence around the table, although Sam could almost feel the question, "Duh! What else is there? Hasn't he read our job description lately?" None of them had read it either, but that was beside the point.

"I want to know from you—I'm not kidding—why our department is so average." Sam looked at each member of his team briefly before adding, "Our numbers don't exactly inspire." The team members shifted in their chairs. The silence felt *un*comfortable.

Sam saw the "What's he up to?" expression on their faces, but they also seemed to sense his interest. He'd heard about the "beat the team up" mode they had grown accustomed to with their previous manager.

"What would it look like if we were kicking butt?" Sam continued. "Start by imagining this as a really cool place to work, like you just can't wait to get here in the morning." That comment raised a few more eyebrows and flared a nostril or two. "What would be in place that's absent now?"

Sam sat back and waited. He remained silent even as some people shifted in their chairs, glanced at their feet, furtively stole a glance at him, and cleared their throats. He just waited.

And then aimless Joe, the last one Sam expected to take the initiative, asked pointedly, "Do you really want to know?"

"I do," Sam replied without hesitation.

"I don't know if it's anyone else's opinion, but it's mine," Joe began. "I think that with the way we do things now, nobody's happy. I think the clients' problems could be solved a lot faster than we're solving them right now."

"Tell me more," Sam encouraged. "Ground that assessment." He leaned forward.

"Well, ideally, given the intricacies of the software and the client's particular challenges, whoever logs the problem would take the issue from start to finish," Joe began. "I know that's not always possible, but we could develop the protocol that would make that happen more often than it does now. Right now it's standard practice that whoever is available will take the call. That may mean that three or four of us could get involved. And there are lots of downsides to that."

There were nods among the team members.

"Why do we do it that way?" asked Sam, his tone of voice announcing this was a fact, not a fault-finding mission.

"It's policy to take the call immediately when possible, but we guarantee a call-back within an hour."

"So our intention is to be quick and responsive. We want the client to know we care."

"Yeah." Joe nodded. "That's the intention, but it doesn't work out that way. For example, the client often winds up explaining his or her problems more than once. That's a pain for them, and it's annoying to me when I can't finish the job I started." Sam saw more nods and heard a few "uh-huhs."

"Worse yet," added Joe, gathering steam, "Someone else may have taken them in the wrong direction trying to solve what I had already set up and worked so hard on. And then we have the issue of incomplete data on problem-resolution progress. Some people are better than others in entering the support notes."

Sam listened for the next forty-five minutes, asking an occasional question as one team member after another weighed in. He noticed that in forty-five minutes he'd gotten a clearer picture of how his people experienced their challenges than he had in his entire first quarter.

"I appreciate what you brought up today," he said, noticing that people seemed vaguely at loose ends. This had not been a standard meeting.

"We apparently have some opportunities for streamlining what we do—and in the process make everybody happier." Then he added with a chuckle, "I'll take that," which seemed to lighten the energy in the room.

"So, here's the deal. I want several well-thought-out scenarios which will solve the problems you brought to light. I'd like to see a sub-group who'll work on best-case scenarios identifying the real or potential obstacles. Get creative with consulting the rest of the team or whoever else you think is a resource for ideas to first identify, then reduce or remove obstacles. Who's willing to work on this and get me something substantive no later than in, let's say, seven work days?"

Several hands shot up. The previous manager had never asked for help with identifying problems never mind designing solutions.

"Who's willing to take the lead?" Nobody volunteered.

"I didn't ask who *wanted* to take the lead," Sam said in a matter of fact tone of voice. "You may not want to. Maybe you're worried that you might do a poor job or fail. I got it. But I want you to put that aside. I suggest you consider this a project we take on because we're committed to continuous improvement."

Sam let his words sink in then added, "It's evident to me how committed all of you are to our clients. If you weren't, you wouldn't have brought this up. So look and see if you're the point person on this. One way you can tell is if you're *willing* to do it even if at this moment you don't want to."

He looked around the room, somehow confident that a leader would emerge. Sam noticed with both satisfaction and detachment that he had put the distinction between "wanting'" and "being willing" into practice.

"I'll do it," Joe said, turning to those who had raised their hands. "I'll get with you guys after this meeting to talk about next steps."

A trace of a smile was the only sign of Sam's pleasure. Joe didn't look so aimless now. Sam thought he might have to remind himself often that "Things aren't always as they seem."

"Thanks, Joe. Thanks everyone."

People filed out of the room talking. Sam watched them go, filled with amazement—not only about Joe's leadership, but also about what else the meeting had revealed: his direct reports were not clear about their jobs, and they didn't have tools they thought they needed.

But what fascinated Sam most of all was the quality of the meeting. After their initial risk-averse behaviors, they had been forthcoming. Russell's flippant tone had vanished. Sam was convinced they had leveled with him and had foregone the usual "cover your ass" behavior. What accounted for *that*? He crossed his intended meeting with Joe off his to-do list. He didn't need it anymore.

He looked at his yellow note pad where prior to this *un*usual meeting he had written down some questions for his team. But he was more interested in the five words he had put in the top left-hand margin. *Courageous, clear, open, receptive,* and *truthful* were the attributes he had chosen to demonstrate at this meeting. He recalled the butterflies in his stomach as he had thought about the meeting. "I really need to call on these qualities, if this meeting has a chance of being extraordinary," he remembered thinking.

Sam was struck that he had actually exhibited behavior that was outside his comfort zone. He had been direct and clear in stating what he wanted from the team. He had asked questions that he really wanted the team's input on. When he got the input, some of it difficult to accept, he had listened with respect, without trying to change anybody's point of view. "I was truthful, courageous, clear, open, and receptive," he concluded.

"I was different, and they were different too!" he kept saying to himself, doing mental somersaults in celebration. His being different had to have something to do with it. He couldn't wait to talk to Coach Zabar about it.

"I got it! Dammit. I got it! Yep, I got it!" played like a chant in his mind. He got the 'C' in the COSA process. He knew what the fuss was about. It really *was* big! His experience was proof.

It was almost time to go home, but Sam found it impossible to leave. He grabbed the phone and pressed extension 6021. It belonged to the third name on the list of four great managers he got from Coach Zabar's office. "Tom Pierot," he heard, and introduced himself. "Come on over" was the reply.

†*†*✝*†*†

Five minutes later Sam stood in front of a bald, six-foot man with a boyish face and a fifty-ish body. Tom Pierot had managed the marketing department for many years. He had a reputation for being tough and for getting results.

"Thanks for seeing me," said Sam. "I appreciate your time. This *un*-game is really something, isn't it?"

"Yes indeed," said Tom, with a smile in his voice. "You've *un*covered a few rules other managers follow but great managers ignore, have you?"

"I have, and I'm jazzed about that. But right now I'm even more jazzed about the COSA process. I finally get it about the 'C.'" Sam recounted the story about his meeting and how having chosen five qualities had produced the extraordinary result. "I said I'd be those qualities, and I was," he said with pride.

"That was lucky."

"What do you mean, lucky?" said Sam, immediately suspicious.

"Could you actually guarantee that you'd demonstrate the qualities that you chose?"

After a pause Sam replied thoughtfully, "No, I suppose I can't really guarantee it."

"What, if anything, *can* you guarantee?"

Sam was silent, struggling to come up with an answer.

"What are you seeing?"

"Well, if I'm choosing, then I do that freely. So..." Sam looked pensive. He leaned back in the chair. "Hmm, so I *can* guarantee that I'm *willing* to be truthful, courageous, clear, and so on."

"Good, Sam. That's important. It won't always turn out your way, and if you thought you had to demonstrate those things, you'd turn a marvelous, powerful principle into a rule. That would take the power out of the principle."

Sam thought about what Tom had said. Coach Zabar and the managers he'd visited were so precise, so clear. 'Clear' was one of those qualities on the list he and his coach had *un*covered. Sam decided it would be one of his favorites to choose. It seemed to him that it all began with clarity.

"So it sounds like you had a very important conversation with your team on many levels," said Tom. "Is there anything else you want to say about that?"

"Yes, thanks. I'm pumped about the process improvement I'm going to get. And the team will own the process because they're leading it. But it also became apparent to me that my team members are *un*clear about their job. They all can have their own notion of what support is. They didn't seem to know how it was going to be measured. There are performance standards attached to their job descriptions, but they're not actively trying to demonstrate them."

"Can you give me an example of a performance standard?"

"Yes. For example, they're supposed to use the customer's name in their conversation with them. They're pretty spotty about that. Another one is to smile because people can hear a smile over the phone."

Tom nodded. "Yes, those are pretty standard expectations, but they just don't work. Look and see if you can give me some loopholes in the thinking that would use the support staff's smiles as a measurement for excellent support."

Sam scanned his experience. "I know when people call, they're often agitated. Smiling could be seen as not taking their concern seriously. It could be interpreted as callous and disrespectful. I hadn't thought of it like that."

"Yes, and how many times have you been a customer yourself, and the sales or support person just kept using your name over and over again? What was that like?"

"Crappy. I felt manipulated most times. Like it's not real. They're just doing it because in their training it said to do it."

"Right. So what are you seeing about this?"

"It seems that there ought to be a better way to set expectations than to outline the desired behaviors and define the steps the employee should take to get to the desired results."

"I agree. So what comes up for you when you consider that?"

"Well," replied Sam and stopped.

"That's a very deep subject," teased the older manager, his grin fitting his boyish face. Sam's thought that Tom was using this well-worn joke to lighten things up was confirmed by his next statement.

> Great managers are clear about setting expectations, but they do it by defining the right outcomes, not by defining the right steps.

"It's a serious subject, but we don't have to take ourselves too seriously, do we?" Without waiting for an answer Tom asked, "What do you want customers to feel like after they get off the phone with any one of you?"

"Like a million bucks on a whole lot less."

"Spoken like a great manager, Sam. If you do as you propose, you'll be developing performance standards that demonstrate customers experiencing your services as worth a million bucks when they pay a whole lot less! You'll be among the great managers who ignore the rules lesser managers follow. Great managers are clear about setting expectations, but they do it by defining the right outcomes, not by defining the right steps. *And*," he added, "they don't hide behind the assertion that some outcomes can't be defined. Yes, they can!" Tom was obviously passionate about what he had just said.

"I'm all over that," said Sam, trying to disguise…just a little…the pleasure he experienced at the older manager's compliment. "That would give me a lot of breathing room, and I bet it would give my people breathing room too. They could do it their own way, so long as they produced the right outcome."

He hesitated for a moment, trying to organize his unruly thoughts.

"Come to think of it, I just did exactly that! I just told my team what outcome I wanted regarding this process improvement they're working on. I didn't tell them how to do it!" Sam's face was one large smile as he looked at Tom.

"Good for you," said Tom. "You mentioned 'breathing room.' Look and see what's present for you when you experience what you call 'breathing room.'"

"I just feel energized and motivated. As if I can come up with answers that are unique. They're mine. And they're good," replied Sam. "And that's going to be true for everybody on my team. They're no different. Their unique contribution can come out, because each one of them would be working from their strengths and not try to squeeze themselves into a one-size-fits-all set of behaviors which might play to their weaknesses. The one-size-fits-all stuff would be very de-motivating."

Sam picked up speed. "And that means I wouldn't have to remediate, fix, cajole, whatever. I'm not in the business of controlling or correcting. I can be what I'm supposed to be—a catalyst! That's way more fun!"

"Aha," said Tom, laughing. His fifty-ish middle jiggled *un*self-consciously. "You're getting the hang that management can be a game, eh?"

"Yeah, I can tell Coach Zabar I'm having fun the next time she asks that question," grinned Sam.

Sam was thrilled with this new awareness. Conventional wisdom defines one of a manager's core activities as selecting a person for a job based on experience, intelligence and grit. What he'd learned from Marguerite Chan was that great managers don't ignore experience, but they look more for talent when they select a person for a job. That was especially cool because it gave young people like him a chance. Provided that he was talented, of course, which he was beginning to think might be more than just his fantasy on steroids.

The second core activity was about setting expectations. Sam had just learned from Tom Pierot that poor, average, and even good managers generally set expectations by defining the right steps. Great managers, on the other hand, set expectations by defining the right outcomes. And that made the third core activity, motivating, infinitely easier. Sam was certain of it from his team meeting of just an hour ago. In that meeting he had been deliberate in listening—not criticizing and correcting. In reviewing what his team members had said, the possibility that motivating them had something to do with focusing on their strengths rather than on helping them identify and overcome their weaknesses became a probability. It had extraordinary implications.

> Conventional wisdom defines one of a manager's core activities as selecting a person for a job based on experience, intelligence and grit. Great managers don't ignore experience, but they look more for talent when they select a person for a job.

Sam looked at his watch. It seemed an eternity ago that he had walked into Tom Pierot's office. The building had emptied out. Sam tore himself away. "Before I go," he said, "I know we can't talk about both these things any more today, but just tell me two things. As a manager it's also my job to develop my people. Conventional wisdom tells me I should help my people get promoted. Do great managers do that?"

"Not necessarily. And the second thing?"

The "not necessarily" without further explanation took Sam by surprise, but he recovered quickly. "What can you tell me about the 'O' in the COSA process before I make another appointment with Coach Zabar?"

"I can tell you a lot of things, but they wouldn't make a difference." Tom said this cheerfully.

"Why not?" Sam blurted out.

"Let me ask you something," said Tom, ignoring Sam's question. "How did you make your '*un*coveries' in your conversations with Coach Zabar and the managers on her list?" He emphasized the word "*un*coveries."

"They asked questions, and I thought about…" Sam left his sentence *un*finished.

"No," he corrected himself. "I looked for answers without thinking."

"What specifically *did* you do?"

"I looked into my experience and then saw stuff that led me to the answers. So I'd say I observed. I took a look from the position of an observer." He remembered being complimented by Coach Zabar for having made excellent observations. "So," he ventured, "the 'O' stands for OBSERVE, doesn't it?" Sam looked to the older man for confirmation.

"Indeed it does, Sam. Indeed it does. And now it's time to eat. The hell with observing." He laughed that impish laugh and waved Sam away. Sam took no offense. It wasn't hard to tell Tom liked him.

After thanking Tom and shaking his hand vigorously, Sam walked to the door with a purposeful stride. Before opening it he turned around. "Thank you," he said again. "You've made my life a lot easier today." He saw Tom's eyes light up. Then he closed the door on the meeting. But not on the possibilities that flooded his mind and heart.

Dear Reader

1. Do you recall a conversation which opened your eyes to
    new and exciting possibilities? What makes that specific
    conversation memorable for you?
2. Have you had situations at work or at home where you were
    *un*clear about what was expected of you? What did you do to
    resolve the tension? In what ways was your strategy successful?
    *Un*successful?
3. The young manager clearly is a talented observer. On a scale
    of 1 to 10, how important do you think this ability is for people
    who are managers? Why did you choose your number?

Chapter 6

FIRST MEETING OF THE *UN*-TEAM

W hen Sam left the office he decided to have a quiet
dinner alone. He wanted to replay his team meeting
and the coaching conversations that had led up to it. It
seemed like such a roller coaster ride. In the space of a few days he
had gone from the depths of despair—well, maybe not quite that
bad—to the sweet anticipation of infinite possibilities. He needed
some time to cool his over-heated brain.

After dinner he stopped at the bookstore to have a latte and just
walk around. He thought about COSA and how effective his team
meeting had been after taking Step One—choosing qualities he was
willing to demonstrate.

"I wonder if coaches have meetings to discuss the people they're
coaching." Sam pictured Coach Zabar and the managers discussing
him. Preferring to be thought of as modest, he was glad his
thoughts were his own rather than flashing on a neon billboard.
What he didn't know was that the managers and Coach Zabar *did*
meet to discuss their new "great-managers-in-training," as they
sometimes referred to them.

Sam finished his latte and walked home, still envisioning Coach
Zabar and the managers in a lively discussion of the next generation
of great L-4 managers, the greatest of all being him, of course. But

he knew nothing of next day's real meeting in Coach Zabar's office where he would be discussed.

⁎⁎⁎⁎⁎

"All right, then, let's start the meeting," said Coach Zabar, motioning the assembled to take their seats. Present were Peter Black, Marguerite Chan, and Tom Pierot, all the managers their protégé Sam Adler had already visited. Maria Nordstern, the human resources manager, was there too. Sam had met her during his hiring process.

"Who am I willing to be in order to make an extraordinary contribution to this meeting?" began Coach Zabar. She then listed five qualities beginning with "I'm willing to be." Each member of the assembled group of great managers did the same. Then the coach asked a few other questions, each of which she and the group answered in unison with a strong "yes."

If Sam had been privy to the meeting, he would have assessed it all as a bit surreal. Upon reflection he might have observed, however, that the questions the coach asked were related to the COSA process. They clearly invited those present to be in their hero's heart—in the ontological space, that is. They chose five qualities from a list he would have recognized. With a few additions they were the qualities he and Coach Zabar had generated together in their last session.

"OK, *Un*-team," said Coach Zabar with affection. "As a way of starting our review of the great managers-in-training, let's just remind ourselves of our very own chatty little internal critic— monkey mind. Don't you just love that descriptor? And the fact that we're not immune to its mischief?" She laughed amiably.

"Suppose we go around the room and identify our game-wrecker monkey mind chatter. It'll help keep us humble. I suspect it may be helpful to remind us that we're all a work in progress, and that our commitment is to a learning environment in which each of us, no matter where we are on our path, can continually improve. Let's hear it for progress, not perfection."

The group nodded, and an "indeed" and a "right on" could be heard. They went around the circle beginning with Peter Black. Sam Adler would have been astonished to hear what came next.

"The monkey mind chatter that takes me out of my game is 'I'm stupid.' It just makes me crazy and I forget everything," the quality control manager with the laugh wrinkles said with a flare.

"Mine is around when I'm not sure," said self-assured Marguerite, the programming manager. "It makes me nuts, and I get obsessive about getting certainty instead of keeping my eye on what's important."

"For me it's when I'm dead certain there's something wrong with me," said the jolly marketing manager, Tom Pierot.

"And for me it's when I'm convinced that people are jerks. When that happens I just want to go home and either kick something or somebody, or pull the covers over my head." As she delivered that comment, Maria Nordstern, whose appearance some thought matronly, looked anything but.

> We're all a work in progress, and our commitment is to a learning environment in which each of us, no matter where we are on our path, can continually improve. Let's hear it for progress, not perfection.

"What takes me out of my game, as you all well know, is when I'm having an 'I can't' fit," reported Coach Zabar, laughing. "It isn't pretty since I really have to prove that I can, and my driven behavior makes people want to give me a wide berth. And, *Un*-team," she said after a brief pause, "is that chatter ever going to go away?"

"No," shouted the group in unison.

"But you want it to go away, don't you?" Coach Zabar knew what was coming.

"Oh yes, oh yes. Oh, please, Coach. Can't you make it go away?" The group's exaggerated pleading ended in roaring laughter.

"You're having entirely too much fun." Coach Zabar's mock criticism only prolonged the laughter. She became serious as she continued. "Aren't we all grateful for the *un*-game that allows us to *un*learn so many things—like thinking we can actually get rid of our monkey mind. Instead we're learning to use it to do good. Let's just acknowledge ourselves for that."

Coach Zabar's voice was gentle and her words warm. "You are *un*commonly courageous and compassionate," she told the group. They smiled in appreciation and looked expectantly at their coach. We'll use our usual process to review each candidate and to see if action might be called for. Are we on the same page?"

Everyone nodded. "Let's start with Sam Adler from Customer Support," said Coach Zabar. "Isn't he just the best? I really like him. My sense is that he's definitely a long-term, viable candidate." The group agreed.

Maria joined in, clearly pleased with herself. "So I did pretty good in helping select young Sam, eh?" There were nods and smiles all around.

"Let's take stock. Has he gotten the CHOOSE in COSA at the level of principle, or is it still academic for him?" asked Coach Zabar.

"I saw him just yesterday after a team-meeting he was jazzed about," said Tom. "I think it's now in his DNA. He experienced not only the power of the choice he made for this team meeting, but that he can do it again. A lot of people don't ever get what an incredible power that is and that it's theirs to call upon at will."

"Yes. That's my sense about him too. In our second session I got that he saw possibilities to use the qualities of being like a compass. I told him the 'wolf you feed' story," reported the coach.

"Does he get the difference between the ontological and the psychological self?" asked Maria.

"Not at the level of effective action. He'll need to get beyond the conceptual level. But he's aware that those qualities of being come from a different place in us, and that it's a place *un*affected by circumstances in his outside world," responded Tom.

"I agree," said the coach. "He's on his way. As a Joseph Campbell fan, he understands we all have the potential to be more than psychological beings ruled by our emotions. He gets Campbell's hero archetype, so the door is already open for him to see that we can all be heroes—when we accept our psychological selves, but choose at the same time to also access the higher self that is so much more mysterious to us."

"I'm glad to hear that, Sophia," said Tom. "I have no hard evidence for what I'm about to say. My sense is that for Sam people are either at the mercy of their feelings, or they deny them in order to act rationally. As we know, both scenarios constrain. They don't allow for authentic, powerful action. And for Sam Adler, authentic, powerful action is a coveted prize."

"You're on the money, Tom. The ability to exercise conscious choice in order to call forth qualities of being is a new possibility for Sam. To act in alignment with those chosen qualities rather than blindly following societal dictates becomes much more likely as well. I suspect he loves having an actual list of qualities of being, which he got with the wolf story I told him and by reviewing the work you all did with him."

"Well," said Tom, "he demonstrated the qualities he chose in his team meeting yesterday, and he got some results he wouldn't normally have gotten—such as his team having a pretty *un*guarded conversation with him. And they willingly took on a process-improvement project. He didn't manipulate them. They own the project."

Coach Zabar nodded. "Great. So let's talk about Sam's strengths before we consider what might be next as he moves his attention to the 'O' in COSA. What do you see as his strengths?"

"Well, he's eager for the coaching. He dislikes ambiguity of course. While it makes him *un*comfortable, he's nevertheless quick to search out his lessons. I like that a lot about him," said Peter Black.

"And he's resilient," Peter continued. "He goes up and down, waxes hot and cold, but keeps coming back. He's able to regain his focus. We need resilience like Sam's in these times of cataclysmic change. *I* sure need it." Peter knew well that quality can suffer during times of dramatic change.

"And he has a keen sense of language and making distinctions in language. I think he speaks German and French fluently, and some Spanish," offered Maria Nordstern as she recalled her Sam Adler file and her interview with him.

Peter said, "He hung in there with me as we teased out the distinction of 'discovering' and '*un*covering,' even though he wasn't clear how that would be useful to him."

"He's a quick study," said Tom, remembering how alert, attentive, and observant Sam had been. Several of the others nodded.

"I see him as quite determined," offered Marguerite. "He goes after what he wants. He really wants to be a great manager and learn whatever it takes. I like his being willing to be vulnerable and ask questions. I bet that's not how he was the first time he saw you, Sophia. And he's got the makings of a sense of humor," she added, recalling Sam's comment about having an "I don't wanna" fit.

"You're right, Marguerite. He was quite guarded in our first session. But now I'm impressed with Sam's enthusiasm and commitment," said Coach Zabar. "I've rarely seen someone who's as focused on acting in alignment with his words. He's going to make that his number one priority, I suspect. That will make him a brilliant coaching client for us and a huge asset for L-4 now and down the line. And yes, he's a quick study. He demonstrated being able to shift his focus, for example. Plus he consciously applied some of what he had learned. You all have been doing a great job in helping him make distinctions that will support him in doing really well with the OBSERVE part of COSA," she added, smiling at her protégés.

They returned their coach's smile.

The group was comfortably silent. "What are some of his challenges?" the coach asked.

Marguerite was quick to respond. "His budding sense of humor notwithstanding, he takes himself quite seriously. It's likely that his standards around perfection and his own performance will get in his way of achieving the level of performance he wants, unless he becomes adept in observing his monkey mind."

"Yes, he's eager. That's good, *and* it may get in his way as he worries about being judged negatively. But we should be able to make that visible to him. He'll get beyond it," remarked Peter.

"I agree," said the coach. "He's hard on himself. And mostly he sees that as a plus."

"His other challenge, of course, is his show-stopper monkey mind chatter," offered Tom.

"What do you think is the monkey mind conversation that takes Sam out of *his* game?" asked the coach.

There was some laughter among the *un*-team. "It's too early to tell. We'll know better at our next meeting. All I have are my suspicions—and we know what they're worth," said Tom, grinning broadly.

"OK then, let's move on to tools he has, so that we can give him what might be next."

For the next ten minutes the group reviewed what they had contributed: the distinction between "wanting" and "being willing," "discovering" and "*un*covering," the psychological and ontological self as demonstrated by the 'C'—CHOOSE , and the metaphor of monkey mind as the self-limiting chatter that tests the hero's heart.

They also listed some of the *un*examined assumptions—also known as rules that great managers ignore or break—that Sam had been exposed to in conversation with them. Sometimes it was only a surface reference. Sometimes they reported a deeper conversation around the assumptions. The assumptions list was as follows:

Conventional *Un*examined Assumptions
- Managers should control and correct.
- You can reach your dreams if only you try hard enough.
- People need to be given good answers. They don't have their own.
- The American call to quick action is normal and every culture's "driver."
- Managers should select employees based on their experience, intelligence, and will.
- There's one best way to perform each role.
- Some outcomes defy definition.
- Employees should follow required steps to insure customer satisfaction.
- Managers should develop their people so that they can be promoted.

"Sam did pretty well, given we have three more steps in the COSA process. I would have never gotten all that in such a short a period of time," said Peter Black.

"Why? Because you're stupid?" teased Maria Nordstern. They all laughed at the reference to Peter's game-wrecker monkey mind chatter.

"Peter, the only conventional assumption he's challenged deeply is 'Managers should control and correct.' The rest we've just touched on. They still live as concepts for him. But the door to reflection and observation is open. Let's move on," said the coach.

"All right, getting back to the rules great managers ignore, are there any particular rules we wish he would *un*cover in future conversations?" asked Tom Pierot.

"Yeah, but you know we don't lead. He does," responded the

coach. "This is like a dance, remember?" She smiled. "But it's not the Texas two-step. It's more like a Judith Jameson's Alvin Ailey Dance Company dance."

Marguerite looked *un*comprehendingly at the coach. Peter and Maria both burst out laughing. Maria finally said, "That dates *you*, Sophia. I bet Marguerite, being so young, doesn't even know Judith Jameson. She's about sixty now," Maria reminded the coach.

"Oh well, I made my point," said the coach, taking the jab in good spirits. "When Judith Jameson dances with a partner, Marguerite," she explained, "they create a rich story together. There appears to be nothing predictable about it, except that one partner influences the other. Not *un*like our coaching." It was obvious the *un*-team was enjoying themselves, each other, and the work.

"Yeah, but humor me," Tom Pierot insisted. "Just name a few rules. I want to be ready in case I see them lurking in Sam's conversation. They brainstormed some of their favorite rules to ignore. The list included:

- Managers should not play favorites.
- Managers do things right. Leaders do the right things.
- People work for companies.
- Talents are rare and special.
- Excellence is zero defects.
- People are broken and need to be fixed.
- Treat people like you'd like to be treated.
- The shortest distance between two points is a straight line.
- No news is good news.
- People need to be promoted to stay motivated.

"Now I know I don't need to say this to you, but it makes me feel better. Don't try to force any of these in your eagerness to be supportive. It's only support when the 'supportee' says it is," the coach warned. "Don't try to make things happen. Allow them to happen."

"What else would we do, Coach? We're catalysts not controllers, remember?" Maria Nordstern got up and put her arms around the coach. "Relax, Sophia. We know how much you care. Who taught us to remember that all is well? Oh, it was our master coach," she said with an exaggerated emphasis on the word "coach." "Now I remember." She smiled sweetly, and everyone laughed.

"Thanks, Coach Maria." The master coach smiled gratefully. "Before we close the meeting today," she continued, "I want to talk about two more things. The first is about the second step in the COSA process, 'O' for OBSERVE. Does anyone have anything to say about that?"

"I think Sam's well positioned to go into the OBSERVE part of COSA," said Tom. "He's clear about Step One—CHOOSE. He's coachable and *un*likely to get hopelessly mired in his feelings. He's willing and able to focus away from them when coached, and he's already demonstrated good observation skills. In addition he has a strong need for knowing. My guess is he'll come after the coaching with a vengeance. Obviously he's already done that a time or two."

"Nothing for me really," said Maria. "As you said, the client leads, the coach follows. I think we can all make a contribution." The other three *un*-team members agreed.

"OK, and the second item before we move to our next great manager-in-training, Samantha Osler, is support. Is there any way we can offer appropriate support to Sam at this point in his development?" The coach scanned the group for responses.

"Why not offer to connect our two Sams—Sam to Samantha," Peter suggested. "They could be accountability partners and reinforce what they're learning. It'll support both of them. After all, future conversations with both these managers are surely going to include support."

"That's a great idea," said Marguerite. "Sophia, will you take care of that?"

"Yes. I'll look for an opportunity to suggest it," agreed the coach. Their attention turned to Samantha Osler, the second manager on their list.

Had he listened in, the meeting would have seemed a bit lax to Sam, and certainly *un*conventional. His thoughts would likely have been something like "The client leading and the coach following? What kind of coaching was that? And offering a support partner didn't sound like much of a conventional development plan."

*Un*conventional? Yes. Lax? Some would say so. The *un*-team, however, was satisfied with their meeting. *Un*conventional wisdom was all part of the *un*-game, they would probably say. And then they would laugh merrily.

Dear Reader

1. Coach Zabar and the great managers make a big deal out
    of the 'C' – CHOOSE in the four-step COSA process that
    *un*leashes a manager's power to produce *un*common results. If
    you agree that choosing qualities you wish to demonstrate in
    challenging situations is a powerful act, be prepared to back
    up your assertion. Can you recall a work situation in which
    you consciously did that? If not, will you experiment? What
    qualities would you choose that would make success for your
    experiment more likely? Is this process of choosing who one is
    willing to be limited to managers, or is this skill-set transferable
    to personal situations?
2. Some people find it extremely difficult to choose qualities of
    being and then measure their actions against those qualities
    to see if their walk and their talk are a match. What skill must
    people cultivate in order to make the process less difficult?
3. Coach Zabar asks her team for their assessment of Sam
    Adler's strengths and challenges, or his areas for growth. In
    conventional settings some of Sam's "challenges" might be
    considered assets, for example, being hard on himself. Some
    of his "strengths," such as his willingness to be vulnerable,
    might be considered liabilities. Where can you align with
    the team? Where do your assessments differ? Will Sam be a
    great manager in the rapidly changing corporation of the 21st
    century? Or will you withhold judgment until you see how he
    handles himself in the other three steps of the COSA process?

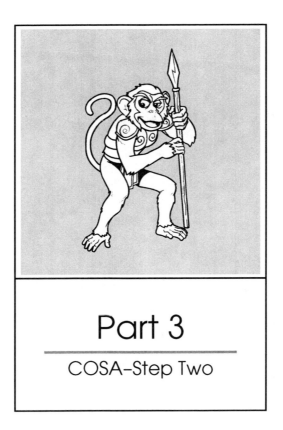

Part 3

COSA–Step Two

Chapter 7

THE POWER POINT

S am was to see Coach Zabar at 10 o'clock. Could he hang on to what he had learned? He could clearly see that the CHOOSE step of the COSA process was powerful when he felt *un*restrained by doubts and worries. But what about when he felt weak and vulnerable? He'd always been able to put up a good front. That was the norm in corporate America. He knew he looked calm as a duck on a still pond. Yeah, right—if people only knew he was paddling like hell underneath. Things are not always as they seem.

Sam felt weak and vulnerable when he didn't know something he thought he should know. It made him nervous. He was a little nervous now. But his curiosity and desire to be a great manager trumped his discomfort. He thought about some of his favorite authors and management experts: Block, Blanchard, Peters, Senge. He speculated that all of them would agree that self-observation in the face of self-doubt is important. They would support corporate norms that encouraged the authenticity that becomes possible through accurate self-assessment. Authenticity—feared as much as it is desired—actually provides a much needed experience of safety. You know where you stand. Sam decided that authenticity may be the prize of competent self-observation.

When Sam was nervous he had a penchant for theorizing. He still had a little time before his session. His musings shifted to a global perspective. "In a time of shifting global paradigms there are so many *un*knowns," he thought. "Would present business practices survive the 21st century demands? If business has to reinvent itself—and it *does*—the reinvention begins with the individual. And COSA, with its emphasis on self-observation, was a source of solid support and power." Sam didn't notice, but his thinking had already expanded beyond the customer support department woes that had so completely absorbed his energy until recently.

Closer to home again, Sam recalled some of the stories he and his Wharton friends traded about managers from hell. They were certain then they'd never be one of those. But that was before he'd started with the coaching. Surely he wouldn't see the situation differently now, would he? He thought about the quality control manager he'd had in a previous job. Every day this guy did "a little coaching" on quality control. He talked about the importance of quality and said all the right things. But then he went back to his real job—getting product out the door. He couldn't understand why the product-quality record in his department was so bad.

"People are boss-watchers," Sam thought. They knew that in order to get product out the door when the pressure was on, this manager ignored some scratches or minor defects. Needless to say, his actions spoke louder than his words.

"Did this guy have a clue how powerful a teacher he'd been for the boss-watchers?" Sam concluded that this clueless manager, not to mention the company, was paying a high price for his blindness. Self-observation would call into question this manager's staunch assertion that his commitment to quality was a ten. Sam imagined him saying, "It's X or it's Y. It's not my fault. If only…"

Sam had heard "It's not my fault" labeled as the shadow side of innocence. He liked the term. When people have a vested interest in staying asleep—in staying *un*conscious because being awake would be too painful, too inconvenient, or too perturbing—that is an example of the shadow side of innocence.

Sam came by his philosophizing naturally. His family not only routinely talked about literature, philosophy, sociology, psychology, economics and world events, but made links from them to their own lives. Being conscious, responsible global citizens was important to Sam's immigrant parents.

Sam remembered one animated dinner table discussion in which his father had criticized Americans, who only represent five percent of the world's population but blithely use twenty-five percent of the world's resources. "Waking up to that inequity would be too inconvenient, too perturbing for many Americans," his German father asserted. Sam saw parallels to the quality control manager and his *un*conscious behavior.

He looked at his watch. Time to make a note of what he wanted to ask Coach Zabar. He was sure that self-awareness was a skill great managers needed. "Where do *I* need greater self-awareness?"

> When people have a vested interest in staying asleep—in staying *un*conscious because being awake would be too painful, too inconvenient, or too perturbing—that is an example of the shadow side of innocence.

he wondered. His thoughts went to one last disturbing story he'd heard from a Wharton friend just a few weeks ago.

This story was particularly meaningful for Sam because the story's villain supervisor was, like him, in charge of customer support. Relationships with key internal customers were strained. There were breakdowns and inefficiencies. The supervisor had family problems that spilled over into her work. The support team members saw themselves mostly as fire fighters. "Team" was really an inaccurate description. Even a casual observer would not have called them a team.

The supervisor held important information close to the vest. Rumors that her yearly performance review resulted in a largely ignored development plan were confirmed. She gossiped, running roughshod over a core company value. The situation was dire. Confrontation, the one thing that was absolutely necessary and long overdue, had not been initiated.

The boss-watchers were all saying, "What the hell are they waiting for?" And their own performance tanked. Morale was in the basement.

It was rumored that the boss, who sometimes joked about managing with benign neglect, said he was waiting for the right time to confront the ineffective supervisor. Kindness and compassion supposedly drove that decision.

"Why was he *un*able to see that kindness and compassion had nothing to do with it?" Sam thought. The manager's bad decision came from his desire to satisfy personal needs without regard to the moral consequences. Simple as that. If comfort and courage were waging a war, comfort would be the winner. Truth, as always, was the first casualty of war. The manager couldn't tell the truth.

"Self-awareness gained from self-observation surely would have made for a different outcome in this story," Sam concluded. He would have been able to find a way to be truly kind and compassionate to the errant supervisor—for example, by having regular meetings with her to discuss progress toward specific goals, or even finding a position for her which was a more natural fit. Nothing will change in that scenario until the manager is able to see with new eyes."

He'd ask Coach Zabar about that. Time for his coaching session. Outwardly he was calm, but inside he was on high alert, ready to take the next step in the COSA process. Five minutes later he was seated in Coach Zabar's office.

"Good morning, Coach. How are you?"

"Just fine, Sam. How goes it with you?" The coach seemed glad to see him.

"Great. Can I ask you a question?" Sam wanted every minute of his hour to count.

"This is your time. Go ahead. What's on your mind?"

"You said that choosing attributes or qualities of being comes from a different place than the rational mind, namely from our hero's heart—from the ontological space. How does that square with someone who says, for example, he's compassionate by not confronting an ineffective supervisor? According to him he's waiting for the right opportunity. It has never come, by the way. So it seems to me he's fooling himself, and his 'compassion' isn't really…chosen. Do you know what I mean?"

Coach Zabar smiled and replied, "Why don't we each take a deep breath and choose some qualities we're willing to be?"

Sam was struck by her response, especially that she was going to choose qualities too, but he took out his notes. He was ready. When the coach asked, "Who am I willing to be in order to make an extraordinary contribution right here, right now during this session?" she immediately followed with, "I'm willing to be present, clear, appreciative, empowering, and supportive."

"I'm willing to be clear, focused, receptive, courageous, and open," said Sam. His voice sounded strong.

"What do you notice about having chosen your qualities?"

"Hmm. I notice that I'm truly willing to be those qualities."

"Different from 'I'm willing to be petty, fearful, stingy, hateful, and obstructive'?" The coach smiled.

"For sure. Anything I'd do coming from those qualities would have failure written all over it. I'd just be following my feelings. And that's actually what I worry about. Some feelings just shouldn't be expressed in action."

"Is this what we'll coach on?"

Sam thought it odd that the decision was left up to him.

"Yes. I want to learn about what I'm not seeing about these managers. I just get mad every time I think about them," he replied, not missing a beat.

"What makes you mad?"

"The support manager just flat out lies to himself. Admitting he doesn't have the guts to do what has to be done is too much for him, I think. Instead of confronting an incompetent supervisor, he's hiding behind his all-too-generous assessment that he's compassionate!"

"What do you notice about how you're seeing this manager?"

"I think he's a jerk and a coward. And that's being kind."

"That's an interesting judgment. How are you experiencing your energy right now?"

This was not going the way Sam had expected it.

"I'm irritated you aren't agreeing with me."

"Look and see what's so important about my agreement."

Not wanting to respond, Sam nevertheless said, "I'd feel validated."

"Can you see a parallel between you and the manager you criticize?"

Sam was stunned. He wanted to say, "What the hell do you mean? There's no parallel between that jerk and me!" But he took a deep breath and tried with moderate success to *un*clench his jaw.

"So what just happened between the time I asked you the question and now? You seemed very irritated, and now you appear less so," Coach Zabar asked, narrowing her eyes as she looked at Sam.

"I was really pissed off. I strongly dislike that manager. I have no respect for what he does and doesn't do. Then I remembered choosing 'courageous' as one of the qualities I was willing to demonstrate in this session. It was hard to think that he and I have anything in common, but I was willing to look. What I saw was that the manager wants to feel validated too—just like me. He just chooses different means. He validates himself by describing himself as a good guy even though he's doing things that aren't in the interest of his department. That's really very interesting."

"What makes that interesting?"

"Well, I came in here concerned about strong feelings like those that blinded that manager. And then, before I saw that he and I aren't so different, my feelings almost got the better of me. Finally I saw that he and I both just want to be validated. You brought it back to what's important, namely seeing there's a lesson for me and not for the manager who pisses me off."

"There might be a lesson for that manager, but *you*'re here for coaching. He's not. Would it be all right with you to know that everyone wants to be validated?"

Coach Zabar's words lingered in the silence that followed.

"Yeah," Sam replied, almost to himself. "But you better be aware of it so you can manage it and not let it manage *you*!"

"Well said." The coach looked at Sam with smiling eyes. "OK, Mr. Adler," she said. "You've come to the right place for some tools to prevent you from being a feather blowing in the wind of your feelings. And you've just had an experience in which you were the wind rather than the feather. Can you see how that happened, besides trying to demonstrate some qualities you chose from your hero's heart?"

Sam was pleased to see hear himself referred to as the wind rather than a feather, although it continued to jar his brain to hear phrases like "hero's heart" and "feather blowing in the wind" bandied around in L-4.

"You asked me questions that had me look at what I was thinking and experiencing right then and there—what was important to me about your agreement, for example," he answered, looking straight at the coach.

"Very good. So the questions had you observe your experience. Observe, rather than...?" The incomplete sentence hung in the air.

Sam looked at the coach, his mind racing.

"Observe rather than analyze," he responded. "Wow. That's a really important distinction. And it's the 'O' in COSA—OBSERVE.

There's power in observing." He let that thought sink in.

"You got it. Would you like to have some tools that will make it easier for you to observe—so that you may *have* your feelings rather than worrying your feelings will have *you*?"

"For sure. That would be a relief. Being subject to my feelings and being a great manager are probably mutually exclusive."

"Yes, Sam. Keep that in mind when the going gets tough." The coach paused as if searching for another thought.

> We aren't our psychology, that is, we aren't our thoughts, beliefs, opinions, conclusions, and body sensations. And that's excellent news—except people are in a fog about it. They agree it's true but say, "Well, that's just how I am. I'm hot-headed."

"People are psychological beings," she said, having found it. "That means we have feelings, thoughts, and body sensations that influence our decision-making. Some thoughts are rational; many are not. We're hard-wired that way. We have no choice about it. And anyone who thinks they can keep people's feelings off the corporate playing field is woefully naïve.

"The good news is that we *have* a psychology. As psychological beings we are subject to ruminating and to asking 'why.' These questions get us off track and bog us down. Still, no matter how convinced we are to the contrary, we *aren't* our psychology, that is, we aren't our thoughts, beliefs, opinions, conclusions, and body sensations that have such sway over our emotions. And that's excellent news—except people are in a fog about it. They agree it's true but say, 'Well, that's just how I am. I'm hot-headed.' Or, 'I'm kind and compassionate' like the manager you described."

"True enough," Sam thought and added aloud, "Yes, and that usually ends any real conversation you can have with them."

"Indeed," replied the coach. "If you think you are a certain way, then that's it. End of story. Unless you've had the kind of experience you had just a moment ago, in which you were put in the position of observer. If it's true—and it is—that you can't be that which you observe, then I have to ask you, 'Who then is doing the observing'?"

"*I* am. There must be a trick to this," Sam thought.

"But who is the 'I' if you aren't your thoughts? Who's the observer observing your thoughts and emotions?"

Seeing Sam's puzzled look, the coach said, "Don't try to understand it. Can you just see it? Can you see there's a 'you' observing your own struggle with the two managers you mentioned to me?"

Sam nodded. "Understanding may be the booby-prize," echoed in the recesses of his mind. He *did* see the judgments he'd made and his feelings toward the two managers. But who was the observer who noticed this, if the observer wasn't his psychological self? Sam was stumped.

"Just imagine yourself," the coach said, "as this circle." She got up and walked over to the easel, turned the page with the *un*-words over, and with a black marker drew a large circle on the blank page, labeling the graphic "ME."

"Pretend that's you here at the periphery, you who are concerned about the situation with your former quality control manager." She paused then said, "Seeing people whose actions don't match their words really bothers you, doesn't it?"

"Yes, it does," replied Sam without hesitation.

The coach drew a line away from the circle and wrote, "Who I pretend I am" on it. In parentheses she wrote, "I walk my talk." "This is your public persona," she said. "How you want to be perceived." She pointed to the "I walk my talk." Next she drew a smaller circle in blue within the first one, saying, "Then there's the 'you' who's worried that you're not good enough, not in control, probably not right or smart enough. Do you have those thoughts sometimes?" Coach Zabar smiled.

"Yeah, like I might talk about having integrity and then be like the managers that piss me off!" Sam felt close to the coach. She obviously was an expert on pretense as well as the "put your conqueror face on" mentality that still dominated the male corporate landscape.

Coach Zabar labeled the line she drew away from that circle, "Who I worry I am." In parentheses she wrote, "I'm a phony."

"You could say that this second circle inside the first one is your psychological self. Mine too, because this graphic could be any of us."

Sam couldn't imagine Coach Zabar or any of the great managers having any of these psychological concerns. Surely they were beyond that. But he observed that he felt comforted, especially when he pictured the other outwardly self-assured junior managers "calm as ducks but paddling like hell underneath." He was not so different after all. "Sweet," he thought.

"So that second circle is the 'me' who's afraid I might be someone who doesn't walk my talk?" he asked.

"That's right. Of course that's just one example. We have lots of worries, and they all reside here. But happily that's not the end of our story."

"At the center," she said, drawing a red circle that made the graphic look like an archery target, "you'll find neither 'who you pretend you are' nor 'who you're worried you are.' You're going to find 'who you *really* are' in your hero's heart, as Joseph Campbell would put it." The coach punctuated the word "really" and with the determined stroke of the red marker wrote "Who I *really* am" in the innermost circle. In parentheses she wrote, "I am a contribution."

"Who you *really* are is *un*affected by circumstances. It's forever. It's *un*changing and *un*changeable."

The coach spoke passionately and with great certainty. "Nothing and nobody can take 'who we really are' away from us. All of us have that core even if for some of us it seems inaccessible. Nevertheless, at our *un*assailable core we are as solid and deep as Earth itself."

She took and let out a deep breath. "We call that our ontological self. The ontological self is the domain of being. It's where 'who you're willing to be' resides. It's *you* at choice. You, the dispassionate, wise observer.

"The ontological self doesn't ask 'why.' Or 'Do I want to? Don't I want to?' Instead each of us asks, 'Who am I really?' 'What am I to contribute?' 'What am I to learn?' The bottom line is this: our psychological self is no match for our ontological self."

Sam stared at the graphic. "What's coming up for you right now?" asked the coach.

"OK, let me try to make the connection. The manager I brought up earlier, the guy who says he's being compassionate, really isn't. He's in his psychological self and in the fog about it. If he had this coaching, he might see he doesn't have to lie to himself to feel good about himself. He wouldn't need to allay his fears about whatever negative assessments his psychological self is entertaining. He might be able to choose being compassionate, for example, and just notice that he *has* feelings that get in the way of action that's aligned with his real intention—which no doubt is to deliver stellar customer support. The results would be very different, it seems to me."

"There you go, Sam," replied the coach with a wide smile. "You've just coached yourself. How great is that?"

Sam couldn't quite hide his glee at the compliment, looking younger than twenty-five. "It's great," he said. "Coaching is awesome." The comfortable silence that ensued was broken by Coach Zabar's next question.

"You're clear how what you just learned applies to those other managers. How does it apply to you?"

Clearing his throat, Sam experienced a brief moment of annoyance that he had once again focused on someone else first.

But he recognized the annoyance as coming from his thought "I should have known better." He decided that the interpretation "I'm practicing new skills and doing it well" was a lot more interesting. He relaxed.

"The 'ME' graphic will support me in observing. It'll also allow me to see if my actions reflect my values." He noticed the presence of possibility and the absence of the defensiveness he might have felt earlier.

"You've underlined for me how important self-observation is, Coach Zabar. That's really what I'm interested in right now. The 'O' in the COSA process stands for observation, and it's clear to me that the ability to self-observe is an important skill." He frowned suddenly.

"What's your biggest concern about being an observer, Sam?"

"Well, blindness is a distinct handicap."

"Say more about blindness being a handicap."

"My concern is that I don't want to be like the managers I told you about—deluding myself so that I can keep my illusion that I'm a great manager while other people suffer, talk behind my back, and do crappy work. That's worrisome."

"What worries you the most about that? You're doing great, Sam."

"I'd feel like such an ass once I saw it. I'd feel stupid."

"Let me get this straight. You're worried you might have a blind spot, and people will think you're stupid?"

"Yeah, that too. But mostly *I'd* think I'm stupid." He slumped forward.

Coach Zabar ignored Sam's dejected expression and probed, "Is there anything you feel stupid about right now?"

"Well, I have an employee I often see not talking to clients when he should be. I've been putting off talking to him about it."

"So what's the conversation you're having with yourself?"

"I'm not sure."

"Good. Go look."

Sam was silent. Coach Zabar waited.

"I want to confront him well, and I'm afraid I won't," he admitted.

"So right now you're holding back. Like the support manager you told me about."

"Uh...I'm not proud of that."

Coach Zabar ignored that comment.

"What's the worst thing that could happen if you didn't hold back?"

"If I didn't hold back?" Sam stalled, waiting for his brain to rearrange itself. "I'd probably botch it and look like a jerk."

"Terrific. So are you seeing how well it serves you to not confront your employee?"

"Not in terms of being a good manager it doesn't!" Sam's voice was indignant.

"This is true. But it serves another commitment you have, doesn't it?"

Sam raised one eyebrow as he looked at the coach. "Well"—the word seemed to have two syllables rather than one—"I play it safe. That way I don't look like a jerk," he said.

"You're being very courageous, Sam. So you're seeing you want to be a great manager, and you also want to look good and play it safe. So where are you in the 'ME' graphic we just talked about?"

Sam stared at the newsprint. "I'm not in my hero's heart. I'm worrying about being found out. I'm in that second circle." He pointed to the "Who I worry I am."

"Very good, Sam. You're observing that you have worry thoughts like 'I'm a jerk and I'm stupid.' *Are* you a jerk?"

"Not if I'm not that which I observe, but I sure feel like I am," Sam said slowly.

"Brilliant, Sam. You *have* thoughts and feelings, but you aren't them, no matter how much you think 'But that's really me. If only people knew what *I* know about me'!" The coach smiled.

"Would it be all right with you if this were easier?" she asked gently.

"Yes, it would," Sam sighed.

"Well, I suspect this is the first time you've not only seen that you have competing commitments but you've admitted it to someone else, namely me. Is that right?"

"Yes. That's true."

"So let's assume for the time being that you don't have to do anything."

"Is that what Marguerite Chan meant when she said 'Don't just do something. Sit there'?"

"Probably so. Observation may be curative all by itself. However, there are some safe things you can do with what you've become aware of."

"Like what?"

"Like looking at what it's costing you to not confront, because it's clear that not confronting an under-performing employee isn't in your department's interest, nor does it serve your goal to be a great manager."

Coach Zabar referred to her notes. "Ah, yes. Let's look at the qualities you've chosen for this session. Of course. What might someone who's willing—let's say, to be 'open'—do in the situation you describe?" Sam looked at the coach for a long time before he took a deep breath. Then, with a determined look, he said, "He'd take his attention off playing it safe [Sam was applying the question to himself] and he'd remember who he *really* is." He pointed to the center circle on Coach Zabar's "ME" graphic. "He'd focus on what's important and how he could produce the results he cares about. He'd keep an open mind, talk to the employee, and be prepared to confront him if it became clear that he wasn't doing his fair share of the work."

"What are you getting from what you're saying?"

"Two things. One, you essentially just asked me to switch my point of view. From that vantage point I see possibilities I didn't see before, like it might not even get to a so-called confrontation. And two, that in the 'Who I worry I am' circle I have a lot of mischief-making thoughts."

"What about your thoughts is mischief-making?"

"What do you mean?"

"Well, thoughts are just thoughts. They're just blips. Little wisps. Neurons firing in your busy brain. What makes them so powerful that you label them mischief-makers?"

Sam studied the graphic.

"My thoughts get their power from the meaning I attribute to them," he replied, having found his answer. "Until this conversation, I was sure that my worry thoughts were not only the truth, the whole truth, and nothing but the truth, but they were bad and should be hidden from others." He stopped and marveled at how easy it had been to say that to the coach.

"But if I were open, I wouldn't make my worries mean the same things," he added.

"So are you saying you don't have to believe everything you think?" The coach leaned back while studying the young man's face.

"I really *don't* have to believe everything I think. Hmm. How obvious. But what a relief!" Sam was quiet for an *un*usually long period of time.

"Something shifted for me," he said, breaking the silence.

"And what was that?"

"It's like you and I are on a quest together to learn something rather than you attacking me or trying to correct a flaw in my management style. So it was easier to look at my experience than prepare myself to defend against your questions."

"You're doing great, Sam. Anything else?"

"You're a catalyst, not a corrector!"

"Anything else?"

"Yes. Even when I *do* believe something I'm thinking, I can change my mind! For example, if I have the thought I should already know how to confront expertly, I could ask 'How would someone who's being compassionate think about this?'".

"Somebody who didn't feel the need to be hard on himself,

maybe even you?" The coach winked at Sam, and he recalled their earlier conversation about being hard on himself.

Sam laughed. "Yeah, why not?"

"Good work, Sam. The fact is you and I are meaning-making machines. We can't help it. But that doesn't mean we have to believe everything we think, right?" Both the coach and Sam burst into appreciative laughter.

"Yeah, that's right. I could just notice my thoughts, even have fun with them and say, 'Thanks for sharing, but I'm more interested in being open than in listening to myself whine about what an ass I am.' Ha! I like this a lot. Yes, I do."

Sam sat back looking pensive now. "Could it be said that the moment I stopped to consider being open, I was no longer embroiled in my psychology?"

"Very good connection, Sam. Yes. Anything more?"

Nodding he said, "When you asked me that, it allowed me to literally inhabit my ontological self. I seemed to have…yes, uh…to have shifted into my hero's heart." He pointed to the center ring on the "ME" graphic. "That's extraordinary. Really extraordinary. Hmm." He squinted, still focused on the center of Coach Zabar's graphic.

"It's the best, isn't it? Is it safe to say that your doubts and worry thoughts have stopped you a time or two in the past from producing extraordinary results?"

"That would be more than fair," Sam said, remembering the worries he had before his coaching session.

"Your being truthful is courageous."

"Thank you."

"It's not a compliment. It's the truth." Sam sat up straighter. He noticed Coach Zabar's mischievous smile. It wasn't the first time Sam experienced himself off-balance in the presence of this woman. Things that should stay steady and solid often felt like shifting sand. For sure they weren't as he expected. "Hmm. Kind of like the italicized "*un*" in '*un*cover' or '*un*common' or '*un*leash.'" He got it now. Being *un*settled was OK with Sam at the moment. He experienced a sense of possibility and adventure, not threat.

"I suspect if future similar situations were easier to navigate, that would be a boon, yes?" The coach's question interrupted his reverie.

"Definitely."

"Good. We have to end this session, but I want to alert you to a major point of power." Coach Zabar paused to let her words make their impact. "And you've been practicing it a lot in this session. Observation is your second point of power. It follows right on the heels of choosing who you're willing to be.

"To increase your power exponentially, you must consciously choose to observe what I'm about to identify for you." Sam and Coach Zabar simultaneously leaned forward, he in anticipation, she to communicate gravitas.

"Without your vigilant and relentless observation, it's just an interesting concept. *With* observation it's more valuable than all the gold in the world, more dynamic than the fastest plane, more powerful than all of our advanced degrees put together."

Sam was on the edge of his chair. "For God's sake, what is it?" he wanted to yell, but he restrained himself.

"I learned this when I studied world philosophies and religions."

"Not exactly the background for a developer of great American corporate managers," Sam thought.

"My Buddhist friends call it monkey mind." The coach suppressed a faint smile. "You've heard me or one of the managers mention it, but now you'll get to know and love it. It's that chatter we hear in the background that you alluded to a moment ago. You know, that voice which says 'What chatter?'." Coach Zabar chuckled. She liked talking about monkey mind.

"Monkey mind is the voice that second-guesses you. The voice that tells you you're stupid, or the one that rationalizes and makes excuses. Even the one that makes comparisons between yourself and someone else where, incidentally, you usually get the short end of the stick." Her eyes were smiling again. Sam loved his coach.

"That chatter is what stands between you and your hopes and your dreams. It's the biggest opponent between you and the goal post in your work and in the rest of your life. This opponent never leaves you alone. But he's not your enemy—although most people make him that.

"He gives you valuable information, just like today when you became aware that you're perfectly positioned to *not* get what you dearly want!"

> That chatter is what stands between you and your hopes and your dreams. It's the biggest opponent between you and the goal post in your work and in the rest of your life. This opponent never leaves you alone. But he's not your enemy—although most people make him that.

The coach's words "perfectly positioned to *not* get what you dearly want" echoed in Sam's mind. He had to make an effort to keep listening.

"You can learn to outplay monkey mind. But you must be able to see the little trickster. Coaching will empower you to recognize monkey mind symptoms, observe them, and even use them to help you move forward on the path to your goals."

"Outplay?" wondered Sam aloud. "Is this part of the *un*-game?"

"You bet. With practice it can become a lot of fun to outplay monkey mind," responded Coach Zabar. "Unless, of course, you decide to empower the thought that it will be a lot of hard work." She suppressed what might have become a giggle.

"Are there ways to recognize specific monkey mind symptoms—

like those that the manager who doesn't confront people displayed?" asked Sam.

"Yes."

"Oh good. And for the one who thinks his commitment to quality is a ten when in reality he sucks?"

"Does that manager really suck, or is that the meaning you give his actions?" She winked at Sam, clearly enjoying herself.

"Damn. We're always attributing meaning, aren't we? And a lot of that is probably monkey mind, huh? Amazing. Our brain is really something."

"True enough, Sam. You can observe and examine. And you can do it again and again! It could be said that this is what the *un*-game is—identifying our most closely held thoughts, beliefs, opinions, and conclusions, and examining them to determine if they still serve us. *Un*covering *un*examined assumptions with *un*flagging consistency positions you to produce *un*common results, often in an *un*usually short span of time. Pretty good, huh?"

> This is what the *un*-game is—identifying our most closely held thoughts, beliefs, opinions, and conclusions, and examining them to determine if they still serve us. *Un*covering *un*examined assumptions with *un*flagging consistency positions you to produce *un*common results, often in an *un*usually short span of time.

"Yeah. I'm up for *that* game." Sam was having fun. His picture of the *un*-game was coming into much better focus.

Looking at her watch, the coach said, "Is there a lesson you learned from our conversation today that you're able to articulate?"

Swallowing his momentary disappointment at having this great session draw to a close, Sam answered, "Just having a label for the self-limiting conversation is awesome. I don't feel so alone and stupid anymore. If everybody has monkey mind, then we're all in the same boat. If others can learn to deal with the monkey trickster, I can too. And there's a powerful antidote to monkey mind, namely the hero's heart. It's just so thrilling"—he didn't even hesitate to say that word—"that I'm *not* my feelings. I really get it at a whole different level. I *have* feelings. That has enormous implications."

"Because of your observations, what you just said now lives for you at a level beyond your intellect. I can see that. You're doing great, Sam. I really admire how willing you are to engage in this process including when it's *un*comfortable for you. Can you see yourself promising some actions to demonstrate what you've learned here today?"

"Well, I'm going to make an appointment with Maria Nordstern no later than Tuesday. She was part of my hiring process, but I haven't been in to see her since we started the coaching. It really helps me get clearer when I talk to somebody other than myself.

"And I'm going to spend some time trying to identify some of my specific monkey mind talk before our next session, especially around this confronting stuff. Armed with what I know about monkey mind, I have a good chance to become better at having tough conversations. It may even help me be the manager I want to be.

"Could you do me a favor? We've talked before about rules great managers ignore. And the *un*-game is supposed to be about *un*covering rules great managers ignore or break. I can see that consciously looking at our closely held thoughts, beliefs, opinions, and conclusions facilitates that process tremendously. But could you just email me a couple of rules? I'd like to see if I can come up with why average and good managers follow them while the great ones don't."

"OK, I'll email you three. That sounds like a good exercise. Well done, Sir." The coach got up.

"Thank you, Coach. See you next week?"

"That's fine. Work it out with my assistant."

Flashing an open, grateful smile, Sam said, "Thank you so much, Coach Zabar. I really appreciate you working with me." He bent down to shake her firm hand before moving on to meet the challenges and opportunities of the week ahead. He felt seven feet tall.

Dear Reader

1. What does the statement "You're not your psychology" conjure up for you? Does it provide an opening? A new way of seeing? How so?
2. Have you ever lied to yourself about something you did or didn't do that you later cleaned up? What helped you perform this courageous act?
3. How does French philosopher Albert Camus' statement, "In the midst of winter I discovered I have within me an invincible summer," reflect that we have a hero's heart? Do you recall a time when your hero's heart (your ontological self) triumphed over your psychological self?
4. Can you think of an example where you had once been blind or in a fog but then could see? What was the best thing about that? Do you agree that self-awareness through self-observation is important to gain? Why or why not?

Chapter 8

UNCOMMON MANAGERS

S auntering through the hallowed halls of L-4 whistling the theme song from *Rocky*, Sam arrived at his office ready to change his world. His whistling devolved into a quiet humming as he scanned his emails before setting up his day. He stopped humming and groaned instead when he read one of them. "What? Russell is quitting?" he exclaimed aloud.

"He can't do that to me. I need him. This can't be happening," Sam muttered, a crestfallen look splattered like raw egg all over his handsome face, his get-up-and-go gone.

"What's wrong with him?" he muttered. "I bet he wants more money." He was about to grab the phone to call Russell in when he saw another email, this one from Coach Zabar.

"You're doing good work, Sam. I'm pleased to be your coach. Here are three 'rules' great managers ignore," he read.

For a moment Sam remembered his "*un*coveries." The manager's role as catalyst rather than as controller and corrector, setting expectations through outcomes rather than listing activities, and the false premise that you can achieve anything if you only work hard enough. The momentary pleasure vanished as he shifted his attention to the three rules on the monitor:

1. People work for money and for companies.
2. The shortest distance between two points is a straight line.
3. People are broken and must be fixed or the company's PPPsT is impacted.

"What the hell is PPPsT? And who says people don't work for money?" Sam thought belligerently. "What does *she* know anyhow?"

He got up, paced, then sat down and reluctantly took a deep breath. He remembered Coach Zabar saying it would bring oxygen to his brain. "Focus, Sam Adler," he heard himself say.

*Un*clenching his jaw he said, "All right. I don't wanna, but I'm nevertheless willing to be…" He fumbled for the qualities that seemed so far away at this moment. He heard a little voice chattering "Don't bother. That's not gonna help you. Who's inventing that crap of a hero's heart anyway?"

Having found the qualities, he looked at them, not as eager as he had been in his coaching session, but he willed himself to keep going.

"OK," he said after asking, "Who am I willing to be in order to make a contribution right here right now?" Scanning his notes, he decided. "I'm willing to be receptive, alert, open, clear, and compassionate."

Sometimes Sam's hyper-focus, as others called it, irritated people. But it was an *un*beatable asset, and the young manager was *un*deterred. His tense shoulders relaxed, and he looked at the screen again. What he saw threatened to rob him of his newfound calm.

"How have you been doing in observing your monkey mind in the last thirty minutes?" read the rest of the email from Coach Zabar.

"How have I been doing with my monkey mind?" he repeated in exasperation. "Damn good. Thanks for asking. But that stuff with Russell is different. It's the truth." Gathering steam for a second tirade, he stopped short and said, "Stop it. Stop and look at this, you idiot."

"Is that what someone who's demonstrating being compassionate would say?"

This time the voice had Coach Zabar's image attached to it. It lacked the agitated quality of the first one. Sam asked with a hint of defiance, "Why should I only be compassionate with others? I don't see any reason not to be compassionate with myself." He didn't know the coach would agree whole-heartedly with him. Having always been rather hard on himself, this was far from easy for Sam. *Un*observed habits don't die.

"OK, Sam Adler, look at this as a former idiot," he said to himself, having found his lost composure. He recalled his self-talk and observed that there was a lot of monkey mind. There had to be. He figured he'd be able to recognize a monkey mind fit coming on. Wouldn't likely triggers be the so-called negative emotions—like anger, frustration, fear, resignation? "Add feeling victimized and impulsive to the list of triggers," he harrumphed.

> To recognize a monkey mind fit coming on, look for heightened emotions generally called negative: anger, frustration, fear, resignation. Add feeling victimized and impulsive.

"My conversation had some of those," he thought, satisfied that he'd seen it. He no longer remembered being angry at Coach Zabar for even raising the question. If he had, he might have seen that his misdirected anger was another example of monkey mind on the prowl for a taker.

Sam turned his attention to the three rules, having decided to talk with Russell later. He was glad he hadn't called Russell in as soon as he'd read the email. Instead he crafted an email thanking him for his communication and requested a face-to-face meeting the next work day. He added that he hoped Russell's decision wasn't set in stone and that he was looking forward to learning from the conversation.

Sam silently thanked Coach Zabar and the managers. Their support and tools like learning to observe monkey mind were powerful—he liked the term "monkey mind" for the self-limiting chatter in his mind. The tools increased his capacity for self-awareness. "Self-awareness rules!" he thought as he turned his attention to Coach Zabar's email.

Still reveling in "Score 1 for Self-Awareness, 0 for Monkey Mind," Sam read Rule One Great Managers Ignore—*People work for money and for companies.*

The first part of that seemed easy. There's agreement in management literature that people aren't motivated by money. While they have to have it, of course, it's a negative satisfier—never enough by itself. What's strange is that neither company nor employees seem to pay attention to that. As soon as people are *un*happy, many either ask for or are offered more money. Sam felt he could talk intelligently about that part of the rule. Great managers simply remember, even under the pressure that causes others to forget, that people don't work only for money.

"I'll have to remember that when I talk with Russell."

But what about *People work for companies?* He himself had chosen L-4 for its reputation and its promise for advancing his career. That part of the rule just didn't make sense to him. Much as he thought about it, he couldn't make any headway. He decided to look at Rule Two Great Managers Ignore—*The shortest distance between two points is a straight line.*

It helped Sam that this rule came from a trusted source. If Coach Zabar says great managers ignore this rule, then he'd start from that premise and look for evidence for its fallacy even if it felt completely counter-intuitive. He didn't make much headway here either. He could point to so much evidence. How could this not be true? He pondered for a while, eventually deciding he needed to go on with the rest of his day's work. He'd come back to that one. But before abandoning the rules he took a look at Rule Three—*People are broken and must be fixed or the company's PPPsT is impacted.*

Sam puzzled over *PPPsT.* "Must be an acronym. Oh, you jerk," he exclaimed. "Oops. Jerk designations, like idiot designations, aren't allowed in the domain of compassion." Sam rolled his eyes at his silliness while pleased that he had caught himself. "Score another point for self-observation." The score was now 2 for Self-Awareness, 0 for Monkey Mind.

It occurred to Sam that he was using the language of games. He concluded that this was part of the *un*-game.

"*P* stands for Profits, the second *P* for Productivity," he mused. "What the hell is the third *P*? People are broken and must be fixed or the company loses profits and productivity. The third *P* is not just *P* but *Ps*. What is that little s? Oh, I know—the third *P* must be People.

"Aha! These are the four major business outcomes against which all performance measures have to stand up. *Ps* stands for customer satisfaction if you consider not only external customers, but employees as internal customers and service providers to each other. Coach Zabar just made it into *People's satisfaction—Ps*—to remind me of that. OK, and the *T* then has to stand for Turnover. That settles that." The mystery solved to his satisfaction, Sam pondered the rule again.

"What if Russell's wanting to leave is an example of an internal customer's dissatisfaction? I'll find out during our meeting. And if Russell was dissatisfied, how was it related, if at all, to the assumption, *People are broken and must be fixed?*" Feeling like a sleuth, he went to the file cabinet and removed Russell's folder. He opened it and glanced at a few documents, then settled on a review of Russell's performance appraisals.

"Hmm, interesting." Sam closed the folder. He looked again at the third rule and decided, "People are de-motivated when others see them as broken and needing to be fixed." He recalled how

Coach Zabar and the managers treated him. They were there to support him and help him learn in an environment of personal safety and professional challenge.

Sam recalled his conversation with Marguerite Chan about talent. She said talent can't be taught. Skills and knowledge can. And that a mistake managers often make is to try and remediate what can't be taught. That they'd do better to support employees in what they have no talent for with systems and focus their efforts on what they *do* have talent for.

Sam's realization rushed at him like a waterfall. He got the breaking of the third rule. Great managers know that people are heroes! They're not broken! They don't need to be fixed! Like him, everyone on his team—Russell, Joe, even Bob—they all have a hero's heart and a monkey's mind!

> Great managers know that people are heroes. They're not broken! They don't need to be fixed.

Sam choked up a little. He was glad he was alone. He glanced at the door and confirmed it was completely closed.

Out of this *one* realization—this *one un*covering of the gigantic lie of that third rule—he could change his world. He now was very clear that this *un*conventional wisdom, "People are whole and complete as they are," was the truth. They don't need fixing.

People need great managers who with *un*remitting commitment can elicit the absolute best from them, a best they can't even conceive of themselves. They need the freedom to try and the courage to fail. They need the *un*common support of conscious, courageous, and compassionate managers who help them demonstrate their talents and who, with *un*flagging consistency, treat mistakes as learning opportunities, not punishable offenses. They need managers who rigorously challenge the status quo. They need *un*common managers.

Sam felt as if he could bench-press two hundred pounds. "This feels like a big game and one worth playing," he said, drumming on his desk. The *un*-game was making more and more sense to him now. He began to speculate that *un*conventional management wisdom and *un*conventional thinking were the keys to creating and maintaining a vibrant 21st century workplace. It would, however, be a massive shift in the current corporate environment. Locked doors sheltering pretense and inauthenticity needed to be opened not only in the offices of L-4's great managers.

"How appropriate," he thought, calmer now. "We live in an extraordinary time. The never-before-experienced challenges of the 21st century—technological, economic, sociological, cultural, environmental, personal—they all call for examining our *un*examined assumptions of how to 'do' relationship, work, community, service, communication—everything. It's all up for consistent, *un*flinching examination. Albert Einstein's famous quote 'You can't solve problems with the same level of thinking that created them' is what should guide us as we proceed."

He hadn't thought about it before, but L-4 was a self-declared player in that game. The company's stated commitment to the triple bottom line was *un*usual. No large company he knew of had structures and practices in place that made that work. L-4 didn't have them either, but few pioneers did. It occurred to Sam that the coaching he was getting was part of the process of re-imagining how business would do business. It needed its managers to challenge everything, beginning with how and what they think. He was part of something very big.

Sam decided to leave the three rules and follow his desire to talk to the fourth manager on Coach Zabar's list, Maria Nordstern, the human resources manager. Ten minutes later he was in her office.

✶✶✭✶✶

Maria Nordstern welcomed him warmly, as if she had been expecting him. Sam guessed her to be close to retirement age.

Matronly described her appearance well. He wondered what rules Maria Nordstern broke. After all, she was on the list of great managers, and they didn't adhere to a lot of the conventional rules.

"It's good to see you again, Sam. I've heard good things about you," Maria said in a sonorous voice. "What can I do for you today?"

Basking briefly in Maria's acknowledgment, Sam said, "Thanks for seeing me on such short notice. You're on Coach Zabar's short list of managers. I've been learning about the *un*-game. It's amazing, isn't it? My understanding of it just keeps expanding. It's beginning to make some sense to me, and I've had a lot of new realizations that are going to make a difference in how I do my job. But I'm wondering if you can help me see why great managers ignore certain rules. I have a lot to learn."

> You may have more to *un*learn than learn.

"That may be so," said Maria Nordstern. "But might I suggest that you may have more to *un*learn than learn?"

"*Un*learn? Aha! That's part of the *un*-game, then…*un*learning things. I think I've already done a bit of that. But yes, I'm up for that." Sam thought about having *un*learned setting expectations for his team.

"Does learning the rules of the *un*-game and familiarizing yourself with the playing field interest you?" Maria asked.

"You bet it does," was the quick answer. "I feel as if I've been on a fishing expedition. I've hooked *un*-game pieces on my line, but I can't put them together into a coherent whole."

"Maybe it's time to give the *un*-game a real shape. What's your understanding of what it is?"

"It seems to be a systematic challenging of our *un*examined assumptions that get in the way of reaching our goals for producing change in a complex world. It seems to promote leaders' capacity for self-reflection and observation to make the complexity more or less manageable." Sam was surprised. His answer had just tumbled out.

"I'd modify that only to say that the *un*-game promotes an organization-wide capacity for self-observation and reflection, but leaders can provide the framework for it. What framework does your coaching adventure offer you?" Maria asked.

"The COSA process is the framework. Coach Zabar introduced me to the observation part of COSA. Observation is a very big deal. But we sure didn't make it a big deal in grad school or anywhere else."

"No, but that has to change. We can no longer assume everything is a technical problem that can be solved by technical solutions. It's people who solve problems, and we're convinced L-4 has people who are capable of what's needed, namely a quantum shift in transforming their own mind-sets once they see them. Isn't it grand?" Maria's eyes lit up at the thought.

"It really is."

"Very good. What are some of the *un*-game concepts you've hooked on your fishing line, Sam?" Maria settled back in her chair, giving Sam her *un*divided attention.

"Well, there are some players on the playing field, namely me and some team members. Coach Zabar is on the side lines, and you, Marguerite Chan, Peter Black, and Tom Pierot are on my team."

Maria laughed. "That's a good team. Anything else?"

"Yes, there's an opposing team, but I've met just one player, although I suppose it could be said that he has many uniforms," Sam said playfully yet earnestly.

"I like that description. And who would your opponent be?"

"Monkey mind," Sam shot back. "And he's cunning. Coach Zabar says it's my job to outplay monkey mind. So obviously he's on the opposing team." Recalling his monkey mind outburst when he heard about Russell, he said with urgency, "I'd like to kick his butt so he'll disappear forever. He seems to wreak nothing but havoc."

"Oh really?" asked Maria, raising one eyebrow. "If monkey mind were to disappear, what would happen to the game?"

"Uh…" Sam stopped, confused. Then a flash of recognition spread over his face. "Geez, I can't believe what I'm about to say, but…if monkey mind were off the playing field, there'd be no game!" He looked pleadingly toward the HR manager. "But surely you can get rid of monkey mind. I bet Coach Zabar doesn't have any. Or Marguerite Chan, or…"

His voice trailed off, and he looked at Maria, remembering Coach Zabar's words. "Everyone has monkey mind."

Sam recalled that he'd felt less alone, but it hadn't occurred to him that Coach Zabar really, like no kidding, meant everyone, with no one left out, including her.

> You need monkey mind. It has the same function for the mind as pain does for the body.

"Wow, he said, still *un*able to let in the full impact. "Game called because the opponent didn't show. Man! This means you actually need monkey mind!" Somehow Sam couldn't get his mind around that at all.

"So you expected the *un*common managers to be exempt from monkey mind? All they told you, I suspect, is that you have to learn to outplay monkey mind, if you want to be an *un*common manager too. Isn't that correct?"

"Yes, it is. And I sure as hell want to outplay monkey mind. I can see why I shouldn't want to get rid of him, but he's such a pain in the butt. Isn't there a better way?"

"Sorry, but you need monkey mind. It has the same function for the mind as pain does for the body," Maria said.

"You mean as a signal that I ought to take care of something?"

"Yes, monkey mind is there to remind you that you're up to something big. Its job is to keep you in the familiar rut of the status quo, because to change something means danger to monkey mind who protects you from harm and gets you, among other things, what it thinks you deserve. Have you ever noticed that you don't hear monkey mind when you're at the movies enjoying the film, eating a barrel of greasy popcorn, and guzzling a soda?" Maria laughed.

"That's true. I don't think about important stuff at the movies. I'm just there to chill out. But what do you mean by being up to something big? I might have a different meaning than you do." Sam recalled his lesson on attributing meaning to facts or thoughts that had gotten him all wound up.

"Every time you consider something new, you're up to something big. Monkey mind is on high alert, telling you 'Don't be interested in that. It could get you into trouble.' Staying out of trouble is another of monkey mind's jobs. Don't ever, and I mean ever, expect monkey mind to be reasonable. That's not its job."

> Don't ever expect monkey mind to be reasonable. That's not its job.

"This is mind-boggling. Coach Zabar and I started to talk about monkey mind. I can see better now why some of my managers from hell didn't fire people when they should have, and told themselves stories about why it was OK to let shoddy quality go out the door even though they coach on quality control. Monkey mind is a helluva powerful opponent. Knowing this will focus me on improving my game."

Maria smiled, clearly enjoying Sam's passion and enthusiasm. "Sounds like you might have a talent for making connections, Sam.

"And yes, it will definitely help you improve your game, but wouldn't you like to know the rules and what the playing field is like?"

"Yes, I would. Can you describe them to me?"

"Yes, I can," said Maria who loved to teach eager learners. "I believe you'll be able to take the concept and apply it to your affairs here at L-4 and in the rest of your life."

"Let's use a metaphor," she said briskly. She seemed very clear about where she was going with all this, which inspired confidence in Sam.

"In the *un*-game we're big on metaphors. Imagine a football field and call it 'Life's Playing Field.' Don't get distracted by the cliché. This works very well." Maria drew a crude graphic on a sheet of plain paper. "By the way, you can play the *un*-game any time anywhere, not just at work."

Sam nodded, paying close attention.

"*Un*like on a golf course, you have clear, chalked outlines, right?"

"Right."

"If you think about life, aren't there really two distinct realities? Imagine the two realities as the two parts of a football field." The HR manager drew a line dividing the rectangle into two squares resembling a football field. Sam just nodded.

"One part of the playing field is the day-to-day reality, your outer world." She wrote "My Outer World" on the top part of the divided rectangle. "And the other is a bit more hidden."

"The reality of my mind," contributed Sam.

"That's right," Maria affirmed, and then named the lower part of the divided rectangle "My Inner World."

She proceeded, "How do I bring something from vision, which occurs in my inner world, down here, to action in the outer world of my day-to-day reality, up here? The two realities have very different characteristics, don't they?"

"Yes, they do. It's a lot harder in real life to fly to Hawaii than it is in my mind. Ha, ha, ha."

"Very fine, Sam. It's light and airy in your mind. Thoughts and feelings come and go. Those wispy thoughts can flit from here to there and back again, can't they?" Maria didn't wait for a response.

"It's where your hopes and dreams and your longings live, like your longing to be a great manager. You're hard-wired that way so that you can generate lots of excitement and enthusiasm for ways to demonstrate those longings. It's for the mind the same as for the body when it puts out pheromones to make you irresistible." Maria was enjoying herself.

Sam recalled that the other managers seemed to have fun too. "Nothing would happen without pheromones," the HR manager continued. "And similarly nothing would happen, except maybe purposeless activities, if you didn't have longings you want to demonstrate. But you can't demonstrate your longings in your inner world. You must bring each longing into your outer world in the form of a specific, measurable, and achievable goal."

Maria stopped then asked, "And what's the difference between the light, wispy energy in your inner world and the energy of your day-to-day outer world?"

> You can't demonstrate your longings in your inner world. You must bring each longing into your outer world in the form of a specific, measurable, and achievable goal.

"Plenty. If your dream is to assure your team is on the same page with performance expectations, you can make that happen in an instant in your inner world. But it's a whole lot of steps when it's in day-to-day reality. It takes time. There'll be breakdowns, misunderstandings, mismatches between people's talents and the job's requirements. Things are not predictable in one's outer world. They change."

"Correct. And very perceptive, Sam. Would it be fair to say that we'll be disappointed if we think it'll be as easy as our mind tells us it will be?"

"Absolutely. It's ten times harder than we think."

"Indeed. And in order to bring the longing to be an *un*common manager forth as a demonstration, what do you have to do?"

Sam pictured the life's playing field graphic and himself at the fifty yard line. He saw it as the border between the two realities. "I have to cross the line," he said without hesitation. "And that'll feel like I'm going from a rocket that's in space back to earth. It'll be a rude awakening after being in my weightless inner world for so long." Sam was having fun.

"Yes, and who do you think awaits you at the line?"

"The opponents, of course." Sam's answer was quick and sure. "Oh Geez," he exclaimed just a moment later. "I'm going to meet monkey mind! That's why it's so easy to get distracted from goals and why it's so hard to reach them. Monkey mind has a different agenda. It has other commitments. By the way, I notice you refer to monkey mind as 'it.'"

"Yes, because it's really a conversation. We try to be precise. But we aren't always successful. So anyway," Maria said, "it's there to greet you and say, 'If I were you, I'd turn back.' Monkey mind doesn't want you to achieve your goal."

"That explains everything. That explains why people, including me, get stuck at the line. We have trouble crossing over. We get push-back. That is priceless, Maria. Monkey mind sends us a message. 'Stop Advancing Pal!' I think I'll use the acronym SAP —because I'm a sap when I stop myself from achieving my goals. Man, I'm all over this!"

Sam was a tightly wound spring. He got up and paced. "This is awesome!"

"I'm glad you see so many possibilities. You're recognizing you'll have to decline monkey mind's request to stop advancing." Maria giggled. "I can see that monkey sentinel standing on the line *un*successfully urging you to turn back," she said, her eyes flashing.

"But that's not the end of the story. Monkey mind just keeps coming back." There was a plaintive note in Sam's voice. He was sure by now that monkey mind was implicated in his present departmental woes.

"Naturally. Would you expect your opponent to stop playing after the first tackle? Monkey mind is your faithful, loyal opponent whom you can count on to have commitments that are perfectly designed to assure you don't reach your goals. No different from your football team opponents.

"Let's assume, Sam, you're across the line of scrimmage. If you're skilled and lucky, you gain yardage. The line moves. You move closer to the goal post. That means you encounter monkey mind again and again. Being aware of monkey mind's goals for you and keeping your eye on yours is the strategy that wins you the game."

A pregnant-with-possibilities silence pervaded the space.

"Let's make this real," resumed Maria. "What's a goal you have? It doesn't have to be gigantic. Just make it small and sweet. What would delight you as a demonstration of your longing to be a great manager, for example?"

> Would you expect your opponent to stop playing after the first tackle? Monkey mind is your faithful, loyal opponent whom you can count on to have commitments that are perfectly designed to assure you don't reach your goals. No different from your football team opponents.

Sam thought for a moment. "Easy. An authentic conversation with an under-performing employee. I already know what my monkey mind's commitment is. So I have a leg up."

"Tell me about that."

"Well, my monkey mind opponent is committed to me not looking like a jerk. So the assumption is that if I confront my employee I'll do it badly, and therefore I'll look like a jerk. But that's just monkey mind's story. It may not be the truth. I can surely test it out."

"Fabulous, Sam. Go for it. If you can make monkey mind visible like that more often, you'll blow the *un*examined cultural assumption that people don't change much right out of the water. You'll enter the hall of fame of *un*common managers who *un*leash their power to produce *un*common results.

"So show me where you are on the playing field graphic in your example," she requested.

"Right now, it's just an intention, so it lives in 'My Inner World' quadrant. The moment I pick up the phone to set up the meeting, I'm at the line dividing the two quadrants where I can expect monkey mind to be alarmed and to tell me this isn't important or whatever. When I've made the call I've crossed the line. I score a point. I'm in 'My Outer World' quadrant because I've taken action. When Bob walks in I'll probably be at the line again with monkey mind urging me to talk to Bob in the usual way that doesn't get us anywhere. At some point, though, at least in that conversation, monkey mind will get the message that I'm not turning back, don't you think?"

"Yes, monkey mind eventually retreats in the face of your *un*relenting focus, and you're likely to score that goal. Just how thrilled will you be on a scale of one to ten?"

"Oh, that's at least an eight for me. I think it's going to make a big difference in my team's morale."

"An eight is great," said an enthusiastic Maria. "For it to be a game, it's got to have some juice for you. Otherwise your 'I don't wanna' monkey mind is practically guaranteed to obliterate—not forever, of course—your 'I am willing' hero's heart, and you might do what you've always done. Does that make sense?"

"Yeah. It does. This is great. Thanks so much, Maria. I can get my mind around this playing field metaphor. Can I keep the graphic?"

Maria handed the crude drawing to him. "I love supporting

people who are eager to learn the *un*-game. What else is on your mind, Sam? I have a little more time."

Sam told Maria about the rule great managers ignore that he didn't get—*The shortest distance between two points is a straight line.*

"I just don't get it." Sam slouched back against his chair. The managers he admired had a goal and went for it with laser focus. They went from Point A to Point B—from vision to result—in a straight line.

Maria said nothing. "Tell me," he said, clearly frustrated. But she remained silent.

"I hate not knowing," he mumbled.

"What's the worst thing about not knowing?"

"It makes me feel inadequate," Sam said, resignation creeping into his voice.

"I see. And I imagine that means you have an interpretation of 'not knowing' that's pretty dismal." She was silent again.

"Oh." Sam's voice was already more upbeat. "That's a trigger for me being in my monkey mind. This feels like a familiar 'you're a jerk' conversation."

"Good, Sam. You're doing fine work here in seeing it and bringing it forward. There's a monkey mind conversation that centers around insufficiency—that is, around 'not enough-ness,' if you will. Not everyone has that conversation. For many people not knowing is just an adventure or an opportunity to be surprised. Obviously that's not the meaning you attach to not knowing."

"I can't imagine anyone feeling that way about not knowing," Sam said, shaking his head.

"Of course not. For *you*, it's a conversation that takes you out of your game the exact moment you experience this insufficiency around 'not knowing.' Do you recognize it right now in what you're saying?"

"I do. I hear the chatter: 'If I knew more, I'd be smarter. I'd have this sucker figured out.'"

"Well that's an interesting conclusion, but is it the truth? In the *un*-game we define the truth as 'facts.' What we make the facts mean is a whole other ball of wax."

"No, by that definition it's not the truth. Besides having a respected graduate degree, I'm taking advantage of opportunities like this coaching to meet the challenges my work puts in my path. That's the truth."

"Very good, Sam. You just told the truth, and the truth shall set you free, *nicht wahr*?" The tone of her voice was light-hearted as she used the German words for 'isn't that so?'

"Remember, I'm the HR manager," she continued in the same up-beat manner. "I know a lot about you. I know you have your eye on L-4 Germany. I bet you'll achieve that goal. Just keep your eyes on your goal, and tell that monkey sentinel 'thanks, but no thanks' when it shouts 'Stop Advancing, Pal!' Then look for the path of least resistance to get from your longing to be a great, well-traveled manager to the goal of being in Germany. And get yourself supported. Everything goes easier with support."

> In the *un*-game we define the truth as "facts." What we make the facts mean is a whole other ball of wax.

"Thank you for your confidence, I appreciate that. I…" Sam stopped abruptly. "What did you just say?"

"What do you think I said?"

"I think you said I should look for the path of least resistance to get to goal, to get from point A to point B. So the shortest distance between two points is the path of least resistance, not a straight line. That's true when you think of it. The most efficient route that nature has found from point A to point B is rarely a straight line. It's always the path of least resistance. A river cuts through where it's easiest. A cow will graze around a tree, not push it over to stay straight. It's a no-brainer. I can't believe I didn't see it."

"Great. So, can you take what you just learned and apply it to the challenges you're experiencing?" Maria Nordstern asked gently.

"You bet I can. For example, my team's work on improving our customer support process. I'll be looking at this through the questions 'What's the most efficient way to turn someone's talents into performance?' and 'How can I help them find their own path of least resistance toward the desired outcomes?' My job as catalyst is just that—to help my team find that path. When I'm firmly focused on the right outcomes, I can avoid the monkey mind temptation of correcting their actions according to some standard mold. Instead I can go with each person's flow, simply smoothing a unique path toward the desired result." Sam beamed. "I'll enjoy doing that. It'll be great."

"You're on a great path, but don't assume you can avoid the monkey mind temptation. That would be underestimating your opponent."

"Duly noted, Maria. Thanks."

"So it's a cool game, this *un*-game, eh?"

"No, it's hot. It's really hot," Sam chuckled.

"Did you get all your questions answered, Sam?"

"Well, I have one more. Why do great managers ignore the standard assumption that people work for companies? I came to work here because I wanted to work in a forward-looking company with staying power."

"You think you came for that reason, but I bet we could put that to a test. What are reasons you would leave? Look and see what's at the top of your list."

Reflecting only briefly Sam said, "I'd leave if I didn't know what was expected of me, if I didn't have the materials and equipment I need to do my job well, if I didn't have the opportunities to put my talents to work, if nobody noticed I was doing good work. Should I go on?"

Maria nodded.

"I'd leave if nobody cared about me and if the company

didn't encourage my development. There are probably other things, but these seem the most important to me. If these things were true over an extended period of time, I'd leave. I'm certain about that. Yes, no 'I guess' about it."

"I believe you, Sam." And who would be responsible for helping you meet those important needs? The company?"

Sam looked intently at her for about twenty seconds, then grinned, delighted with the recognition. "I get it! Ultimately this is about solid, satisfying relationships. It's about being connected. I don't only work for money. It's a negative satisfier and becomes critically important only when I don't have it. That's true for others too. And we don't work for the impersonal entity called 'company.' The company's values must be reflected in its managers' behaviors. We work for our *manager*. If the relationship sucks and the manager ignores our fundamental needs, it's all over. No wonder great managers don't buy that assumption. You've made my day, Maria. Thanks. Thanks a lot."

"It's my joy, Sam. Like you, I love supporting people."

Sam noticed again the odd language his *un*-game coaches used. That's part of what makes it the *un*-game, he decided—*un*usual language, reference to stories, heroes. Odd? Yes. But intriguing. "Hell, I'm just going to go with the flow," he decided.

The HR manager got up, signaling the end of the meeting. As she walked with Sam to the door she said, "It would be useful for you to know what kind of equipment you have for playing the *un*-game on life's playing field. If you were playing football, you wouldn't want to show up with baseball equipment, now would you? Coach Zabar or any of the other managers you've seen can show you the equipment, if that interests you. Have a nice weekend." With that the HR manager and the customer support manager went their separate ways.

Dear Reader

1. Monkey mind is the self-limiting chatter everyone has. Do you recognize some monkey mind chatter in yourself? If so, what do you do with it? In what ways has the chatter constricted you at work or in other areas of your life? Do you have a sense that you can do something about it, or are you frustrated or resigned?

2. At the very moment we have a monkey mind conversation, we're certain it's the truth. Only when we can stand back and observe can we see we've been tricked. Can you think of one or two examples in which you've been able to see later that you've been tricked by your own mind? What did you learn from that?

3. What's your reaction to the assertion that we need monkey mind? That there would be no game without it for the hero*— you—to play? What ramifications do you see in your role as a manager and in the rest of your life?

Note: An archetype, such as the hero archetype in "The *Un*-Game," is different from the male hero and the female heroine found in many contemporary narratives. An archetype represents both the masculine and the feminine.

Chapter 9

THE ALPHA AND THE OMEGA

Sam walked into his office after a weekend of fun, relaxation, and reflection about COSA and all the conventional rules that begged to be broken. He opened his email just as he was wondering who else was being coached by the famous Sophia Zabar.

"Well, well, seek and you shall find," he thought, whistling.

"You might want to contact Samantha Osler," the email from Coach Zabar suggested. "She's responsible for employee communications. The two of you could support each other and enhance your learning." The postscript read, "Everything is easier with support."

"Coach Z and the managers must talk to each other," Sam thought. He was curious. He looked at his schedule and decided regretfully he couldn't fit anything else in. But to set up a meeting would just be a quick phone call. He pressed Samantha Osler's extension, got her voice mail, and left a message.

"I like her voice. And she sounds young. Maybe in her twenties like me."

Turning to his work he dismissed all thought about a support meeting with the woman attached to the arresting voice and replaced it with preparation for his meeting with Russell. At this point he was more curious than upset about Russell's supposed decision to leave L-4.

The phone rang, interrupting his thoughts.

"Hi, this is Sam Osler from employee communications. So you're being coached too, I understand. I got an email from Coach Zabar and then your voice mail. Looks like we're destined to meet."

Sam liked the sound of her laughter.

"Sam squared, eh?" he said. "My name is Sam too. Sam Adler."

"Well, mine is Samantha, but I go by Sam. Where I grew up we needed to get right to the point. It looks like we're the Alpha and the Omega. That's pretty cool."

There were those peals of laughter again.

Sam Adler noticed she seemed to appreciate her own savvy and the not very humble reference. He liked her self-confidence.

"Why don't we meet for coffee at Starbucks at 5:15 today? We can work out what this support from each other will look like. I'm definitely up for it. This *un*-game stuff rattles my brain," he said.

"Sounds good to me. Ditto on the brain challenge. But I suspect that's what the COSA process is all about. If we're operating with the wrong assumptions, all the fancy footwork, programs, 'this-es' and 'that-s' ain't gonna matter." There was a hint of a southern accent in that *un*self-conscious voice.

"OK, see you later." Sam put the phone down, his preparation for his meeting with Russell once more claiming his *un*divided attention.

† †★† †

Sam arrived early at Starbucks. He wanted some private time to review his meeting with Russell. He found a table in a relatively quiet corner and claimed it to enjoy his coffee and replay the meeting.

He recalled with amusement a Mark Twain quote which was applicable to his concerns preceding his meeting with Russell. "My life has been full of terrible misfortunes, most of which never happened." He had been worried that Russell intended to leave

L-4. Russell had a job offer elsewhere he was considering.

Choosing some qualities of being and a few deep breaths had calmed him. The conversation had led to Sam asking Russell "What would have to happen for you to feel supported in your ongoing development here at L-4?"

Sam didn't know this was *un*usual, and that many managers avoid that conversation because it invariably surfaces complaints, many of which the manager shouldn't, can't, or doesn't want to do anything about. What happened next was something Sam recalled with satisfaction.

"So I hear you saying you're tired of people not talking to each other, tired of people running each other down behind their backs, and tired of taking on more than your fair share of the work. It's obvious that you care a lot about what's going on," said Sam, showing that he saw Russell not as a complainer but as someone with feedback worth noting.

The fact that his manager took such an *un*conventional approach didn't escape Russell. "Well, it has improved a little since our last team meeting," he admitted. His answers to Sam's further questions were a revelation to both him and Sam. With Sam's capable questioning Russell said that he wanted direct communication and a functional team that routinely coordinated actions effectively.

"Thanks, Russell. We both want the same things," said Sam, his enthusiasm apparent, his appreciation genuine.

They spent the rest of their meeting talking about ways in which direct communication within the department could be achieved, beginning with what Russell himself would do, which included a direct and active participation in the team's current process-improvement conversation.

Sam reflected on what had happened. He had turned Russell's wish to leave into a development opportunity. He had also met the fundamental need of his employee—to get recognition as well as encouragement to develop beyond his present capacity. Sam assumed Russell's decision to stay was the result of their

conversation. And how had he done it? By listening and asking
questions whose answers not only genuinely interested him, but
which also helped him turn Russell's complaint into a commitment.

"Hmm, complaint to commitment. Good job, dude." Sam
thought as he looked up and saw a woman in her twenties enter and
get into line to order. She was small, wiry, and tanned. Definitely
not New York, Sam decided. The young woman had short, closely
cropped dark hair framing an attractive, somewhat tomboyish face.
There was a certain toughness about her that was not *un*pleasant.

As Sam Osler moved toward him, a questioning smile on her lips,
he saw that she had an open, friendly face. Sam Adler waved, and
the slight hesitation in her step changed to confidence.

"Hi, Sam," she said. "I'm Sam."

"Nice to meet me," replied Sam, and they both laughed.

Sam Osler was from Texas and had grown up on a 6000-acre
ranch belonging to Dallas oil tycoons. Her mother and father
managed the ranch. As a teenager she had trained horses. For Sam
Adler that explained her wiry, tomboyish appearance, as well as that
touch of toughness. And he was right about the southern accent,
although it was slight. She was a University of Texas graduate with
a major in international studies and a minor in business.

"A feat to have landed this L-4 job given that she only minored in
business," Sam thought. Aloud he asked, "So you're responsible for
employee communications. Do you like it?"

"I love it," she responded. "When you think about it,
everything happens out of relationship, and I love relationships.
And if management isn't about relationship, then I don't know
what it *is* about."

As the two young managers talked, they discovered they had
each seen Coach Z, as they referred to her, twice, and they had met
the same group of managers. They shared some of what they had
learned with *un*bridled enthusiasm. It seemed as if they had known
each other for a long time. After a while they picked up and went to
Giovanni's, a small Italian restaurant across the street, to continue

their conversation over dinner.

"So, what did you learn that I didn't?" asked Sam Adler. "Maybe we could provide each other with some shortcuts."

"I doubt it," she replied. "My sense is there are no shortcuts. Think about how we learned stuff in college. What distinguished your best classes from the ones you can't even remember?"

"That's easy. The ones I remember were the fun ones. I had to do something, not just read stuff and regurgitate it. Like the simulations. They were a blast." He added, "But I'd still like to know what you learned. I can usually use something."

He remembered that he and the HR manager, Maria Nordstern, hadn't finished their conversation about the equipment that was available on the corporate playing field.

"Did you get coached on the equipment on the playing field?" he asked. "I like that metaphor, don't you?"

"Yeah, and we're using it right now," teased Sam Osler with an 'I'm in the know' kind of grin.

> Everything happens out of relationship, and if management isn't about relationship, then what *is* it about?

"We *are*?" Sam stopped stabbing his salad. "What equipment are we using?"

"Support. The equipment is our ability to focus our *relationships* on behalf of our goals. You and I are talking because it serves goals we have, whether we've articulated them or not. At the very least it's a demonstration of our intention to be great managers."

Sam was intrigued. He told her about his interaction with Russell. She whistled appreciatively. "Great job. Most people would have been pissed off with him on two counts—one for wanting to leave, and two for complaining. What specifically did you apply in that conversation that you learned from coaching?"

"Oh, I was pissed off all right when I first saw he wanted to leave." Turning to the second part of her question, he said, "I'm not sure. I just know I was feeling a lot more charitable toward him once I got a helicopter view of my initial monkey mind reaction."

"That probably helped. But your cool conversation with him didn't come out of nowhere. What was it that had you start the conversation with a greater sense of generosity?"

"Oh, now that you mention it, I *did* choose 'generous' as one of the qualities I wanted to be. But..." Sam stopped.

"But what?"

"I was just thinking about the conventional assumption that great managers don't buy into."

"Which one is that?"

"'People are broken and need to be fixed.' I think I started out with 'The guy is OK.' I doubt I would've been able to mine his complaints for the hidden commitments they contained if I'd harbored a secret 'He's an ass.' You know what I mean?"

A far-away look in his eyes, he added, "By God, I was seeing him as a hero with a hero's heart, and I didn't let any of his monkey mind distract me. I used his monkey mind stuff to gather information. OK, Sam Osler, tell me what a great manager I am," he said flashing a wide, self-satisfied grin.

"Super, Sam Adler. You're the best." His new best buddy gave him a thumbs-up.

"Yeah, I didn't do so badly. I bet that's what Coach Z meant when she said you needed monkey mind. It can give you some really good information."

After a brief pause he asked, "So are you saying how we interact with others is one of the pieces of equipment on the corporate playing field?"

"Yeah, but I widen the playing field to include the rest of my life. Anywhere I want to accomplish something," she replied.

"So what else could I have done? Just apply the golden rule?" Sam threw her an expectant look, chewing a bite of steak. He anticipated she'd say "yes." Judging from her ease with him, he had a sense that this interesting woman was pretty competent in relationships.

"If by 'apply the golden rule' you mean treat the guy like I'd want to be treated, hell no!" the tomboyish brunette replied, her tone as feisty as her taunting smile. Sam stopped chewing.

"What do you mean? What could be wrong with treating someone like you'd want to be treated? With dignity and respect?" he said, hoping his twinge of irritation didn't show.

"There's everything right with treating your guy with dignity and respect. But not like you'd want to be treated. Haven't you heard of the four-year old who gave his mom a red toy truck for her birthday? He treated *her* like *he* wanted to be treated, all right!"

Impressing Sam O had been more fun for Sam A. Self-satisfaction wasn't all that easy to give up. But he regrouped, then replied, "I can't believe I didn't see that. Of course we don't want to treat our people the way we want to be treated. We need to treat them the way they want and deserve to be treated. We have to put ourselves into their shoes."

Suddenly he remembered a story. "Let me tell you about one of my buddies," he began. "He's a competitive sales manager, and he had a guy who despite great training had no fire, no burn. He was just plain bored. Not competitive. He was an achiever and he just wanted to beat himself, not anybody else. So Rick started asking him what he was going to do this month to better himself, not who he was going to beat. The guy wound up opening up, getting excited, and in the long run turned out to be a big producer for the company. It was awesome. Rick just was smart enough to see he needed to speak his language."

He stopped. "I bet that's one of the rules great managers ignore," he said a moment later, doing what his talent—making connections—made so easy for him.

"That's really clever. I bet you're right," said his female counterpart whose greater talent was relationships. "You're really smart, Sam." She said this with an easy generosity and grace.

Sam A was having a wonderful time. "Do you have any insight into what managers are *un*aware of such that they offer more money to a valued employee who's contemplating leaving? The management literature is pretty clear that money is not the most important thing people work for. But the first thing we do is offer them more money anyway." He remembered his first knee-jerk reaction to Russell's email—even though he knew better!

"I'm not sure, but the questions we talked about could provide some answers. Managers might be oblivious to the causes of the person's *un*happiness. For example, the employee might be *un*happy about his or her development prospects. Or the lack of tools. Or their talents aren't maximized. You know. But if the manager doesn't know that or thinks it's *un*important..." Her voice trailed off.

The Alpha and the Omega sat a while in silence, both reflecting on how great it is to *un*self-consciously talk to someone else who's passionate about management.

Sam remembered a connection he'd made about people's actions not matching their words. He told Sam Osler the story of his former QC manager. "If people don't walk their talk, then these people are having some hidden commitments which their monkey mind is keeping them *un*aware of," he said.

"Yeah, I think you're on to something." Sam O signaled the waiter she'd have the tiramisu for dessert. Sam A seconded the request.

"I just read about a study of top executives who were asked the question, 'What do you value most in life?'," she continued. "Because the question didn't say 'What do you value most at work?' the answer could be broader. 'Children' was their answer. When they were asked to reflect on how much face-to-face time they spent with their children per week, it turned out they spent a whopping one to eight minutes per week! As you can imagine, it was an eye-opener for the execs.

"Clearly, leaders and managers who care to reduce the risk that their actions contradict their stated values must, if they want to be great, take an *un*flinching look at themselves," Sam Osler asserted, now on a roll. "This is why COSA is so terrific. They get a chance to observe what's really going on with them right then and there. They get to see not only their stated commitments but the hidden ones that have them veer off those stated commitments, often to their great surprise and shock. Let's face it. The coach isn't going to let them off the hook. Has Coach Z or any of the managers ever let *you* off the hook?"

She didn't wait for an answer. "In coaching they'll get to see—did Tom Peters or Scott Peck say this?—that any closely held value, no matter how well hidden, even from yourself, inevitably prompts action that's consistent with it." She paused.

Sam felt almost mesmerized by Samantha's voice as well as her message. "How true," he thought, but he didn't speak. She wasn't quite finished making her points.

"I remember a meeting I had when I was twenty-two," she said. "It's as if it happened yesterday. I really had an epiphany. I was in a group, hanging back listening to my monkey mind chatter. Only I didn't have the words for it then. Anyhow, I wasn't going to put myself out there in any kind of leadership position, lest they find out how stupid I really was. And this despite the fact that I knew I was *un*doubtedly more skilled than the people leading the meetings!

> Any closely held value, no matter how well hidden, even from yourself, inevitably prompts action that's consistent with it.

"I don't even remember what happened, but at some point during the meeting I got crystal clear that I couldn't hide from people, no matter what. People would know if I had a hidden agenda. I couldn't conceal that fact. Granted, they wouldn't know my exact agenda. But they'd know I had one, if I did. People can sense hidden agendas like dogs can sense fear."

Sam A just nodded.

"It was cool. I decided since I couldn't hide anyway, I might as well solve all of my problems, so that I could go out there and just be me! And that's what started my whole process of self-discovery and self-observation. It's been quite a ride and obviously still is." She smiled.

Sam looked at her. It hadn't been lost on him that Samantha had made herself vulnerable. On the "ME" graphic she was in the center circle—"Who I really am," he thought. He interpreted her self-disclosure as wanting to be known, and he appreciated that.

"She's tough-minded and tender-hearted," he concluded.

"So you've decided to be the change you want to see, eh?" he asked, in a gentle tone.

"Yes I have, and I'm not looking back."

After pondering what she'd just said, Sam asked, "So what's more important to you, being a great manager or being an effective communicator?" He took a bite of the tiramisu that had just arrived. "Mmm, this is good."

"In the bigger scheme of things, 'being an effective communicator,' but it's not an 'either/or.' There are a number of intentions that provide the fuel for my goals."

Sam Osler was clearly observant, a talent that she shared with him, Sam thought immodestly. They had a lot in common. Everything he cared about right now had to do with being a great manager. But being an effective communicator ranked high too.

Everything happens out of relationship, and he had to catalyze great relationships. As a manager in general and as the customer support manager in particular, there was no getting around it. One simply had to be interested in relationships.

And as far as relationships go, he was certainly enjoying this one with his new-found friend and colleague.

"We sure got a lot of mileage out of you telling me about one piece of equipment on the playing field," Sam marveled, adding,

"It's *un*familiar to think of our ability to be in relationship as equipment that's available to us to achieve our goals. But it makes a lot of sense. Please tell me about the others, if you remember them."

"I do remember them. But relationship came up first because I love relationships, and I haven't always been very good at using this piece of equipment," she added wistfully.

"Well, live and learn, right? Practice makes what?" he inquired mocking his emphasis on the "what."

"Progress!" the two young people almost shouted in unison. No one noticed; the Italian restaurant was filled with gesticulating people talking loudly. "Very Italian," they said in unison again and laughed.

"This *un*-game sure is fun," said Sam O.

"No kidding. I love it," replied her male counterpart. "I really get it." His first tense, *not* freely-chosen session with Coach Zabar was long forgotten.

"The other equipment you can use on the playing field," Sam Osler said, shifting back to Sam A's request, "is always available to us. We just have to know what it is. Mostly we never think about it as equipment. Therefore it isn't available for conscious use."

She continued in her best stage voice (she had been a thespian in high school and college), "What did you do once…you… knew?" No doubt about it, Samantha sure knew how to keep Sam's attention.

"I'll give you an example," she said. "What do you use in any situation to move from vision to action? Let's say I wanted some new tracking software in my department. What do I do to make it appear in my office?"

Sam jumped right in. "Well, you'd take some time to research options. You'd ask some people who you think have something similar or have a similar need. If you've made a decision, you'd contact purchasing to give them a heads-up. If you don't have the budget, you might have to get creative, but if you do, you'd authorize the money. Then you'd go out with me to celebrate knowing the tracking software will soon make life easier, which is definitely all right with you."

Sam made the last comment with a flourish hoping she wouldn't connect the mention of going out to celebrate with his reddening face. The petite brunette was very attractive, easy to talk to, and a lot of fun.

"Well there you have it, my man," Sam Osler said in her charming southern accent. "So the equipment on the playing field of life, be it at work or at play, are relationships, also known as support, as we said before. Then there's time, money, and believe it or not, creativity and enjoyment. Implicit, of course, is that you need your body's physical vitality.

"Without the bod, you ain't goin' nowhere fast, so you best take good care of yourself," she added.

"Hmm. So you're saying that we can use this so-called equipment consciously each time we make a 'play' on the goal."

"Yeah. The key word is 'consciously.'"

"What would be doing it *un*consciously? Give me an example for, let's say, the equipment of 'time.'"

"That's a good one. So, for example, when people say 'I don't have time,' that's not true. They have as much time as everyone else. It's how you allocate the time to advance your agenda. You can do it consciously, or you can notice you play cards on the computer rather than designing an effective staff meeting. Or you can notice how often you say 'yes' when you should say 'no.' The first would be an example of the *un*conscious use of your equipment of time, the second of your equipment of relationship."

The young woman seemed to enjoy sharing.

"That has all kinds of incredible ramifications," said Sam. "People do the same with the 'money' equipment. There's never enough." Both Sams nodded and fell silent.

"But what do you mean 'creativity' is another piece of equipment? And 'enjoyment?' I don't get that," said Sam A, breaking the silence.

"I don't know what Coach Z would say, but the way I've used that to move myself off 'stuck' is to see with new eyes. You know how the questions Coach Z asks always have you look at things differently?"

"Yeah, and the managers do that too. Go on."

"So I ask myself when I'm stuck, 'What would I be doing with this challenge, if I were being creative? If I were enjoying myself?' Try it some time. I literally can change my point of view. I can observe from a different place. It's like changing position in a room. The room looks different from the couch than from the rocking chair. Plus just knowing that creativity and enjoyment are considered valid equipment for me to use for the game gives me more room somehow. It expands my answers."

"I'll have to try that out, said Sam A, fascinated. "What I'm getting from what you're saying—and it's a reinforcement of what I've been getting with Coach Z and the managers—is that one way to change your thinking is to first observe what you're thinking right here and now, and then observe it from a different perspective. Like first from the 'stuck' place and then from the point of view of someone being creative, let's say."

"I think that's right," said Sam O. "Otherwise you'd come up with same-ol' same-ol.' No cheese at the end of *that* tunnel. Speaking about enjoyment, isn't this a beautiful meal? Let's do this again. I don't know about you, but I think this is very helpful. There's something about talking out loud that beats my own thinking about stuff. I mostly have the tendency to go 'round and 'round."

"You too, huh?" Sam was relieved he wasn't the only one. This talking out loud seemed to lead somewhere—a question here, a comment there. It wasn't a vacuum. Even though he didn't see himself as an extrovert who liked to process things out loud while simultaneously driving the introverts in his life crazy, he *did* experience the difference.

"Maybe the going 'round and 'round is what happens when you stay too long in the inner world of the playing field. If you want to get somewhere, you have to go across the line of scrimmage, so to speak, and bring your intention to where action occurs, namely physical reality," he said, appreciating even more Coach Zabar's suggestion to meet with this new colleague.

Sam didn't want the evening to end, and this wasn't even a date. "Let me ask you one more thing before we get going," he said. "What the hell does the 'S' in COSA stand for? I have no clue."

"Well I don't either. We're about in the same place, I guess. I haven't had a chance to visit any of the managers about it, but I'm going to."

> Going 'round and 'round is what happens when you stay too long in the inner world of the playing field. If you want to get somewhere, you have to go across the line of scrimmage and bring your intention to where action occurs—physical reality.

"Maybe the 'S' stands for SEIZE," ventured Sam A.

"Yeah. Seize the opportunity to act. What else could it be? After observing you have to do something. If you don't, you'll stay in your inner world—in metaphysical reality. And if you do *that*, you'll meta-fizzle."

Both Sams felt like kids playing a guessing game.

"No, it's SIPHON," she guessed. "Siphon the learning from the observation."

"No, that makes sense, but the word is too *un*common," he said. "Not after CHOOSE and OBSERVE. It can't be."

"Oooh, *un*common. OK, that may be it. This is the *un*-game, after all." Having exhausted their repertoire, Sam and Samantha became silent.

"Phew," said Sam A. "I think I'll make an appointment with Coach Z. This is about to drive me nuts. I think I'll feed the nuts to my monkey mind and get my mind right." They signaled the waiter for the check. It was close to 9:00 o'clock. They'd been talking for nearly four hours.

Dear Reader

1. The "equipment" that allows the young managers to move the ball up the field toward a goal in the game of life is an *un*conventional metaphor for what's at our disposal to make things happen. How does consciously identifying the "equipment" like "relationship" or "time" when a challenge arises provide a greater opening for reaching your goals at work, home, and in your community? Might you experiment with the "equipment?"

2. Reflecting on your experience, do you agree that the concerns the young woman manager expresses on behalf of employees— Does my manager care about me and my development? Do I have the tools I need to do a great job? Am I using my talent?— are key concerns which managers must address in order to have a vibrant, highly functional work environment?

3. Can you contradict, or do you agree, with the following well known statement? "Any closely held value, no matter how well concealed, even from yourself, inevitably prompts action that's consistent with it." Can you think of a situation in which you once tried to hide a value from yourself, but then it (the value) was revealed to you through your behavior? What changes, if any, did you make upon finding out that your talk and your walk weren't a match, and that you had hidden commitments that were in the way of achieving congruence between what you said and did?

4. It has been said that the most important and the most difficult job people have is to become more themselves, that is, more who they really are in their heart. Samantha Osler is clearly dedicated to the goal of becoming herself. What are your thoughts about that statement? Are you totally who you really are? If so, you may be *un*self-conscious. Is that part of the *un*-game, do you think? Why do you say so?

Chapter 10

SECOND MEETING OF THE *UN*-TEAM

Coach Zabar's office was abuzz with laughter and loud talk. Evidently no one there had heard of the "no cross-talk" rule.

"OK, let's get into the ontological space," said Coach Zabar, and everyone took a seat around the large conference table: Peter Black from Quality Control; Marguerite Chan from Programming; Tom Pierot, Marketing; and Maria Nordstern, HR.

"I'll do it," volunteered Peter. "Who am I willing to be in order to make an extraordinary contribution to this meeting?" They all presented five qualities they were willing to demonstrate. They had each written them in the margin of their note pads. For working in a high-tech company, they were a low-tech bunch.

"Am I willing, in a clear and focused manner, of my own choosing, to observe my closely held beliefs, opinions, and conclusions, no matter what?" was the next question Peter asked.

The group said "yes" in unison. An observer familiar with the COSA process would have recognized the questions relating to choosing and observing. The last two questions covered the 'S' and the 'A' in COSA. The casual observer, however, would have been jarred by the *un*usual use of common words in the questions.

"Great," said the coach, embracing them all with her warm

smile. "It's wonderful to be with you who are so willing to be a contribution.

"So, how's it going? Are we glad we hired Sam Adler? What do we know about how he's doing? Who besides me has seen him since our last meeting?" Coach Zabar inquired.

"I have," replied Maria. Others had seen him informally or had talked with him on the phone or via email.

"Yes, I think L-4 has made a good investment in Sam Adler. He's competitive with himself and intuitively collaborative. A great combination of head and heart. I was impressed with his definition of the *un*-game. And he's got a good grasp of its implications," said Maria.

"Give me an example of how he's being competitive and collaborative, Maria," requested the coach.

"He's competitive with *himself*! I see that in how eager and able he is to put the pieces of what he's learning together. He's getting clear that the *un*-game is about challenging conventional wisdom.

"In terms of the propensity for collaboration, his team is at this very moment genuinely engaged in a process-improvement project they own. The team apparently got the message that he values their contributions. And while I haven't heard him make applications that go beyond his team yet, I'm certain he's capable of seeing the possibility of the quantum mind-set shifts that become available to practiced *un*-game players. He sees COSA as the vehicle to do it. I experience him being on high alert—in a good way."

Maria stopped and looked around the room.

"The other thing I saw," she continued, "is that he's smart. He makes distinctions easily and sees them as important to empower himself. For example, having to *un*learn. And he gets the definition of 'truth' as we define it. There's more. He's quick to connect what he learns from us to the *un*resolved questions he struggles with."

The others nodded.

"Additionally, I admire his being willing to be vulnerable. This is a quality we need desperately if we're going to shift from entrenched positions to taking a stand for what supports the highest good. For example, when he saw that 'the managers from hell' were really about him too, he was shocked but perfectly willing to look, see, and tell the truth about it. Not an easy thing to do." Maria smiled.

"Finally," she said with gusto, "he just sees possibilities everywhere. He's fun to work with. I could probably keep going."

"I agree that he's capable of seeing the big picture," affirmed Coach Zabar. "And I see the competitiveness with himself through his eagerness to outplay monkey mind. That automatically increases his chances of becoming a fabulous observer.

"I also see the facility he has with making distinctions. He's enamored with the distinction 'We have a psychology; we aren't it.' And although I suspect it'll get him into trouble a time or two or three, he sees the difference between observing and analyzing. He observed his thoughts quite a bit and saw that they derive their power from the meaning he attributes to them. That they're often not true as we define 'truth.'

> Being eager to outplay monkey mind automatically increases the chances of becoming a fabulous observer.

"Anyone else have anything to share?" invited the coach.

"He called me about the rules you sent him, Sophia," offered Peter.

"Yeah, he had a huge 'aha' with 'The shortest distance between two points is a straight line,'" Maria added.

"So, do any of you have any more thoughts about what his monkey mind show-stopper is?" asked the coach.

Tom said, "I think it's either 'I'm stupid' or 'I don't know.'" Maria nodded.

"He really wants to know, and if he doesn't, he has a tendency to be self-deprecating. It's hard to tell, but if I were a betting man, I'd say that 'I don't know' is the one," concluded Tom.

"Well, let's just be on the alert, so we can help him recognize it. He'll be glad when he can have this monkey mind show-stopper, rather than *it* having *him* as often as it does right now," said the coach.

The whole *un*-team laughed. They all had to corral their own personal show-stopper monkey mind from time to time. Before knowing what it was, however, each of them had been the target of its mischief…often!

"So it sounds like we're on schedule. He gets the 'C' and now the 'O' at more than the conceptual level. I can tell from what you said that he's gotten some tools. Any tools that weren't mentioned?" Coach Zabar asked.

Peter said, "During our rules conversation he mentioned that he'd learned the playing field metaphor which enabled him to put the *un*-game in a frame that will be very powerful for him. Especially the principle of moving from vision to action and what one can expect from one's monkey mind. I suspect that knowledge will be like a compass for him. He has a talent for applying in action what he's seen in himself even just once. I think he'll be our poster child for promoting self-reflection and self-observation company-wide."

"How *un*-American," joshed Tom Pierot. "Americans are so quick to move to action." The rest of the team acknowledged the *un*-American comment by nodding or chuckling.

"Indeed. And I hope we don't lose our penchant for action. But as we know, informed observation and self-reflection will produce better results," said the coach.

"The 'ME' graphic I showed Sam really got him engaged with self-observation and reflection," she recalled.

"Yes, and he did a lot of self-observation in relation to an employee who was going to leave and now isn't. He emailed me to tell me of his success with this employee—he really handled that conversation fabulously," Marguerite chimed in.

"Apparently he teased out the commitment behind the employee's complaint. I think that's not just an example of making distinctions and applying them, but indicates the level of complexity in thinking that we're hoping to develop throughout L-4. I like seeing it in someone so young. My experience with this generation is so often they're subject to sound bytes and reductionism. Yes, I think he'll go far in L-4," Marguerite concluded.

"Careful about generalizations, Marguerite," warned Maria who was older than the forty-ish Marguerite.

"Duly noted, Maria" was the programming manager's appreciative response.

"What about conventional assumptions he's challenged?" Tom Pierot asked.

"Well, with the rules that he requested I send him," the coach answered, "he's examined 'People work for money,' 'People work for companies,' 'People are broken and need to be fixed,' and 'The shortest distance between two points is a straight line.' But there are a lot of other assumptions he's challenging. That's another thing I really like about him. He's willing to challenge."

"Does anyone know anything about if or how he's using support?" asked Peter.

"Yeah. I spoke with Samantha Osler the other day," replied Marguerite. "They had a terrific meeting. Seemed to deepen the learning. And they had fun. My sense from talking with Samantha is that they both did some good observing during their meeting. She shared with him the equipment on the playing field since she'd learned that already. He was particularly impressed that 'enjoyment' was part of the available equipment. The conventional wisdom 'Work is not fun' got a blow to its head at that meeting."

They all laughed, affirming the value of enjoyment.

"Not-in-the-know" observers would have been shaking their head at this strange *un*-team.

"OK, so we're on schedule," Coach Zabar said. "What we're hoping for is that Sam Adler gets a few more tools in the process of learning COSA, but most of all we want him to get the COSA process itself. So we're ready to move to Step Three of our four-play to business as *un*usual, right?"

"Yes, Sophia. And not to worry. They'll lead, and we'll follow," teased Maria. "But I think we can be pretty sure that we'll be able to shine a light on their conclusion about how one reaches conclusions."

They laughed at their inside joke.

"As for Step Three, Sophia," said Marguerite, "Samantha and I talked about it a little. They were both speculating about the 'S' in COSA during their meeting. They're ready, so get ready."

"OK, let's talk about Samantha Osler and then be on our way. Are we glad we hired her?"

The group appreciated Coach Zabar not only as their coach but also as a great facilitator. They continued their conversation, and in another fifteen minutes their agenda had been completed. Amidst animated conversation, laughter, hugs, and backslaps, the *un*-team filed out of Coach Zabar's office.

Dear Reader

1. An assertion is made in this chapter that the practice of challenging conventional wisdom can result in quantum mind-set shifts. How would you define a quantum mind-set shift, and do you agree with the assertion? What might be an argument against the practice of challenging conventional wisdom?
2. What was the most important thing you *un*learned as a manager or in your personal life? Why was it so important for you?
3. The qualities the *un*-team admires in Sam Adler are not the conventional qualities associated with a high-level manager. Being vulnerable, for example, is seen as a strength. Is that a mistake? Why or why not? Can you recall a time in your life where being vulnerable was a strength?
4. Marguerite Chan talks about L-4 wanting to develop a higher level of thinking throughout the company. Couldn't it be said that we, as a culture, are already demonstrating an incredibly high complexity in thinking as evidenced by our technological achievements? How might the level of thinking Marguerite talks about be different, if at all?

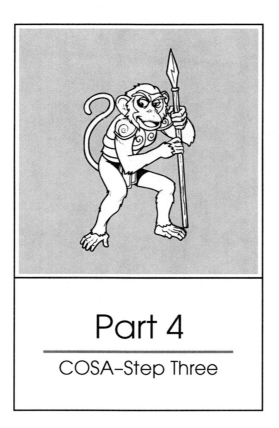

Part 4

COSA–Step Three

Chapter 11

THE ULTIMATE CHALLENGE

"Hi, Jane. Could you check for me when Coach Zabar is available?" Sam asked the coach's receptionist the morning after his meeting with Sam Osler. "Great. A cancellation? See you at two then. Thanks a lot."

Sam hung up the phone, shifted a non-urgent appointment he'd scheduled for 2:00PM, got himself some coffee—go-go juice, as a corny Texan friend would call it—and sat down with old-fashioned paper and pen to get clear on what he wanted coaching on.

Smiling, he briefly thought about his new *un*corny friend from Texas, Sam Osler. *Un*corny, *un*common, and for sure *un*expected. He remembered how much fun they, the Alpha and the Omega, had had and how much they were *un*covering—the COSA process, the *un*examined assumptions great managers didn't buy into. He loved thinking about it all.

But back to COSA. What did he want out of his next coaching session? First of all he wanted to find out what the 'S' stood for and get to know whatever principle the 'S' represented. And maybe he could get some feedback on setting clear expectations. The meeting with his team had been productive. Still, it might be useful to talk about it. Or maybe he could bring up his hesitation to talk to Bob about being an airhead. Carrying on at the water cooler as if he didn't know calls needed to be returned in a timely manner. He thought about Bob with mild resentment, his hero image having faded from Sam's mind. Too bad they all weren't like Russell.

At exactly 2:00PM, Sam entered Coach Zabar's office. "So, Sam, what would you like coaching on today?" asked the coach after some friendly preliminaries, the familiar choosing of five qualities, and a second question about being willing to examine closely held beliefs. They both said "yes" to the second question.

"Why would Coach Z be willing to examine *her* beliefs?" Sam still wondered. "She already knows everything."

As soon as he thought that, his face got warm. Of course, she'd want to examine her own thinking. That's how she stays as sharp as she is.

"What I'm most curious about, Coach Zabar, is the 'S' in the COSA process. Even though it's clear to me that without observation I'll always be a feather in the wind rather than the wind, it's equally clear to me that if I stay in observation, I might as well be navel-gazing. It's all useless without action. So it's got to have something to do with action. I can't just follow Marguerite Chan's advice."

"And what advice is that?"

"Don't just do something. Sit there."

"Yes, that's useful in order to hone your skills as a competent observer. You're right, Sam. Ultimately you have to act. Do you have another challenge you'd like coaching on?"

"I do," Sam replied, wondering why she wasn't answering his question about the 'S' in COSA. He hadn't noticed that the coach and the managers rarely answered questions.

"And what might that be?"

"I need to confront one of my team. I'll refer to him as Bob. Bob doesn't consistently do what he says he'll do, and he spends a lot of time on breaks. I've noticed I find all kinds of excuses to not confront him. There must be something about this I don't see. Otherwise I'd go ahead and take the plunge, don't you think?" Sam declared rather than asked, looking as frustrated as he sounded.

"It's courageous of you to be willing to meet this challenge. Many managers will offer up all the reasons why they don't confront. Alternately they'll just barf all over the guy."

The coach's choice of words distracted Sam for a moment as he envisioned what this grandmotherly woman had just said.

"What is it that you're seeing about not seeing something?" Sam heard her say.

He thought this was a weird question, but he answered after the brief hesitation that meant he was scanning his experience for the answer. "I'm seeing that I'm both frustrated and curious about finding out what I'm not seeing."

"So if I asked you 'Why aren't you talking to Bob about your concerns?' what would you say?"

"I'd say it's because I'm in the fog," Sam replied cautiously.

"That's interesting. Didn't you say that Bob's behavior warranted confrontation?"

Coach Zabar was clear and focused as she and Sam began the process of systematically *un*packing his beliefs around his challenge with Bob.

"You sound pretty clear to me. So if you were to penetrate your so-called fog, what would you see about what's stopping you from having this conversation with Bob?"

"I want to do it right. I don't want to cut him off at the knees, but I want this stuff to stop."

"There's a right way to do this, and if you knew what that was, then you could proceed, is that correct?"

"Yeah." Sam shifted his weight and tapped his fingers on the armrest of his chair.

"What's happening right now, Sam?"

"There *is* a right way, just like there's a right way to set expectations, and I'm getting the feeling you're going to tell me there is no right way."

"And what's that like for you, thinking that?"

"I don't like it."

"I get you don't like it, but what's that like for you thinking that? What's your experience, not your assessment of your feelings?"

The coach's questions showed her *un*flagging commitment to help Sam *un*cover how he had constructed his mental model about doing things right.

"Truth be told, my gut's constricted. I'm *un*comfortable."

"Very clear. That's the truth, and you don't like it. What do you see about your discomfort?" she asked in a matter-of-fact tone of voice.

"I don't want you to change my mind."

> The worst thing about changing my mind is that it's *un*comfortable. It's as if there's a void where the old thinking was. The void will make a new demand of me.

"I see. What's the worst thing that would happen if you changed your mind about 'there's a right way to confront'?"

"I'd have to change." Sam heard the hint of a whine in his voice.

"Very good. What do you see as the worst thing about changing?

"It's *un*comfortable. It's as if there's a void where my old thinking was. It'll make a new demand of me."

"And what would that be?" Coach Zabar leaned forward, her voice conveying only interest.

"I might have to give up a belief I'm comfortable with."

"And what belief might that be?"

"There's a right way to confront," Sam answered, but he was worried he might have to give up some other 'right' ways of believing things.

"And you're not up to it?" Sam could hear the amusement in her voice.

"Yeah, that's what I'm afraid of. But saying it out loud, I'm thinking 'That's stupid thinking.' Being able to give up outmoded beliefs is not only good but necessary."

Coach Zabar chuckled. "Breathe, Sam."

Sam reluctantly did as directed. It calmed him a little.

"When you look, who do you see having the thought 'It's stupid'?" Coach Zabar asked, still smiling.

There was a moment of silence, then a look of recognition. "Oh, it's monkey mind." His brief smile morphed into a frown.

"Do you see it?"

"Yes. I see it. Damn. No doubt about it." Sam tapped the armrest of his chair.

"So what's the truth about what you've been telling me, remembering that truth as we define it is just the facts and not what we make the facts mean?"

Sam sat in silence before saying, "The truth is that whether or not there's a right way to talk to Bob, I haven't talked to him. I've made the thought 'there's a right way' important. It's also true that I've wanted to hold on and protect the notion that there's a right way to do things—period."

"Brilliant observation, Sam, and you're courageous to boot! Out of what you've learned about yourself just now, how would you language the lesson that's available here for you?"

Sam lingered on the acknowledgment and how the coach used "language" as a verb rather than a noun. Then sifting through his experience for the lesson, he said, "Well, I've focused on all the reasons why I shouldn't have a face-to-face with Bob, and how else I could do it while preserving my fragile comfort level. That's not useful. It doesn't move anything forward. I could just keep my eye on the prize, namely that a great manager wouldn't let this go, because it wouldn't be in line with motivating and developing his people. Nor would it be consistent with the expectations that are in place."

"Very good. Anything else?"

"Yes. My hanging on to 'there's a right way' to do things is pretty confining. There may be many right ways to do it, and I imagine more than one could work if I'm coming from the right place. If I'm clear and one hundred percent committed *not* to manipulate people."

"Fabulous. Anything else?"

"Yeah, that monkey mind is one cunning little sucker. I better be alert, or it'll outplay me," laughed Sam. He seemed to have recovered from his disappointment at failing to recognize his monkey mind.

"Well done, Sam. Out of what you've become aware of, is there an action you're willing to promise which would be a small demonstration of what you learned here today?"

"Sure. I'll set up a meeting with Bob when I get back to the office today." Sam's reply was quick and transmitted the clarity he had achieved during the coaching.

"Good work, Sam. I appreciate how determined you are to create value out of our sessions together. Being coachable is one of the key characteristics of being a great manager. Good for you."

The coach relaxed into her chair and asked, "Would you like to learn about the 'S' in the COSA process now?"

"Yes. Thank you, Coach." Sam was ready to listen.

Coach Zabar began, "As you reflect on our session, would you tell me what you see about how this session was structured, that is, did it have a structure, and if so, what structure can you identify?"

"No rest for the weary," Sam thought, as he realized he'd hoped the coach would tell him about the 'S.' Then he saw what a lie that lamentation was. He was immediately engaged, alert, and attentive.

"Well, we began by getting ourselves into a frame of mind that would facilitate, although not guarantee, that we'd be successful in meeting the challenge I brought to you for coaching. We did that by choosing five qualities we were willing to demonstrate in our interaction with each other."

"Go on."

"Then you asked me a question about being willing to observe, which we both answered with 'yes.' That in turn further framed the session; we are both willing to make it great."

"Yes. Go on."

"Then you asked me a bunch of questions that had me observe. In other words we did the 'CO,' the first two steps in the COSA process."

Sam paused, stroking an imaginary beard.

"At the end you asked if I saw anything actionable and if I was willing to promise an action based on what I had observed. So I speculate"—Sam was *not* going to say 'I guess!'—"that the 'A' in COSA is about taking action.

"But we're not here to talk about the 'A.' There was something in between the observation and the invitation to take action, Coach, but I'm having a hard time identifying what that was."

"Hmm," was the coach's only response. They sat together in silence.

"You asked me some more questions," Sam said, filling the void.

"Do you remember what questions I asked you?" The coach's calm questioning communicated interest and that she had all the time in the world and no more important place to be.

"You asked me something like, 'So what's the truth about what you've been telling me'?"

"What is it about that question that stood out for you?"

"I remember that something shifted for me as you asked it. I can't put my finger on it except that something shifted," Sam replied, feeling relaxed but alert. "You also said something like 'I should remember that truth is just the facts and not what we make the facts mean.'"

"You said that something shifted in your mind. Was there anything else that either you or I said which alerted you to a shift?"

Sam took a deep breath and said, "When I started talking about the facts, I experienced myself as strong. It was great telling the truth, that is, the facts, and experiencing the difference between what I *think* the truth is when I'm having monkey mind chatter and *observing* the monkey mind chatter, knowing that the meaning I attribute to the facts isn't the truth."

Sam reviewed what he had just said. Satisfied that he'd reported his experience accurately, he continued. "The meaning is not the fact. Therefore, by our definition, the meaning is not the truth. I'm allowed to make up the meaning, but the facts aren't mine to make up. In other words—and this is funny—" he said, chuckling, "I have a right to my own opinion, but I don't have a right to my own facts."

The coach chuckled with him. Returning to the description of the shift he had experienced, Sam became serious.

> The meaning is not the fact. Therefore, the meaning is not the truth. You're allowed to make up the meaning, but the facts aren't yours to make up. You have a right to your own opinion, but you don't have a right to your own facts.

"It's so freeing," he said passionately. "Telling the truth is freeing. And then you asked something like," Sam's voice gathered speed and volume, "'Out of what you've learned about yourself just now, how would you language the lesson that's available here for you?' I remember that making an impact."

"What kind of an impact?"

"I felt vulnerable. It was as if you were asking me to make a commitment or something."

"Was I?"

"Not really. Except to say out loud what I've learned."

"That could be seen as a commitment. You're taking a stand for what you've learned."

"Yeah, and it feels like pressure."

"How so?"

"Because if I learn something, then in *my* world I have an obligation to do something with it. So that was significant for me." He took an audible breath.

"Nevertheless you did articulate what you'd learned, right?"

"Yes, I did."

"Well done, Sam. You've just described the 'S' in COSA.

Sam's mouth dropped open. He leaned forward. "I'm not leaving here 'til you explain it all to me."

Coach Zabar laughed out loud. "Now that's what I call being eager for the lesson."

Sam leaned back in his chair, relieved she wouldn't leave him in the lurch. "Thanks Coach," he sighed.

The coach settled back in her chair as well, folded her hands together, and asserted, "I don't have to explain it to you. You already know. I'll paraphrase what you told me. You accurately observed how the session is structured—the choosing, the observing. You then said that telling the truth was freeing and that my asking you to say what you learned had a big impact on you. And that despite your reluctance to say out loud what you learned—since it might require a change in your behavior—you still articulated the lesson. And you didn't stop there. You actually promised to take an action. Did I summarize what happened?"

Sam nodded.

"So which part of what happened is the 'S'?"

"I don't know, but you just described the shift I had earlier" Sam said, flooded with the emotion that often accompanies a profound realization. "I was willing to say 'yes' to the learning. And when I told the truth rather than empowering the interpretation, I also said 'yes' to the lesson and 'yes' to who I really am in my heart, as opposed to going down the usual path that monkey mind urges me fervently to stay on. Like urging me to dazzle you with my brilliant reasoning."

As he heard himself talk, it became clear. "The 'S' is SAY YES. That's the principle, and I demonstrated it," he said, becoming pensive.

The coach nodded. "Pretty good?" she asked.

"No, not pretty good, Coach Zabar. Very, very good. Excellent. No, awesome. Oh, I don't even have the words except to say I'm willing to say 'yes.'" Sam fell silent and relaxed into his chair.

"Well, well," smiled the coach. "That's a rare occurrence for a wordsmith like you," she teased. Then almost tenderly, she said, "I can't think of anything more powerful than to take a stand for saying 'yes' to the lessons that are yours to learn as you travel on your hero's journey. It's a most courageous act."

"Yes. I really get that." Sam swallowed hard then cleared his throat.

> There is nothing more powerful than taking a stand for saying "yes" to the lessons that are yours to learn as you travel on your hero's journey. It's a most courageous act.

"Tell me what's courageous about saying 'yes,' Sam."

"If you say it, you make yourself vulnerable. You can't predict what's going to happen. You don't know how it may change your life and what challenges might be too big for you to meet. You're embracing the discomfort of the *un*known, and you might not even be an adventurer. You probably don't want to enter the *un*known. Nevertheless you're willing. That 'yes' is a very big deal."

"You got it, Sam. It's the ultimate challenge. It has *un*doubtedly been a challenging journey up until this point. Without choosing who you're willing to be and without observation, you will not even be presented with the opportunity to meet the ultimate challenge.

"Most of us think that action is the ultimate challenge. No, it's not. Action is the natural outcome of having met the ultimate challenge! Our thinking around the source of action is incorrect. And rushing into it leads us to a detour, sometimes a very long and costly one.

"Without meeting the ultimate challenge," Coach Zabar said solemnly, "you can't take authentic action. Authentic action is action that's the next, obvious play you make on the goal. It's based on a learning you've become aware of and to which your hero's heart has said 'yes.'

"Yes. Yes. Yes," Coach Zabar concluded with *un*characteristic passion. "The 'S' in COSA, the third point of power, stands for SAY YES. Yes, I am willing. Yes, I am willing to take this as my lesson. I might not like it. I might be *un*comfortable and afraid. I might be clueless about how to do it. Nevertheless I am willing to say 'yes.'

"And the action, Sam, if you look back on all the sessions you've had, what do you notice?"

Sam hesitated only briefly. "You always asked me if I was willing to promise an action, and I always did. But the action was always based on something I learned that had been utterly invisible to me until we had the conversation. The conversation transformed what I was able to do. I went from being powerless to being powerful. Just like a minute ago when I had my 'aha' about the 'S' being SAY YES. Now that I know this, a lot more is possible than when I was guessing what the 'S' meant."

"Yes. You can transform the world one conversation at a time," the coach nodded.

"And the actions you promised, and the results you created,

> Without meeting the ultimate challenge, you can't take authentic action. Authentic action is action that's the next, obvious play you make on the goal. It's based on a learning you've become aware of and to which your hero's heart has said "yes."

Sam, would they have been possible without meeting the ultimate challenge of saying 'yes' to your lesson?"

There seemed to be an emerging awareness in Sam's next remarks. "I could have promised and created results without meeting the ultimate challenge. People do it all the time. But no. My results are qualitatively different. I'm different after coaching than before. And so are the results I produce. Like my team owning the process improvement they're working on.

"I have a larger question about action, Coach Zabar. In the past both you and Marguerite Chan have made comments I didn't understand when I wanted to move into action. You said something like 'Whoa,' or 'How American.' But neither of you ever explained. Is it a cultural norm that we put action in the wrong place in the United States? We seem to begin with the question 'What are we going to do?' We're very quick to act unless we get mired in political showmanship—let's call it monkey mind—designed to delay action."

"You may be on to something although I wouldn't say it's always in the wrong place. Would you be interested in seeing what we've gleaned from talking with L-4 managers around the globe? I can send you the information."

"I'd be honored to see it," said Sam, flattered at the offer.

"Shall we call the session complete then?"

"Yes. Except for one more question, please?"

"Go ahead."

"You made a provocative statement that we can transform our world one conversation at a time. I suspect that those conversations would be rather *un*usual and take into consideration what I learned about taking action and producing extraordinary results. Is it fair to characterize them like that?"

"Of course. This is, after all, the *un*-game we're playing. Transformation depends on the *un*-game. If you want to know the purpose and the characteristics of conversations that transform, you might visit one of the managers on the list I gave you. All of them are skilled in that kind of conversation. That, among other talents, skills, and knowledge makes them great managers."

With that comment, Coach Zabar got up, affectionately patted Sam on the back, and wished him a good day.

✶✶★✶✶

At the end of the day when Sam checked his email, he found a document from Coach Zabar.

"Here are some informal notes from our first global *un*-team meeting," she wrote. "These are the beliefs, opinions, and conclusions of the *un*-team managers. Don't get hung up on what may not be true. No generalization is always true. Not all cultures are included. Find what's valuable and toss the rest. The important thing is that you get a sense of why we examine and challenge our *un*examined assumptions, including those around action."

"What an interesting term, the *un*-team," Sam thought. "And it's global and only about a year and a half old." He opened the document and started reading.

FIRST GLOBAL *UN*-TEAM MEETING
Values that Attract People to L-4:

1. L-4's commitment to reinvent how business does business globally
   a. Recognition of the power of corporations
   b. Recognition that business as usual is not sustainable
2. Expressed commitment L-4 has for the triple bottom line
   a. Structures and practices are not in place, but vision exists.
      i. All business decisions must benefit people, planet, and profits.
   b. Commitment to move from vision to action is real.
      i. COSA process training has begun.

L-4 recognizes that:

1. Americans are five percent of world population consuming twenty-five percent of the planet's resources.

2. In the US people live beyond the earth's means.

3. People in Germany live beyond the earth's means too (three fifths as much as Americans). If everyone lived like Americans, five earths would be needed.

4. India and China are not yet living beyond Earth's means but are emulating the US.

5. This world-wide behavior pattern is *un*sustainable. We only have one earth.

6. A revolution of the heart is needed at home, at work, in the community, the nation, and in the world.

7. Corporations are not exempt. We must lead because we have become so powerful.

8. We must access our individual and corporate hero's heart and subordinate our individual and corporate monkey mind.

9. The COSA process gives us the tools to do that, one conversation at a time.

10. We can transform the world one conversation at a time, and it begins with the individual in your seat!

Different Cultures' Relationship to Action:
Un-Team Brainstorm

1. Americans and the Japanese are known for action. When there's a problem, a challenge, or even an opportunity, the question they're interested in is *What? What* can we do?

2. Not every culture is so keen on jumping into action. The Germans are interested in a different question—*How? How* will it work?

3. The French ask *Why? Why* is it this way?

4. Spanish speaking peoples are interested in the question *Who?* *Who* is involved?

5. Results the people in those cultures value and produce are different than those of any other culture. It's a matter of focus or emphasis.

   a. American: Penchant for acting put a man on the moon and created a lasting democracy. More short-term orientation.
   b. Japanese: "Kaizen"—continuous improvement and long-term orientation. World-famous business models.
   c. German: Scientific know-how, performance upper-end cars like Mercedes, Porsche, and BMW.
   d. French: World-renowned philosophers and thinkers. Think Descartes, Albert Camus, Jean-Paul Sartre
   e. Hispanic/Latino: Relationships to family and community are key. World-famous foods, art.

In a note Sam saw the following: Indigenous peoples like the Achuar of Ecuador and Peru are outside the dominant culture and are not included in this discussion around action. Action in some cultures focuses on preservation not progress. Guiding principle: All is related; we are one with nature.

Sam stopped reading, fascinated by what the first global *un*-team had said about different peoples' relationship to action. He knew that the American thirst for progress was not universal, but seeing it seriously discussed at L-4 nevertheless gave him pause. It showed that the ethnocentrism other countries roundly criticized Americans for was perhaps diminishing. L-4's discussion had enormous implications. But what intrigued him the most was the American emphasis on action. The American relationship to action was particularly poignant in light of the coaching. No wonder he had such trouble with Marguerite Chan's advice "Don't just do something. Sit there."

"I bet the French would have no trouble with Marguerite's

suggestion," he thought. "They have a natural cultural orientation for reflection." This was all very provocative.

Sam left the goal section of the notes for later. "You can transform the world one conversation at a time, and it begins with the individual in your seat" begged for reflection.

"Wow," said Sam and whistled. "This is a big game worth playing. A lot bigger than examining our closely held beliefs about how to produce action in the customer support department. This is about a fundamental paradigm shift. The *un*-game, what a ride!"

Dear Reader

1. Can you think of an example of a closely held belief, opinion, or conclusion you gave up? In the process of giving it up, what was your experience? Sam talked about his discomfort as he gave up "There's a right way to confront." He also spoke about a void where his old thinking was. He said it will demand something new of him. How was your experience the same? Different?

2. Have you ever had a transformative conversation? What made it transformative, rather than ordinary? What were the other person's contributions? What were yours?

Chapter 12

TRANSFORMING CONVERSATIONS

S am walked into his department early the next morning still mentally engaged with his last coaching session and the First *Un-*Team Meeting notes. At the water cooler he ran into Bob. He arranged to meet with him the following afternoon.

"It's interesting," he mused as he entered his office. "Each time I have a coaching session, I leave the session with a higher level of energy and a sense that I can do things I didn't think I could do the day or even the hour before the conversation."

"You can transform the world one conversation at a time," the *un-*team meeting notes and Coach Zabar had asserted. That intrigued Sam. After all, he was a language whiz. Not only did he speak four languages, he had a talent for intuiting the impact of language on himself and others.

"Language dictates your experience," he thought. "Language *does* transform." And he needed a transformative conversation with Bob. That was clear as a Montana sky. Not the same old conversation that produced predictable but tired results.

Sam looked at his watch and decided to call Peter Black in order to get his questions on these *un*usual conversations answered.

"Sure, come on over. I have no fires to put out. I need to be a worse manager so that my department doesn't run itself," he joked. Sam laughed and said, "I'll be there in five."

🧍🧍🧍🧍🧍

"What an education I'm getting!" Sam thought as he sat down across from Peter.

"Hi, Peter. Good to see you, and thanks for seeing me." Sam remembered instantly why he always had a sense that "everything's OK" in the company of this kind man.

"Good to be seen, Sam," said Peter, chuckling at his own humor. Then his countenance changed, and he was ready to attend to Sam's concerns.

"I'm here because I'm intrigued with a comment Coach Zabar made about conversations that can transform the world." Although Sam was concerned Peter might think of him as a megalomaniac for even considering wanting to change the world, or as an idealistic teenager who still had to learn how the world really works, he pushed on.

"Being an effective communicator is important to me. Besides, I don't see how anybody can be a great manager without being an effective communicator."

"Yes, for a manager, the ability to have transformative conversations is critically important. Can't do without it. What do you suppose characterizes a conversation that could merit the descriptor 'transformative'?"

"When I think about 'transform,' I think of a major change—the old form barely, if at all, recognizable."

"Uh-huh. And where have you been having *un*recognizable-by-ordinary-standards kinds of conversations?" the quality control manager asked.

"Right here with you, and with Marguerite Chan, Tom Pierot, and Maria Nordstern, and of course with Coach Zabar. Come to think of it, even with Samantha Osler, the woman responsible for employee communications," Sam added, just having become aware of that.

"And what do those conversations have in common?"

"Well, they're open, not guarded. They're honest. There's no game playing."

"Meaning non-manipulative?"

"Uh-huh. They're also confrontational."

"What does 'confront' mean to you?"

Sam went on alert. The "what does it mean?" part of Peter's question took him back to the pitfalls of meaning-making.

"'Confront' to me announces a tough conversation."

"How would you explain the toughness or the confrontational quality of a transformative conversation?"

Pensive, Sam replied, "It confronts your world view. That's what it does."

"So it could be said that the thing the transformative conversation *does* is interrogate reality?"

"Yes, that's spot-on. For what seems like an eternity, your mind stays still because your world view has been assaulted. Then it sinks in that you didn't have a corner on the truth—despite the fact that you'd been absolutely certain.

"It's weird, but if the conversation occurs in a safe space and you hang in there, then the new reality seems to become spacious, full of promise."

Sam thought of his conversation with Maria Nordstern about the shortest distance between two points not being a straight line but rather the path of least resistance.

Peter Black seemed impressed. "Yes, so transformative conversations, which could probably be described as passionate, *un*bridled, authentic, and clear, *do* interrogate reality. They don't assume things are as they seem to be.

"Willing participants in transformative conversations check out assumptions and even assume that they, concealed or not, are indeed assumptions and not necessarily the truth." He laughed at his quip, and Sam was reminded of his first impression of Peter and his friendly laugh wrinkles. He trusted this good man and his keen sense of humor.

Suddenly leaning forward, he asked, "Have you ever read Don Miguel Ruiz' *The Four Agreements*? One of the four agreements is 'Don't Make Assumptions.' I never agreed with that, because we can't help making assumptions, but we better check them out. Nonetheless, I bet Don Miguel Ruiz knows what a transformative conversation is." He was animated, his eyes bright.

The older man smiled. "I bet he does. I bet he does," he said.

Sam resumed his train of thought. "Well, transformative conversations can be tough because you can't have them without learning something you need to know. And monkey mind, if I understand it, doesn't want you to learn anything new, because it doesn't want you to change or even contemplate change. It hates it, and that might look to the outside world as if you're getting defensive or something. We're defensive if the conversation gets too hot. It's like our brain is overloaded and we trip a circuit breaker. It could be said we're literally out of our mind—our cool, rational mind, that is."

> Transformative conversations can be tough because you can't have them without learning something you need to know. And monkey mind doesn't want you to learn anything new.

"Yeah, that's a great description and a fresh perspective," said Peter with admiration. "Transformative conversations tackle tough challenges. What's tough varies from individual to individual. Each of us has challenges though."

Sam nodded. "Yes, and therefore transformative conversations must provoke learning. Otherwise they wouldn't be able to transform. They couldn't change the world."

"Very perceptive, Sam. You have a talent for making connections, and that's a skill-set the world needs now. It wasn't so critical when there were so few of us on the planet, but now there are seven billion of us. The world has in effect shrunk, and the complexity we face has grown to staggering proportions. What we need now more than ever is what may well be natural to humans, but which many of us have forgotten in an attempt to manage the growing complexity of our world."

"What's natural that we've forgotten?" Sam was always up for a fascinating conversation.

"Being system thinkers, instead of training ourselves to be experts in just one thing and neglecting everything else. Right now many specialists act as if cutting their hand off wouldn't affect the rest of their body. I get images of people sitting in the bow of a boat saying 'We're glad that hole in the stern is not on our side!'."

Sam observed Peter in silence. The quality control manager's speaking reminded him of Coach Zabar's notes of the first global *un*-team meeting. He thought about the American short-term orientation and the short-sightedness of business to only consider shareholder profits, leaving the well-being of people and planet for others to defend. The Ecuadorian and Peruvian Achuar people mentioned in Coach Z's notes came to mind. Their orientation, 'Everything is related,' would make them system thinkers, Sam speculated.

Peter Black would have been at that global *un*-team meeting. Like the coach, Peter seemed to experience some urgency about change on a global scale. "These people are committed to a huge game—the Super Bowl on life's playing field. Or more like soccer's World Cup, a more global event," Sam thought. He got that both Peter and Coach Zabar saw transformative conversations as a means to an important end result.

"So transformative conversations interrogate one's reality," said Peter, breaking into Sam's thoughts. "They induce, even provoke learning, and they tackle the tough challenges. They do at least one more thing. Reflect back on the conversations you've had, Sam, since you said 'yes' to the development opportunity that brought us together. Tell me if you see anything else."

Sam scanned his experience. "I do, Peter. You mentioned that I see connections. I see and feel them too. Like feeling connected to Coach Zabar and you." He stole a glance at Peter, then decided to risk saying "I feel as if we could safely talk about anything, even the tough stuff."

"So the fourth result of transformative conversations is that they enrich relationships, yes?" Peter stated more than asked.

"Yes! Which actually blows a cultural *un*examined assumption right out of the water."

"Which one is that?"

"Well, most people think that tough conversations will hurt relationships. I've heard people say, 'I didn't say anything because I didn't want to hurt his feelings.' I never heard anyone say 'I confronted him because I wanted to protect the relationship.'"

Peter gave Sam a thumbs-up. "That's quite the observation, Sam. Much of the time it's just a very clever monkey mind conversation that goes something like this: 'I'm afraid I might be *un*comfortable. Therefore I don't want to have the tough conversation. I might get hurt or lose face. But hell, I can't say that. That wouldn't fit my self-image as a generous, cool, compassionate, all-around-good-guy. So therefore, Self, just make up some horseshit. Then you won't have to change.'" Peter shook his head.

"Monkey mind keeps its host safely mired in the status quo," he continued. "People won't change as long as they're not aware of its mischief. Phew! Averted *that* one! You see, monkey mind keeps us out of trouble, so to speak. What could be better? Except nothing happens. No transformation. We didn't have a transformative conversation. We had a cover-your-ass conversation!"

"Isn't there a way to make monkey mind capitulate?" It wasn't the first time Sam had asked that question. Nor would it be the last.

"You mean wrestle it to the floor? No, it doesn't work like that. Ever heard the saying 'What you appreciate appreciates'?" The older man relaxed into his chair.

"Uh-huh. But what does that have to do with what we're talking about?"

"Look at it. Trying to force monkey mind to capitulate means you're paying a lot of attention to monkey mind, doesn't it? 'Go away, you stupid monkey. Get out of here, or I'll kick your butt.' What happens to your attention? Do you turn away, or do you strategize how to get rid of monkey mind?"

Sam had experience. "I strategize," he admitted. "I devise schemes I hope will silence that sucker!"

"And?"

"And it follows me everywhere. What I appreciate appreciates. As a matter of fact, it gets louder and more insistent." Sam harrumphed. "Yeah, I *do* see it. I hadn't thought about it," he added. "But the conventional approach a manager might take with, let's say, one of *my* monkey mind beliefs is to convince me that seeing only 'one right way' is a limiting

> Monkey mind keeps its host safely mired in the status quo. People won't change as long as they're not aware of its mischief. Monkey mind keeps us out of "trouble"—except nothing happens. No transformation.

belief. He wouldn't identify it as monkey mind, of course. Next he'd prove that there are many ways to get to Rome, so to speak. That should be it. I would now no longer be bound by my limiting belief. End of story. But Coach Zabar never does that."

Sam silently reviewed snippets of conversations he'd had with Coach Zabar.

When he continued he said, "Coach Zabar's and my conversations use monkey mind to surface hidden commitments, like me insisting on playing it safe or wanting to look good. I become aware of them, and I learn from them. The conversation focuses away from the monkey mind without losing the lesson. It definitely never focuses on removing the monkey mind. Hmm.

Sam had learned that you can have monkey mind without monkey mind having *you!* But you had to see it to be able to use it. He silently congratulated himself before his upcoming conversation with Bob sobered him.

"Excellent, Sam. And the very act of shifting away from the monkey mind chatter after taking the lesson it has to offer is a courageous and significant act. It's huge. I hope you see that," Peter said.

Sam nodded. He recalled his last conversation with Coach Zabar. He got how significant it is to be able to shift your focus away from what monkey mind loves to focus on, like being right or the illusion of being in control.

> Difficult people don't exist.

"So Sam, did you get what you came for today?"

"Yes," he said, although the thought of talking to Bob still made his shoulders tense.

"Peter, would you say that practice is what I need most? I have a conversation with a difficult employee tomorrow." Sam was not quite finished after all.

"You're certain you have a difficult employee, and if I told you there *is* no such thing, what would you say?"

"Hell no. You're wrong!" There wasn't a second's hesitation in Sam's reply.

"So I'm prepared to show you that difficult people don't exist. Really. Are you willing to be an eager learner?"

"I suppose so." Sam was on high alert again. He didn't like this at all—no, not at all.

"That would be a 'no,'" said the quality control manager, simply reporting without judgment. He leaned closer to Sam and looked intently at the younger man, witnessing his emerging struggle.

"Yeah, you're wrong. I have a difficult person, and I have a meeting with him tomorrow. I have plenty of evidence." There was more than a little indignation in Sam's voice.

"I'm sure you *do* have plenty of evidence," Peter said soothingly. "I'm sure you do. Nevertheless, are you willing to be an eager learner?" The fact that no irritation showed in his voice or his manner told Sam that Peter was not invested in a particular answer.

"Well…"

"That would also be a 'no.'" Peter said this matter-of-factly, leaning back again and tapping his fingers together lightly. He studied Sam's face.

"Damn. This is hard." A stubborn resignation had crept into Sam's voice.

"Indeed. That's why saying 'yes' is the ultimate challenge. But are you willing even as it's very clear you don't want to? Even though you think I'm crazy? Even though you're saying to yourself, 'What's wrong with that guy'?"

"Crap. There's really no way out, is there?" He knew the answer from having asked the question several times before.

"Correct. It's either 'yes' or 'no.' Not 'maybe,' not 'I suppose so,' not 'I guess.' It's just 'yes' or 'no.'"

"And if I say 'no'?"

"No problem. A 'no' is just as good as a 'yes,' if you choose it consciously. Just be clear who often answers that question with an *un*conscious 'no.'"

The room suddenly seemed bigger to Sam.

"Oh. Monkey mind. A monkey mind 'no' is not freely chosen. And the 'yes' belongs to the hero's heart," he said. "It's freely chosen."

"You got it, Sam. Congratulations."

Sam experienced no jubilation. Something wasn't right.

"Something's missing," he said. "Yes, I *am* willing to be an eager learner. So why am I not jazzed?"

"Very good. Would it be all right with you if this were easier than you think?"

"Yes."

"That was a clear 'yes.' How come?"

"I knew what I was saying 'yes' to."

"Exactly. So what were you thinking you were saying 'yes' to when I asked you if you were willing to be an eager learner?"

"Duh! I added something to your question. I added that you wanted me to say 'yes' to your conclusion 'Difficult people don't exist.' No wonder I waffled. I wasn't clear."

"Do I want you to share my conclusion?"

"I doubt it's important to you."

"Do I want you to be clear?"

"Probably."

"Yes, because I want you to be powerful. And in the *un*-game, clarity is power." Peter took a deep breath and let it out.

"So let me get this straight," Sam said. "There are really several 'yesses' in COSA so far. 'Yes' to being in the ontological domain by choosing who I'm willing to be. 'Yes' to being willing to observe. 'Yes' to the ultimate challenge of being an eager learner which includes saying 'yes' to the lesson that I've become aware of."

"Yes indeed, Sam."

"This is fabulous, Peter. There's no way I could've met the ultimate challenge given how I have this wired." Sam felt as if he'd just found a buried treasure.

"Tell me more, Sam."

"To me Step Three is about being open to learning generally but also about surrendering to a specific lesson that, prior to Step Three, I'm *un*aware of. I could say 'yes' to the first—being open to learning; but with thinking you wanted me to have the same conclusion as *you* do, I couldn't have said 'yes' to the second—surrendering to a specific lesson.

"I couldn't have said 'yes' because I hadn't done any *observing* about my concern. You need to observe on your coaching concern before you can give a genuine 'yes' to the lesson, don't you? I have no lessons yet to say 'yes' to without observing!"

Peter nodded. "Well, truth be told, I could've made this easier for you. Although I didn't intend it, my comment 'I'm prepared to show you difficult people don't exist,' followed by the question 'Are you willing to be an eager learner,' would've aroused many a monkey mind. When we're in the midst of monkey mind, we can't observe. Your admission that you weren't jazzed got us back into observing, eh? You're a good partner. Thanks for helping me out." He laughed.

Sam was startled then pleased. This great manager had admitted to having been less than masterful in their interaction. The truth was that he had said something *un*intended. That was a fact. But he didn't make it mean he was incompetent, the way Sam might have in a similar situation. Sam saw that Peter had no heat on it. It was clear that it was OK with him to make mistakes. He had said "yes" to being truthful and open. Sam experienced a spaciousness around his heart.

"This is great," he practically shouted. "It's even clearer to me now that SAY YES in COSA is the ultimate challenge. It's tough enough with great observation. But you can't do it at all without observation. You might get to action, but it's not likely to be an authentic action."

"What do you mean by authentic action?" Peter was very interested.

"It's an action that makes sense in relation to what you've just become aware of. It's like 'duh, of course!' For example, if you've just become aware of the senselessness of treating a recurring tooth ache with medicines, the authentic action would be to pick up the phone and make an appointment with the dentist. Of course you'd do that. It's the obvious next step."

Peter said, "Or, when you've become aware of having asked

somebody a dumb question, the authentic action would be to admit it and ask a better one." He chuckled. "Yes. I like obvious next steps. To me they're the reward for having done the work."

"Phew. No kidding!" The 'S' in COSA is something else. I never would have guessed it. I thought it had to do with seizing something. In other words taking aggressive action. For me, after observing came action. But I see what an incredibly important step it is to say 'yes' to your lessons, whatever they may be. It affects the quality of the actions you eventually take." He added, "as we've seen just now."

Peter nodded. "Yes, it's hugely important. All the COSA steps, including Step Three—SAY YES—are always taken by the hero, never by monkey mind.

> Seeing the obvious next step is the reward for having done the work.

"This may come as a surprise to you, but Coach Zabar and all of us fortify ourselves by beginning each day with the COSA questions. They get us into our hero's heart whose aim it is to make a contribution. Sometimes, if we think we have big challenges ahead, we may ask them more often. We enjoy putting monkey mind on notice that we're going to corral it in a nice, spacious corral, but a corral nevertheless. Our message to the little trickster is 'We're ready for the *un*-game.'"

"Yeah. I'm good with that. The *un*-game—the *un*raveling of lies parading as truths. But you were kidding me, weren't you, when you said that there's no such thing as a difficult person? It was just to make a point, right?" There was pleading in Sam's eyes.

"No," said Peter gently. "And when you get that, you will dramatically increase your capacity to live a large life."

Sam wasn't sure he could take much more. This was just too intense.

"Or you could look at it this way," Peter said, laughing. "When you get the tool that will teach you about so-called 'difficult' people, you'll be able to make punch lines when life throws you a punch. And you might even be able to prevent hardening of the attitudes!"

Peter's playful comments shifted the energy in the room. Sam began to laugh too. The mounting tension he'd been experiencing was gone.

After wiping away the almost-tears of their infectious laughter, Peter asked, "Do you see how your monkey mind was just soothed, Sam?"

"Yes, I do. I just can't believe I have something to learn about difficult people other than to deal with them better. When you made the joke just now, my monkey mind about that just dissolved. I'm willing to be an eager learner right here, right now. Laughter may be a great monkey mind tamer."

"You're dead on actually. Norman Cousins in *The Anatomy of an Illness* would agree with that. And for us as managers, we could remember that just because this is serious business, we're not required to take ourselves so seriously." Peter looked at his watch.

> When you get that there's no such thing as a difficult person, you will dramatically increase your capacity to live a large life.

"I'd love to finish this conversation now and show you there are no difficult people. Time flies when you're having fun. But I have a prior commitment in ten minutes. When's your meeting with the 'difficult' person?"

"Tomorrow afternoon." Sam was disappointed he'd miss out on a tool for his conversation with, yes, his difficult employee.

"OK, tell you what," offered Peter, walking to the door. "Buy me a beer and I'll show you. Deal?"

"Deal. How about O'Reilly's at 5:30?"

"OK, and together we'll make mole hills out of your mountain of difficult people." Peter's laughter rang for a long time in Sam's ears.

It had been a transformative conversation for Sam. As he walked toward his office, waves of pleasure and gratitude washed over him. The COSA process was elegant, powerful, sequential, and simple—although definitely not easy. And he had experienced the power of its first three steps.

Dear Reader

1. Do you have an example in your life of how language dictated your experience? What was it?
2. Have you ever had an experience like Sam's in which you were absolutely, positively convinced that you knew the truth and then found out you were way off base? How did you handle that challenge?
3. The conventional strategy most people use when they become aware of a limiting belief in someone else (there's only one right way to do X, Y, or Z) is to convince the person of its fallacy. Have you ever done that? Doing that often produces disappointing results. Can you recall an example, and what would have produced a better result? How might surfacing the hidden commitments that keep a limiting belief in place produce a better result?
4. Are you on Sam's or Peter's side regarding the existence of "difficult" people? Are you willing to challenge your existing beliefs?

Chapter 13

~~BELIEVING~~
IS ~~SEEING~~

O'Reilly's was only beginning to get the after-work traffic, but Sam arrived early and claimed a quiet booth in the corner. He opened a note pad to corral some of his raging thoughts.

"What does he mean there's no such thing as difficult people? That's just flat out wrong." The *un*resolved tension gripped him. His curiosity had to be satisfied if he was to stop obsessing about it. He looked up to scan the sports bar. No, it wasn't time yet for Peter to arrive. However, and this got his immediate attention, Sam saw that Samantha Osler had just walked in. She looked around, spotted him and waved, then went to join someone in another room.

Sam left his paraphernalia on the table and headed in the direction he'd seen her disappear. He spotted her and headed toward her, *un*deterred that she'd joined a table of two other people.

"IIi," said Sam to Sam Osler and acknowledged the others. "Can I see you for a minute?" She nodded, got up, and they walked away from the table for some privacy.

"I'm in a meeting for probably forty-five minutes or so," said Sam. "Could you join me after you're done? It would be OK with me if you joined us while I'm still in my meeting—it's with Peter Black."

"Sure. What's the purpose for meeting him here, if you don't mind my asking?"

"He's saying that there's no such thing as difficult people, and I'm about to bust a gut because he just can't be right, but I want to hear what he has to say."

Sam Osler smiled a knowing, mysterious Mona Lisa smile that reminded him of that time with Coach Zabar. Sam Adler's curiosity went through the roof.

"OK. See you later," she said, returning to her table. Sam was pleased but off-balance. Sam O was intriguing. Plus she was particularly talented in relationships. He wanted to know how she would handle the conversation with Bob.

He looked at his watch just as he saw Peter walk through the door. Sam pointed to the table. "Long time no see," said Peter and slid into the booth facing Sam.

"Yeah," laughed Sam. They motioned the waiter and ordered their beer.

"I've been so curious I can hardly see straight. Please enlighten me, because I'm completely in the dark. Move me from darkness into the light," Sam joked.

"OK, but would it be all right with you if you moved yourself from the darkness into the light?"

"Yes, but with support please. Some of my counterparts like to play the Lone Ranger, but I prefer to do this with ease, if you don't mind, Peter."

"And are you willing to do it with ease, even if I *do* mind? Life is awfully tough when you make your happiness dependent on someone other than yourself. Happiness is an inside job." Peter had a good-natured, mocking grin on his face, one that was perfectly permissible among friends.

Sam considered Peter's comment and broke into a grin too. Peter then asked whether Sam would like to corral monkey mind by choosing five qualities of being and answering the other COSA questions he had learned thus far.

"I've already started the corralling process," Sam told him. "But I'd be happy to have some support—I'm definitely starting to appreciate support in a new way."

The two L-4 managers went through the process of intentionally choosing qualities and asking the questions about being willing to observe and being eager learners. They both took a sip of their beer and then began the conversation about the burning topic.

"I say there are difficult people, and you say there aren't. One of us has to be wrong. I have plenty of evidence that I'm right." Sam rolled out all his evidence about Bob. But from the bland expression on Peter's face, he saw that thus far his evidence hadn't impressed Peter at all.

"Are you noticing how important it is to you to be right at this moment?" Peter asked.

"Yes, I'm noticing. And I'm still right," Sam thought, burrowing into his seat.

"Which is more important to you about this, being right or having a transformative conversation with Bob?"

"I'd really like both. Does it have to be an either/or? What about all my evidence?" A silent "Can't you see what I mean?" hung in the air.

> Life is awfully tough when you make your happiness dependent on someone other than yourself. Happiness is an inside job.

"I'd like to share something with you about this, Sam, but it's not likely that you'll hear it through your filter of needing to be right. The need to be right and the need to control are two of a handful of deadly needs that often mess up the attainment of the most wonderful goals. Does this interest you?"

"Yeah," said Sam, but it sounded more like a "maybe" than a "yes."

"Good. Whose needs are those anyway?" Peter waited for Sam to answer. When the silence persisted he said, "Scan the qualities you're willing to be—courageous, truthful, attentive, open, and flexible, right?" Peter had remembered Sam's choices.

"What do you see about wanting to be right and wanting to control? How do those desires fit in with the qualities you chose?"

"They don't," replied Sam thoughtfully. "They suck the energy right out of me as I hear you say them. One of the managers said one time that you can't be joyous and stingy at the same time. I tested it out, and it's true. This is really the same thing. To answer your question, they're monkey mind's needs."

> The need to be right and the need to control are two of a handful of deadly needs that often mess up the attainment of the most wonderful goals.

Sam let out a breath. "I'll suspend judgment, and I'll simply be willing to be open and receptive. I imagine judging is probably in monkey mind's domain too," he said, sighing again as the door to his mind opened a crack more.

Peter nodded. "By choosing 'open' and 'receptive' you're also saying that you're willing to come from your hero's heart. Do you see that, Sam?"

"Yeah. I see that. All the questions you asked to corral monkey mind get us into the ontological space. I'm with you."

"Very good. Then you're ready to take advantage of this principle and the graphic I'll draw for you." Peter asked Sam for a piece of paper. He wrote "BELIEF CREATES THE FACT" across the top.

"What does that mean to you, Sam?" Peter pointed to the top of the paper.

"It means the same thing to me as it did to Henry Ford who said, 'Whether you think you can or you think you can't, you're right.'"

"Uh-huh. What about managers saying they want to hire more

minority executives or women, but in fact they don't make the corporate culture inviting for women and minorities. They must have a different belief than the one they put out to the public."

Sam said, "People *do* live what they believe. They just don't always, or even often, live what they *say* they believe. Monkey mind is protecting them from themselves through rationalization and justification. They get to look in the mirror and not barf, if they don't look too hard."

Peter laughed. "So you'd grant me that it's already a huge challenge to become aware of hidden beliefs?"

"Yeah, I think we've observed that in coaching," agreed Sam.

"There's a second challenge, and that's our belief about how people make conclusions in the first place. Does that interest you in relation to *your* conclusion about 'difficult' people?"

> People *do* live what they believe. They just don't always, or even often, live what they *say* they believe.

"Absolutely. I believe there are difficult people. I know people who are pretty Pollyanna-ish, and they're always finding the good in people who I think are jerks. It's exasperating." Sam took a generous swig of his beer.

"They're difficult, huh?" Peter was amused. Sam didn't think it was funny.

"So it could be said they have a different view finder than you?"

"Yeah, they must."

"What's the most exasperating thing about the Pollyanna people?"

"I just don't see how they do it—seeing difficult people as *not* difficult. *I* couldn't."

"Yes. I see that you couldn't," said Peter to Sam's dismay. It was one thing for him to say it, but quite another for Peter to say it too.

Sam tapped his right foot vigorously.

"What's happening right now? What's your experience?" asked Peter.

"Right now?" Sam asked, looking for a little breathing room.

"Yes, right now."

"Here goes," said Sam to himself. Aloud he said, "I'm pissed off. You didn't have to agree with me that I couldn't see someone difficult as *not* difficult. I expected you to say something like 'Of course you can.'"

"That would have been standard and customary and would have met your expectation, but that isn't our objective here, is it?" Peter said not *un*kindly. "Who did I remind you of?"

"Duh! A difficult person. That really is ridiculous. All you did was say the same thing *I* did." Sam started laughing. "Man, I could wring monkey mind's proverbial neck."

"What did it say to you?"

"People who don't see things my way are difficult," Sam admitted. He'd never say this publicly because it didn't make sense, but it sure felt right. This was the stuff you thought but never said out loud.

"Good. Let's use that to look at this tool together.

"So we're calling this tool the 'Belief Creates the Fact' phenomenon. It'll make it clear to you what pulls you back time and again into the 'difficult people' conversation. Would it be all right with you if this were easier than you think?"

Peter didn't wait for an answer. "I'll give you this visual to take home, so that you can picture it any time you want to, but first let me ask you this: How do people reach a conclusion?"

Sam thought this was an easy question. Who didn't know the answer to *that*?

"Rational people are going to look to their experience, and after having amassed some experience, they're going to look at all the evidence they have, and if they're smart and logical, they'll use that evidence to reach a conclusion that accurately reflects the evidence."

Sam figured no one would challenge that statement, but surprise was no stranger to him in conversations with his coach and the four managers.

"What if it doesn't work that way?"

"That would turn the world upside down. It would be like stepping out of my house one morning and seeing the trees lining the street with their roots up where the crown should be."

"It *would* turn the world upside down, wouldn't it? The way you have it wired, a lot of people would agree with you. However, how would your account explain your Pollyanna friend who doesn't see difficult people? She must have different evidence or something."

"I don't know. She's just plain wrong. She's not seeing straight." Sam didn't really want to think about it, but he forced himself to pay attention to Peter, remembering he had chosen "attentive" as one of the qualities he was willing to demonstrate.

"All right. Let me ask you one other thing. What kind of car do you drive?"

"What does that have to do with anything?" Sam wondered. Wanting to be seen as more than only practical, he said, "Aside from my Harley, I drive a silver grey Honda Civic hybrid. I bought it when I took the job with L-4."

"Good for you," smiled Peter. "And since you bought it, have you been noticing more silver grey Honda Civics on the road?"

"At first I really did. It's weird, because I doubt that there are more silver grey Honda Civics out there than before."

"No, there aren't. But now that you have one, your mind is conditioned to look for silver grey Honda Civic hybrids."

Peter made a dot on the paper he had titled "BELIEF CREATES THE FACT." "Let's say this is the beginning of a circle," he said. "In your scenario we'd label this dot 'EVIDENCE.' We gather evidence and then we reach a conclusion." He drew the beginnings of a circle and stopped and drew another dot. He labeled it "CONCLUSION."

But I'm going to propose a different scenario," said Peter drawing another dot and the beginnings of another circle.

"Our brain doesn't do what you say it does. Rather, it could be said," Peter lowered his voice and paused for effect, "that we leave the starting block not with the evidence"—evidence hung in the air—"but with the conclusion." He studied Sam's reaction to what had to be an assertion his mind would find troubling.

"It's like when you buy a new Honda Civic hybrid, your mind is alerted to 'Honda Civic hybrid,' and now it starts to look for it. In the same way, your mind starts out with a conclusion. Your mind is now alerted to the conclusion which it then makes front and center."

Sam leaned closer and stared at the graphic Peter Black was creating. He knew that a lot of brain research had been done in the last twenty years or so. New discoveries had been made.

Peter labeled the first dot in the new circle-to-be "CONCLUSION." His speaking had become slower-paced.

"What happens the moment the brain focuses on a conclusion?" he asked. "Which conclusion will we use as an example—'People who don't see things my way are difficult' or 'There are difficult people?'"

"Let's do 'There are difficult people.'" Sam didn't like that he'd given life to a conclusion he would normally not defend. He had a better chance of being right on 'There are difficult people.' "Yes, that'll be better," he said with a decisive nod.

Peter wrote "There are difficult people" next to the first dot which he had labeled in all caps "CONCLUSION."

"So, Sam. Now that you have this conclusion literally in front of you, what are you noticing?"

Sam scanned his experience. "If I'm truthful, I have to say I'm looking for evidence to support that conclusion," he reported very slowly, as if hoping to find something in his experience to contradict what he was seeing and sharing. He hated to be wrong.

"Yes. You're seeing that once we have a conclusion, our mind is duty-bound to gather evidence to support that conclusion." He labeled the second dot "EVIDENCE.."

"What's your best evidence that people are difficult, Sam?" Peter glanced at the younger man staring at the crude graphic on the paper.

"They come in late. Take too many breaks. Sometimes don't treat the client right. Promise stuff they don't deliver." Sam provided a long list, then stopped and looked as if to say, "See?"

"What would your Pollyanna friend have by the conclusion dot?"

"She'd have 'People are fascinating'" was Sam's instant and *un*happy reply. He was thinking about Samantha Osler, the relationship-lover who flashed an enigmatic Mona Lisa smile when he'd asked her whether she doubted the existence of difficult people. It was downright irritating.

"And her evidence wouldn't look like yours?"

"Nope. I bet she'd have stuff like 'They say one thing and do another,' and she'd be endlessly fascinated by the challenge of managing them. She'd see it as a great opportunity to hone her own skills." Sam compared his conclusion to hers and didn't like where this was heading.

"You're bringing me to the next station in my circle," Peter said, outlining a third dot which he labeled "MY REACTIONS/ BEHAVIOR." He drew a line to it.

"What you're saying is that your Pollyanna friend would behave *un*like you given your differing conclusions. Is that accurate?" he inquired.

"I'm afraid that's true."

"So what do you see about how you show up with the evidence you've been gathering? Take the employee you'll be talking to tomorrow. Let's make it real."

Sam inhaled deeply. "I'm going to look for stuff to make me right," he said studying the graphic, a glum look on his face. He saw all kinds of consequences for what he was seeing. "And I'm going to focus my attention on it, like I did with the Honda." It irked him to say that, but what choice did he have if he wanted to look himself in the mirror?

"Hmm. So what might an observer see you doing as you gather evidence?"

"Well, he or she might see me trying and convicting my difficult person, Bob, for being lazy, *un*committed, manipulative, all that kind of good stuff. They wouldn't see me looking at him at the water cooler thinking, 'He's trying to get a strategy for talking to client X, and he's doing that by getting support from others, like I do!'" Sam's cockiness and irritation were gone. A quiet detachment had replaced them. Peter noticed, of course.

Sam wasn't consciously aware that he had said "yes" to the coaching he was receiving. Saying "yes" in the face of hating to look at—never mind let go of—a closely held belief was the mark of an upcoming success. It boded well for personal and professional growth of the person able to do it.

"Yes, and I suspect you could find a whole lot of other examples of evidence, right? Because you want to be sure you have an airtight case, don't you?" Peter looked expectantly at Sam.

"That's for sure. And it affects not only what I see, but also what I do."

"How's that?"

"Well, what you appreciate appreciates, right? My focus makes me suspicious. I look for more evidence. I'm hungry for more evidence. I might be *un*friendly or short, certainly not warm toward Bob. I may avoid him. I may initiate more frequent performance reviews and do them negatively, because I have no hope of him ever improving."

The customer support manager was on a roll. He grasped that with his focus on Bob as a difficult employee, that's what had to happen. His reluctance had morphed into excitement, even though he disliked considering what he might have to give up to learn these lessons. Monkey mind experiences being wrong as dying. No wonder its *un*relenting grip is loosened only by revealing and observing it.

"My God, did you hear what I just said? There's another conclusion I have and that's 'Bob is hopeless.' Crap. The guy doesn't stand a chance with me. I'm bound to build an airtight case."

"Excellent observation, Sam. You're doing great. What you've just described is what happens here at the third dot, "MY REACTIONS/BEHAVIOR," which you've correctly noted as being driven by the evidence you've oh so lovingly gathered. Your brain can't help it. It has to do that."

"So there's no hope?"

"No, there's a lot of hope once you see it. But hold off a sec. Let me ask you another question," said Peter as he closed the circle by placing another dot and drawing a line to connect it. But he didn't label it.

"What are people around you like when you think they're difficult? What would I see them do, or what would they look like?"

"They don't know I think they're difficult. I hide it pretty well."

> Monkey mind experiences being wrong as dying. No wonder its *un*relenting grip is loosened only by revealing and observing it.

"Not well enough, I'm afraid. Have you ever had a dog?"

"Yeah…why?"

"Did the dog know you liked it?"

"Sure."

"Did the dog ever meet anyone he didn't like?"

"Several times. As a matter of fact I was surprised because it was one of my friends Targa didn't like. My friend said he liked dogs… oh, I see where you're going. John might have tried to be nice to me by saying he liked dogs, but Targa knew better. Yeah, that's true. Animals know when you're afraid of them or you have the conclusion 'Dogs are a nuisance.'" Sam easily related the question to the "Belief Creates the Fact" graphic Peter was presenting to him.

"Isn't Targa the name of an old Porsche?"

"Uh-huh. My father had one when he was young, and I liked the sound of it, so I named my dog that."

"Interesting. Well, anyway, what are you seeing about what we're saying here?"

Sam was seeing plenty. He remembered the conversation with Sam Osler and her story about holding herself back from a leadership position because she thought she was stupid. He now knew *she* had discovered long ago that you can't hide your conclusions about yourself or about other people.

Out loud he said, "You can't hide anything from anyone else, because they're just as sensitive as dogs. They may not have the words for it, but they know. This even works for you when you have the conclusion about yourself, for example, 'I'm stupid.' Forget about hiding it from anyone else. Others know. So you might as well face into whatever problem you perceive in yourself and get it taken care of. It takes a lot of energy to hide stuff."

"Does that apply to your situation with Bob too?"

"It does. But I don't know what to do other than hide my conclusion 'Bob's difficult.'"

"Taking a look at your conclusion 'You can't hide,' what do you notice about how the so-called difficult people act around you?"

"They're a bit like my dog Targa. Cautious, suspicious. They might draw a big circle around me. Bob does. They certainly wouldn't want to go on a date with me."

Sam glanced briefly in the direction of the area where Sam Osler was sitting.

"Great. So that's really the fourth dot." He labeled that dot "OTHERS' REACTIONS/ BEHAVIOR."

"While we know we can't control anyone but ourselves, would

you grant me that we *do* influence other people?"

"Of course. So how I show up in the outer world is a reflection of my current inner world which I may be totally *un*aware of, but which nevertheless affects me *and* other people."

"Yes, that's it in a nutshell."

"It's fascinating…the conclusion being placed before the evidence in our mind. That's new to me," said Sam, studying Peter's graphic. His mind was busy making connections and attending to a lot of brain fireworks.

"So it could be that I've just adopted a particular conclusion as fact—namely 'There are difficult people.'" Sam searched Peter's face for affirmation.

"I may have made that conclusion in kindergarten. And from that point on I've just looked for evidence to support it while someone else decided in kindergarten that people were kind and generous, and he or she focused their evidence-gathering on that. And as I go through life, I'll keep looking for that which makes me right. Like with some of my employees. It looks to me if I continue to do that, I'd rather be right than happy. Phew!" Sam stared at the graphic.

His face brightened. "I can see a way out."

"What way out do you see?" Peter asked, raising an eyebrow.

"I see the same way out as before, except it keeps eluding me. Damn monkey mind." His face fell again.

"And which way is that?"

"I can focus my attention on something more appealing than that particular conclusion. Who's to say I can't choose a conclusion that has become more interesting to me after seeing what you showed me? That *is* within my power!"

This was at least the third time Sam noticed that his lesson was to shift the focus of his attention, and each time it felt brand new to him. Momentarily dejected, he wondered how many more times he was going to miss such opportunities to empower his actions.

"That's true. That *is* within your power. And by the way, it doesn't mean that people didn't do what you said they did," said Peter.

"They may have done all those things. It's true that Bob didn't finish the report on time. It just means that you find something else more interesting than the assessment that he's a difficult employee because he didn't finish the report in a timely manner!"

"That's full of profound implications, Peter." Now I can see 'difficult' isn't real. Not like a thing I can touch. It only exists in my conversation. And I've made Bob's actions mean that he's difficult. I could make them mean something else." Sam blinked several times, bit his lower lip, and twirled his pen.

"Yes. It only exists in language, and you could attribute different meaning to the actions, but not very successfully, if you still empower the original conclusion." Peter paused. Then he said, "You can only sustain meaning that is consistent with the conclusion you're entertaining at a given moment. Otherwise it would just be positive thinking, which is different from what we're saying here," he cautioned.

"I see what you're getting at, Peter. Applying positive thinking to the conclusion 'There are difficult people,' is like attacking a gross bathroom with an air freshener. Air freshener or not, it still stinks. Advertisers' claims notwithstanding, it doesn't restore the fresh air of an open window." Sam grinned, and Peter chuckled.

"You're my kind of guy, Sam," he said leaning back, raising his glass as if to toast Sam.

Sam continued. "And if the conclusion exists in conversation, I can observe that conversation with help of someone in-the-know and shift to another conclusion I like better. I don't have to do anything except become aware of the conclusions I'm appreciating. Get outta here! That's amazing."

Suddenly Sam recognized that he'd just identified yet another *un*examined conclusion, namely "Making *un*coveries is hard." He remembered Marguerite Chan's statement, "Don't just do something. Sit there." It had a new meaning for Sam now. He was in awe. "Sit there and observe!" Observation was a powerful light that could reveal how we've constructed our reality. And our reality can be changed.

"People can change, but they have to be interested in seeing the formerly invisible about themselves with tools which make that possible," Sam said. Thinking about corporate training programs, he added, "Despite appearances to the contrary, in tons of corporate training programs, 'People don't change much' is a pervasive *un*examined conclusion." At this present moment he was willing to bet that the COSA process could change that paradigm.

"And, what I appreciate appreciates," Sam asserted. "I'll keep on going 'round and 'round in this circle as long as I don't see that I appreciate *that* conclusion and not another, more empowering one. It's all up to me once I see. The thought of that is a turn-on. Self-observation and self-reflection are sources of power! I see amazing possibilities for action."

"Yes, Sam. What you're seeing will be forever useful to you. You're doing great work here. Speaking about powerful action, what might be a more supportive conclusion you could focus on that would transform your conversation with Bob?"

Sam thought for a while then said, "Ah. Here it is: 'A direct, non-manipulative conversation is just a skill-set away.'"

"Great, are you willing to gather some evidence for this conclusion?"

"Yes, I'd love to practice that. Practice makes progress. It doesn't all have to turn out like the picture of perfection I might have had in my mind before this conversation." Sam smiled at Peter Black who'd given so generously of his time.

"Do you see that you just met the ultimate challenge?" Peter asked kindly.

"Yes. I see it. I said 'yes,' didn't I? I said I was willing. I tell you, this COSA process is sweet. And now I see so much more clearly how that supervisor—you know, the one who wreaked havoc in her department by not confronting—the one who said she didn't want to hurt other people's feelings—had it all mixed up. That wasn't it at all. She had a conclusion called 'Conflict is dangerous to my health' and was gathering evidence for that, killing the whole company in the process! Both she and *her* manager could have gathered evidence for a conclusion called 'A well-managed conflict enriches relationships.' Or, 'Conflict can be the source of rich learning.'" Sam was pumped.

Peter smiled, swallowed the last sip of his beer and said, "You'll do great tomorrow afternoon. See you. Thanks for the beer." He patted Sam on the shoulder and headed for the exit.

"Thanks, Peter, very much," Sam yelled after him. "I appreciate you." The jolly manager waved without turning around, and then he was gone.

Sam sat in silence for a few minutes. Then he ordered another beer and waited for Sam Osler. He was eager to talk to her. After about ten minutes, she slid into the bench seat beside him.

"How goes it?" she asked Sam in that gorgeous voice of hers. "What's up?"

They exchanged some small talk and some news, until Sam O said, "I only have a short while. What did you want to talk about?"

Sam had a hard time hiding his disappointment that she needed to leave. Then he remembered that she'd know anyway what he was experiencing—which was actually a sobering thought—but he just said, "Damn, I want to talk to you. I'm disappointed you have to go. But let's see if we can do this quickly. Maybe we could spend some planned time together. Would you like to go to dinner and a movie Friday night?"

That had just sort of slipped out. Sam held his breath hoping she'd say "yes." Since he'd seen her last he knew that Alpha was attracted to Omega. It was great to have someone his own age around, as much as he loved talking to the managers and Coach Zabar.

"I can't on Friday, but I'm free on Saturday. How about then? I know a really good German restaurant, if you like German food."

"I grew up with it. I'm always hoping to find some restaurant that can out-cook my mother. She's my favorite gourmet chef, if there *is* such a thing as a German gourmet chef." Both Sams laughed. Sam Adler realized he didn't even know where Sam Osler lived, nor did he have her cell phone number, but he figured they'd work that out.

"OK. I'd like your support." Sam explained his situation with Bob as well as what he'd become aware of, being careful to first check whether she'd gotten that coaching about belief creating the fact. She smiled that Mona Lisa smile again, and Sam wondered what she knew that he didn't.

But then he didn't care. "The hell with it," he thought. "I know she's really good at relationship. The more points of view the better."

"I've got just the thing for you," Sam O said and triumphantly pulled a paper out of her carrying case. I just found this in the place that cuts my hair." Her hair *did* look really good. "Look it over in light of what you've learned. It may help you with your conversation. You'll do great. I have no doubt about it. I'll see you Saturday." She flashed him a smile as pretty as her voice, got up, gave him her card which had her cell phone number, and left.

Sam put her card into his pocket, then he looked at the "just the thing for you" paper she'd given him.

The Paradoxical Commandments
by Kent M. Keith

1. People are illogical, unreasonable, and self-centered. Love them anyway.

2. If you do good, people will accuse you of selfish ulterior motives. Do good anyway.

3. If you are successful, you will win false friends and true enemies. Succeed anyway.

4. The good you do today will be forgotten tomorrow. Do good anyway.

5. Honesty and frankness make you vulnerable. Be honest and frank anyway.

6. The biggest men and women with the biggest ideas can be shot down by the smallest men and women with the smallest minds. Think big anyway.

7. People favor underdogs but follow only top dogs. Fight for a few underdogs anyway.

8. What you spend years building may be destroyed overnight. Build anyway.

9. People really need help but may attack you if you do help them. Help people anyway.

10. Give the world the best you have and you'll get kicked in the teeth. Give the world the best you have anyway.

Sam read and reread the commandments several times, finally deciding he would reflect on them in the privacy of his apartment. He didn't know what it all meant for his future. He started for home. But a realization stopped him in his tracks. Great managers, *un*like other managers, didn't think they had any difficult employees.

Dear Reader

1. What was it like for you to hear that rather than use evidence to arrive at a conclusion regarding "how things and people are," we start with a conclusion and proceed to gather evidence to support it? What possibilities do you see out of this?
2. It has been said that you'd be a fool to follow the advice of the author of the Paradoxical Commandments—love people anyway in light of the things they do. Could you make an argument for the "fool" point of view? Or do you believe that people who are able to "love people anyway" live more in alignment with who they really are in their hero's heart? Which path do you follow more often in your own life?

Chapter 14

MANAGER AS CRUCIBLE

S am looked at his watch. It was 12:25. Bob would arrive in five minutes. Armed with the five qualities he was willing to be—among them courageous, creative and truthful—and his awareness that great managers have no difficult employees, he decided he would focus on a new conclusion: "Robust, truthful conversations enrich relationships." He was willing to gather evidence for that conclusion, no matter what. Sam was aware of his loyal opponent, the trickster monkey mind. Nervous or not, he was willing and ready to outplay it.

When Bob's arrival was announced, a new thought occurred to him. "Shift your focus from being enamored with your message delivery, Sam, to having a learning conversation. Remember, in order to be different in what you expect to be a 'difficult' conversation, you have to be willing to think differently." This thought was followed by "If there are no 'difficult' people, maybe 'difficult' conversations don't exist either."

Sam had no time to pursue that train of thought. Bob was in his office. Sam studied the well-built man in his early thirties as if he were seeing him for the first time. After an exchange of pleasantries designed to relax them both Sam said, "Bob, I've called this meeting to learn how things are going for you in your job. On the outside looking in, my sense is that this is a job you're not passionate about. I'd like to support you in playing your best game. It's clear to me when you're able to do that, you'll make an invaluable contribution to our department's success."

Sam looked expectantly at Bob, thinking he'd set the stage for the learning conversation he was willing to have.

After a reflective silence, Bob responded, "It's not a bad job. I'm OK. And I think I'm doing a pretty good job."

"'OK,' 'not bad,' and doing a 'pretty good job' sound as if my assessment is grounded," Sam replied in a neutral tone.

> Shift your focus from being enamored with your message delivery to having a learning conversation. Remember, in order to be different in what you expect to be a "difficult" conversation, you have to be willing to think differently.

"What do you mean?"

"It sounds like you agree that you bring no passion to your work here."

"That's probably true. Is that a requirement?"

"Not legally. However, when I think of my vision for this department, then it's an expectation. What's it like for you to do your job without a fire in the belly for it?" Sam asked with genuine curiosity.

"Well, it puts food on the table, and the weekends aren't bad. It's OK, I guess. As long as I can do it and still satisfy the company, then it's OK by me. I don't expect work to be fun, and I hope L-4 wouldn't make fun a requirement." Sam saw a faint, resigned smile but thought Bob's voice included a hint of challenge.

"That's an interesting belief, Bob, that work shouldn't be fun. So you separate work and fun?"

"Sure. Doesn't everybody?"

"Actually? No. Let me ask you this, Bob. Would it be all right with you if your life at work were easier?"

Bob looked puzzled, as if he wondered why Sam would ask him such an odd question in the middle of a gripe session. Aloud he said, "Sure." But it had a "show me" ring to it.

"Life would be easier if your work were an expression of what you're intensely interested in. You know, the kind of stuff that doesn't let you alone, the stuff you think about at the oddest times."

"You mean besides women?" Both men laughed at Bob's deflection, but Sam only allowed a momentary digression. "Bob's monkey mind is trying to take the attention off something that could get *un*comfortable," he noted.

"Uh-huh. What is it that really interests you, Bob?" Sam genuinely wanted to know.

"I see you spending a lot of time at the water cooler talking to people," he added in an objective, reporter-like tone of voice. "You all seem to be very engaged. I've had the thought more than once that there must be a purpose to these gatherings that I can only guess at."

Sam's neutral tone invited no response, and Bob didn't launch into explanations.

"Maybe you're very good at forming alliances. I'm not sure where that thought came from, but I just wanted to throw it out there as a talent you may be *un*aware of." There was warmth in Sam's tone now.

He studied Bob's furrowed brow. "Talent may be the stuff we do naturally. The things we don't think of as talents at all. But those things, applied to where they're needed, could lead us to paying work, a lot of satisfaction, and maybe even fun!"

"Well, that's interesting," said Bob, now looking like he did in water-cooler conversations. He leaned closer to Sam.

"I *do* like to talk to different people," he said, appearing to Sam as having shed the customary caution that characterized the boss employee relationships. "And I think about forming alliances. What really interests me is how we're all missing the boat, it seems.

Everybody. Business too. This is a changing world. Our troubled economy is just a reflection of it. And it seems that we're looking for solutions in all the wrong places—our priorities for becoming energy-independent, for example. How can we put so little money into developing the new green technologies, like solar and wind power, and fight about spending so much for dirty technology like coal? How can we act as if the world's resources are *un*limited and our American right to consume them greater than other nations' rights? How can we be so penny-wise and pound-foolish with the dollars we spend and the strategies we devise that cause our children to fall further and further behind in the competition with other global players?"

Bob's passion was nothing Sam had seen before. He stared at this new Bob.

"Out of what you're saying, what interests you the most?" he asked, stunned with the *un*expected turn of the conversation.

"The green economy. And for reasons that may surprise you. Being green has been fashionable for a long time. But ask yourself. Who's been interested? It's white, pretty affluent people who can afford to go to the market place and demand and pay for hybrid cars and solar panels for their vacation home.

"But look. Who are we leaving behind? White, middle class liberals have been wondering how come the green movement is so lily-white. How come they can't get people of color interested? The message that global warming will hurt them first and most seems surprisingly lost on people of color who are also poor. They actually *do* know that global warming will hurt them first and most—bad stuff always hits those first who have no means to escape it. But in terms of taking action in collaboration with white environmentalists, they're not interested. I don't think it's any surprise at all."

Revved up, Bob muttered, "Advertising has people think going green is all about saving the polar bears! Tell me, will you be interested in saving the polar bears, if you don't know whether you can pay this month's rent? Will you be interested in a Prius, if you aren't even sure you'll have bus fare? I think not!" His voice had increased in volume and indignation.

"Justice issues would be of much higher concern, don't you think?" Bob was agitated now.

Sam was amazed. This wasn't the conversation he'd expected. Briefly he lost focus berating himself for his own narrow white perspective of the green economy. Bob, as an African-American, was more sensitized to a broader perspective that included social justice concerns. But he, Sam, shouldn't have been blind to that broader perspective. It made sense. And besides...

He took his attention off himself by recalling that he wanted to have a learning conversation with Bob about Bob. He decided against cutting it short and redirecting it to Bob's lack-luster performance. His comment about talent meeting a need had opened a flood-gate Bob had kept tightly closed.

"Am I'm willing to be an eager learner?" was the question he'd asked and said "yes" to in order to produce an extraordinary result out of his meeting with Bob.

Noticing his manager's calm silence, Bob proceeded. "But we could have an incredible opportunity. We have an opening now where we could create a green wave that would lift all boats. With the interest in a green economy...green this...green that—that's all we ever hear about any more—we have an incredible opportunity for poor people to participate in a meaningful way in creating the world of the future. The only way they can participate in the green economy is not through purchasing green products and services, but by providing the man and woman power to work in the emerging green economy. And not in minimum wage jobs either, but in living wage jobs. *Living* wage jobs!

"People can be trained to make and install solar panels. They can retrofit old public buildings to become more energy-efficient. The green economy could be the pathway out of poverty. It needs a bunch of entities working on the same goal. That's what I'm interested in, if you *really* want to know."

Bob stopped suddenly. He stole a glance at his manager. Sam suspected that Bob felt exposed, perhaps embarrassed by his display of passion.

"So given what you're telling me, what would be the goal?" Sam asked, not missing a beat. He projected confidence, courage, and certainty, the very qualities people in an *un*certain environment need from their manager.

Taking his manager's question as an invitation to continue, Bob's response was quick and certain. "Energy-independence and a thriving economy. I want to see us form a strong alliance among all the big players—private industry, education, government, even other nations. All of them committed to defining GDP in a different way than we define it now. If we're *really* committed to our local well-being, then we have to think globally even as we act locally. We're all in this together, and we'll sink or swim together. The way we've been thinking is not going get us to energy-independence and a thriving new

> Confidence, courage, and certainty are the very qualities people in an *un*certain environment need from their manager.

economy. We're trying to solve problems with the same thinking that created the problems in the first place."

"This is reminiscent of Peter Black's concerns of recapturing our capacity to be system thinkers," Sam thought. He marveled that up until now he hadn't known Bob at all. He had simply seen him as lazy, *un*motivated, *un*committed and in the way of making his department a shining example of efficiency, effectiveness, and the envy of all other departments.

"You have a lot to *un*learn, Sam Adler," he thought. "This is a hero in front of you."

He admired Bob's passion. He vowed to choose "open" and "receptive" often as qualities in the COSA process. There was a lot to miss if you weren't willing to be open and receptive.

"What I don't understand, Bob, is why you're here at L-4 and not out there making things happen on behalf of your very strong concern." He reflected back on his sessions with Coach Zabar and his conversations with the great managers. It was obvious that great managers give self-discovery a central role. It's an important goal for the manager and the employee to figure out who he or she is.

In the time it took for Bob to take a deep breath and formulate his answer, Sam thought, "The *un*-game and the COSA process are largely about self-discovery. Plus supporting self-discovery seems right in line with two of the central tasks of the manager's role—motivating and developing."

What puzzled him was that "developing employees" in the usual way of management thinking mostly meant prepping them for promotion.

Sam's thoughts shifted back to Bob as Bob said, "If I tried to get an energy-action coalition going, I couldn't make the kind of money I'm making here." It gratified Sam that Bob was willing to disclose that assessment.

"Do you know that, or are you making that assumption?"

"I know that." Bob didn't hesitate.

"A transformative conversation interrogates reality," Sam said to himself. "How do you know?" he probed calmly.

"The people I know all do volunteer work on the side, just like me. Nobody is making a living at it."

"Nobody? Just because many aren't, does it mean it can't be done?"

Bob hesitated. "I suppose it's possible."

"What, if anything, are you afraid you might have to give up in order to pursue your dream of making a major contribution to American energy-independence?"

"I'm secure here."

"Really?"

Sam knew he was dealing with the monkey mind conversation of someone who probably wasn't aware of such a distinction as monkey mind. Bob had probably never considered that we aren't our thoughts, feelings, opinions, and conclusions.

"Is there such a thing as security, or is it an illusion we wish were real?"

Bob was silent, digesting Sam's question.

"Well, that's a philosophical discussion," he answered, studying Sam's face as if it were the first time.

"Is that so?" asked Sam, nonplussed. "Bob's avoiding something," he speculated in the privacy of his thoughts.

But he was wrong. "No Sir. Security *is* an illusion."

"Can you give me a concrete example from your experience of how security is an illusion?"

Bob shuffled in his seat but answered, "When I was in college I was a gifted tennis player. I was assured I'd get into the pros. Then I injured my back in a motorcycle accident."

"I'm sorry to hear that. And I'm glad you have some other passions now, Bob. So what if you could work yourself into a job that would help you make the contribution you're so eager to make? Would that help you act on behalf of this dream?"

Sam's question had gone straight to what Bob was reluctant to look at. His coaches would have cheered Sam.

"Yeah, I'd be down with that. That would be awesome. But…" Bob looked worried.

"Bob, it seems to me that you could begin to educate yourself about what's possible. Coalition-building means someone has to coordinate the activities of the coalition. Given the keen interest in the green economy means there are people and entities out there that would fund brilliant ideas that have some flesh and bones on them. Yours may be an idea whose time has come. If it were twenty years earlier, maybe people would think you're crazy, but I don't think that's the mind-set now."

Bob was listening, his eyes boring into his manager's.

"Looking at your work here and what you've told me," Sam continued *un*perturbed, "I was initially thinking about where in L-4 you'd fit best. But I can't think of anywhere given your very specific interest. In my department I need people who are as passionate about customer service as you are about the creation of energy-independence and a thriving green economy. I think you and I can both get what we need. How about I support you in transitioning into work that allows you to make the contribution that's yours to make?"

"How would you do that? By firing me?" Bob's question reflected his alarm.

"No, not by firing you. Here's what I think would work for me *and* for you." And then Sam fleshed out his thinking. After some discussion he and Bob had a plan that Sam would run by HR the next morning for approval.

Bob's employment with L-4 would terminate at the end of three months. Until then, Bob would give his best job performance. Sam realized Bob

> Managers can't attain excellence without the right fit for the right employee.

wouldn't catch enthusiasm for this work, but he could nevertheless perform it well. For the interim, doing it well was good enough.

With others, Sam was a pragmatist not a perfectionist. He knew he couldn't attain excellence without the right fit for the right employee.

He told Bob he was counting on him doing the work well. Together they developed a written set of expectations that were specific, measurable and achievable—among them the training of his replacement, whoever that might be. As his replacement was coming along, Bob would still receive full salary but reduce his weekly work schedule by one full day. In the last thirty days, depending on the realities on the ground, so to speak, his work schedule might even be further reduced. It would allow him to create his dream with greater ease.

Bob looked at his manager in *un*disguised wonder. He, Bob, had just told him that he didn't like his job. Instead of reproach or punishment, he'd essentially been given a very generous opportunity.

"Thanks," he stammered. "Thanks a lot. I didn't realize until I said it out loud how much I've dreamed about working on what really matters to me. I won't disappoint you."

The two men shook hands, and Bob left the office.

Sam told his assistant he was not to be disturbed for the next thirty minutes. He needed to reflect on what had just happened. He'd worked himself into a frenzy in anticipation of a 'difficult' conversation. It had been a different kind of conversation, but he wouldn't classify it as 'difficult.' He had indeed been able to be courageous, creative, and truthful, three of the five qualities he'd chosen prior to the meeting.

And he'd kept L-4's as well as Bob's interests in mind. He hadn't tried to control the conversation. He'd resisted the inclination to make the assessment that Bob's talking about the green economy was a digression. It really wasn't. It allowed Bob to *un*cover his passion and share it out loud, clarifying it for him. And he, Sam, out of being more interested in allowing things to emerge rather than attempting to control them, had fulfilled his catalyst role. Bob had the chance to develop into who he really was and would be more able to make his unique contribution. His passion and talents would be directed toward meeting a critically important need. It occurred to Sam that his and Bob's conversation had, in fact, been an example of the commitment to the triple bottom line in action. The expected outcome would benefit people, planet, and profits.

"I'll declare that a success," Sam said out loud, smiling. "And furthermore, Mr. Adler, in three months L-4's customer support department will have a kick-ass rep who loves nothing better than taking care of clients."

Developing an employee doesn't mean preparing him or her for promotion, he decided. What about all those system analysts who were great as analysts and then got promoted to manager? A completely different skill-set for which they often had not the slightest talent, inclination, or preparation. And what about Tom Pierot, the marketing manager who'd been with L-4 a very long time? His terse "No, not necessarily" to Sam's question "Wasn't it his job as a great manager to ready his people for promotion?" now made sense. Known as one of the greats in L-4, he surely could have been promoted, if he'd wanted to be.

Sam was certain he'd *un*covered a rule great managers ignore. He was appreciative of all the support he'd gotten. Still, he'd done it on his own. And he was as pleased as he was sure that Bob would do a good job while transitioning out. In his catalyst role his job was to motivate. He was quietly proud of his achievement.

Even though this hadn't been a difficult conversation, Sam was aware that it had met the criteria for conversations he wanted to be able to have consistently. Their conversation had interrogated Bob's reality as well as his own. It had tackled tough issues. It had provoked learning. And best of all, it had enriched their relationship. He'd created the space for an authentic conversation to occur—a conversation that allowed Bob to come forward, look with new eyes at something, see new things about that something, tell the truth about it, and promise several authentic actions in relation to what he'd become aware of.

"I *did* gather evidence for the conclusion 'Robust, truthful, conversations enrich relationships,'" Sam noticed. "I did what I'd wanted to do." He felt a sudden urge to share this sweet victory with Sam Osler, but he resisted picking up the phone.

Difficult conversations are only difficult when you have no tools," he decided. Granted, this had not been a conversation as tough as the challenges posed by those "Paradoxical Commandments." No one had accused him of selfish, ulterior motives. And Bob, who needed help, didn't attack him as he tried to help him. But Sam had been honest and frank despite the fact that honesty and frankness make you vulnerable. A self-satisfied smile turned into a congratulatory whistle and a spring in Sam's step as he walked outside.

"It really was a learning conversation, both for Bob and for me. I met my goal. When you have the tools," he mused, "difficult conversations are merely authentic conversations that move us forward in the domain of our concerns."

To himself Sam declared that he would commit to robust, authentic, *un*bridled, passionate, intense, powerful conversations— one conversation at a time. They'd be learning conversations that had the power to transform. He was up to it. He could stand the heat. He'd proven that in this conversation.

> When you have the tools, difficult conversations are merely authentic conversations that move us forward in the domain of our concerns.

The metaphor of manager as crucible flashed through his mind. He thought of Coach Zabar and his four mentors. They are crucibles, one and all. A great manager could be nothing less. "I think I'm on my way to being a great manager," he whispered, looking around as if to assure there were no phantom listeners. "Bring it on," he added.

Sam Adler, customer support manager extraordinaire, was ready to tackle his next challenge.

Dear Reader

1. Have you ever worked yourself into a frenzy worrying about a
   conversation that turned out to be easier than you'd imagined?
   What were the roots of your frenzy, and what made the
   conversation easier when you finally had it?
2. What benefits, if any, do you see in having conversations that
   interrogate reality, provoke learning, tackle the tough stuff, and
   enrich relationships? What are the costs you perceive in having
   such conversations? What might you have to give up in order
   to engage in such robust, *un*bridled conversations? Would it be
   worth it to you?

Chapter 15

THIRD MEETING OF THE *UN*-TEAM

Two days after Sam's and Bob's transformative conversation, the *un*-team filed into Tom Pierot's office to have their progress review for Sam Adler and Samantha Osler.

"Sophia has asked me to lead this meeting," said Tom. "She's been called to LA. She's left me her notes. Peter, will you get us into the ontological space?"

"Sure." Peter asked the three questions the two Sams were now intimately familiar with.

1. Who am I willing to be in order to make an extraordinary contribution to this meeting?
2. Am I willing, in a clear and focused manner, of my own choosing, to observe thoughts, beliefs, opinions, and conclusions I cherish, no matter what?
3. Am I willing to be an eager learner?

He added a fourth. "Am I willing to focus, observe, tell the truth, and take authentic action, and when I see I'm not, am I willing to do so?"

As with the first three questions, Peter, Marguerite, Tom, and

Maria said "yes" in unison to the last question.

"Good. Bring it on, monkey mind," joked Tom. His six foot frame settled into his chair. His boyish face matched his jovial "We're ready for you!"

"OK, let's take stock," he said, now all business. "Apparently both managers have completed Step Three: SAY YES. Let's go in alphabetical order. Sam Adler first. Are we still glad we hired him? Throw out what you've seen. I'll record for Sophia."

After the group had created the list, Tom read it back to them.

"So we're saying Sam really gets why SAY YES is the ultimate challenge. As a matter of fact he recognizes the power and the pleasure of the first three steps. He sees that CHOOSE and OBSERVE must precede SAY YES. Otherwise the 'yes' is likely to be inauthentic. He demonstrates competence in having a transformative conversation. He sees transformative conversations as impossible to have without an awareness of monkey mind. Peter is impressed with how willing and able Sam is in letting go of a closely held belief in spite of being intensely *un*comfortable. You're speculating his monkey mind is getting less loud as he's gaining competence in the tools. He's demonstrating power, creativity, and compassion. He's deepening his command of the 'manager as catalyst' distinction. He's a system thinker. And he gets L-4's role in reinventing business."

"So the answer is 'yes,' we're glad we hired him," said Maria. Everybody just nodded.

"While you look at this list and decide which of these you either want to expand or have more info on, let me look at what Sophia wants to contribute," said Tom. He scanned an email from the coach. "Sophia just underscores Sam's capacity to observe and how willing he is to be vulnerable and say things many other people wouldn't say. He gets that the most powerful thing imaginable is to say 'yes' to your lessons moment by moment. He's an opportunity seeker. Sophia also agrees he's a system thinker."

"Can you share a specific example of "He recognizes the power and the pleasure of CHOOSE, OBSERVE, and SAY YES?" asked Maria.

"Yes," offered Peter. "He was jazzed after the conversation about difficult people. He'd tied himself up in knots over this conversation, and he got relief from seeing that with tools everything becomes possible. And he's absolutely thrilled by the power of observation. He practically gloats when he's able to surface the hidden commitments monkey mind has. He's fun to watch."

"I've seen him convert what he sees almost instantly. When he learns something new, he's all over it," said Maria, whom Sam had called to tell about his success in his "not-so-difficult" conversation with Bob.

"Cool. Let's go on. Any *un*examined conventional assumptions that you either made visible together or that you've heard about from Sam?" Tom read a list.

- There's a right way to do something.
- Tough conversations hurt relationships.
- There are difficult people.
- We make conclusions based on evidence we've gathered.
- There is such a thing as security.
- Action is the ultimate challenge.
- People can hide what they strongly believe.
- People don't change much.
- Work is not expected to be fun.
- A manager develops his or her people for promotion.

The *un*-team identified some of the assumptions they had addressed.

"What's one change each of you anticipates will come out of Sam challenging his beliefs about these?" Tom asked.

"He'll have conversations others won't have. For example, 'Tough conversations can *enrich* relationships' will enable what 'Tough conversations *hurt* relationships' can't," said Peter.

"He'll be more creative and resilient. For example, he'll be looking for a Plan B in any situation because he knows the security of the usual Plan A is an illusion. Things will change," said Tom. "He's more prepared for that."

"He'll be very thorough with the first three COSA steps because he knows that authentic action depends on them," offered Marguerite.

"He's sure people *do* change course when they see what once was invisible to them. He's gotten out of the fog so many times with us, and he's seen his own capacity for change. Therefore he's sure at a gut level others can too," added Maria.

"This is good," said Tom. "Sophia will have a clear picture from our examples. Thanks, everyone. What about major tools he's gotten? Sophia says all she did with Sam was have him observe so he could really experience the process of surrendering to the lesson."

"That's all?" asked Peter in mock disappointment. "No one can do that like Sophia. She continues to amaze me."

"No kidding," agreed Marguerite, Maria, and Tom.

Peter said, "We did the characteristics of so-called difficult conversations. I could see the wheels turning. Also 'Belief Creates the Fact.' I never get tired of how surprised and excited people are when they see that the conclusion precedes and dictates the evidence-gathering. Sam was no exception. It was especially fun because he did the circle with the conclusion 'There are difficult people.' It was the 4th of July in his brain, I tell you! You'd have loved it."

"Apparently he really got that you can transform the world one conversation at a time," said Marguerite. "He called me, and we talked about his team and their meeting around expectations. He had them generate what they should be held accountable for. They clarified it together and merged his expectations with theirs. It's tied to outcomes, of course, but I was impressed with the involvement of regular feedback from clients. Bottom line, he, his team, and clients are in frequent communication. His productivity stats are on the rise. I'd bet on it."

"Sam continues to make distinctions which he applies. For example, he sees the power of humor to transform. Taking himself less seriously will serve him and everybody else well," Tom said, and everybody agreed. They'd all seen "Serious Sam."

"Serious as a heart attack," chuckled Peter, oblivious to his use of the well-worn cliché.

"He recognizes monkey mind symptoms, for example, using humor to deflect. He asked me whether his so-called difficult employee making a joke when he faced an *un*comfortable question was an example of monkey mind at work," said Maria.

"He's been sensitized to seeing people as heroes, which in truth has huge ramifications for him as a great manager," said Peter, adding "He's had good support from Samantha Osler."

"Speaking about sensitive, did anyone do any real work with him on 'Language dictates experience'?" Tom asked.

> Surrender for monkey mind is inspired by fear. Surrender for the hero is inspired by courage.

Maria piped up. "Thanks for asking, Tom—I would've forgotten, and this is something to celebrate. No, I'm not aware that anyone worked directly with Sam on that. Correct me if I'm wrong. Here's an email he wrote me. I thought he copied us all. I was very impressed. Clearly Sam has done a lot of reflecting and connecting." Maria pulled it up on her phone. "It was about how language has different meaning in the psychological domain versus the ontological domain."

She began reading to the group. "Surrender for monkey mind is inspired by fear. Surrender for the hero is inspired by courage. This is true for the word 'vulnerable.' Monkey mind would do anything to protect me from feeling vulnerable. Language dictates the belief, then the feeling, then the experience. 'Vulnerable' is weak and fragile in the psychological domain. But 'vulnerable' for the hero just means you're willing to take life as it is. You're willing to be open, receptive, *un*defended."

"Is that the best, or what!" said Maria, proud of their protégé. "He got the holy grail. I can't believe I forgot to mention this. Sam was so excited about the great sessions he had with Sophia and Peter that he theorized, accurately I think, about how people really learn. He didn't mean learning to meet a technical challenge. What he was talking about is learning that's related to an adaptive challenge."

Maria summarized the rest of Sam's communication. "He said that cognition isn't enough to produce the meaningful behavioral change an adaptive challenge requires. In order to be truly motivated, people have to learn more deeply than at the conceptual level. And that has huge implications for the elusive prize of employee engagement. Pretty good, huh?" Maria looked around the room.

"Wow. Yes, that's outstanding. He's gotten that experience with Sophia and you guys, and it will serve him well," said Tom. "Where the hero lives, language has different meaning than it does in monkey mind's jungle. Being such a language lover, he'll keep that front and center."

"OK, so I get that he's ready for Step Four. Agreed?" Tom said looking at his watch. They all agreed.

"What I didn't hear is that he has the blueprint of his personal power." Tom looked around the group.

"For some reason it just hasn't come up, even though this is pretty late in the COSA process," Marguerite acknowledged. "Let's hope it fits when we talk about the 'A'—ACT. Otherwise it'll just have to come up when it comes up." She shrugged her shoulders, obviously not very concerned.

"Yes. Let's just trust the process. It's all OK," suggested Tom.

"Are you ready to take a look at how Samantha Osler is coming along?"

"Sure. We've been doing splendid work with both of them. Yay, *Un*-team," Peter said with his mischievous grin and a thumbs-up. Fifteen minutes later they left Tom's office and amid lively conversation headed for the executive dining room.

Dear Reader

1. Can you think of an example in your experience in which you felt empowered because something that had once been invisible to you was made visible? What was it, and how did it affect your life?
2. The *un*-team talks about the transformative power of humor. How has humor transformed something in your life? Do you use your sense of humor to lighten a "heavy" situation? What example comes up for you?
3. Sam asserts, and experts in adult development agree, that cognition isn't enough to produce a lasting behavioral change. A deeper learning has to occur. Is that your experience? How is your experience the same? Different?

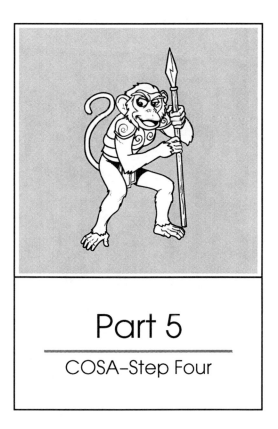

Part 5

COSA–Step Four

Chapter 16

AWAKENING THE DREAMER

While the *un*-team members were having their meeting, Sam still felt as if he was walking on air. In three hours he'd knocked out a project for which a resolution had evaded him all of three weeks.

As Sam reviewed the two days since his conversation with Bob, it hit him that the act of prizing self-awareness in oneself and others was radical in the business environment. It broke an *un*spoken rule. Americans are a pretty driven people. "We're very often in a 'hurry up and act' mode which actually devalues observation," he concluded. He, however, had accomplished more in less time with more energy since beginning his COSA process adventure.

He decided to take the evening off and enjoy some beers with his Wharton buddies. On life's playing field, "enjoyment" is necessary equipment to make a play on goal. Enjoying some down time would support him in what was next. It occurred to Sam that Americans think being driven is a positive quality. He wondered if this was an assumption a great manager challenged.

Walking into the cafeteria the next day, he spotted Marguerite Chan and Tom Pierot. He was suddenly no longer hungry. He walked over to their table. It was just the two of them.

"I'd love to get together with you to talk about the 'A' in COSA.

Any chance either or both of you have some time today?"

"Why don't you join us?" said Tom after his brief glance had been met with a slight nod from Marguerite. "We're in no hurry."

Sam studied the trim, tall programming manager's face. The confidence it reflected had once made her somewhat intimidating. But now he just saw her easy friendliness and remembered how much she'd helped him sort out his early opinions about the role of talent for excellent job performance. Now she was the "Don't just do something, sit there" manager whose comments about taking action he eagerly anticipated. After all, she'd affirmed that the ultimate goal in the *un*-game and the COSA process was action.

"Thanks. You guys are great. I want to tell you…" and he proceeded to tell his story about Bob. Marguerite and Tom didn't say they'd already heard about his success from Maria.

After Tom and Marguerite had shared in the celebration, Sam said, "The *un*-game is a new frontier for me. My life is so different even though it's only been a few weeks. Because of your support I really get the 'COS' in COSA. And I've *un*covered a ton of rules, spoken and *un*spoken, written and *un*written, that great managers break. I'm ready for the 'A.' Let's talk about that."

"Sure. What about the 'A' interests you?"

"So we have 'C' for CHOOSE, 'O' for OBSERVE, 'S' for SAY YES. So the 'A' stands for ACTION, right?"

"The first three are all verbs. 'Action' is a noun. Notice how you experience the difference," said Marguerite.

"The verbs make this more active than the noun. I *do* something with a verb. I choose. I observe. I say 'yes', Oh, the 'A' stands for ACT as in TAKE ACTION. I act. That has to be right." Sam loved to be right.

"You're on the money."

Sam's pleasure was short-lived. He sighed. "I don't know, but I don't feel pumped about the 'A' in COSA. It seems a bit anticlimactic. The other parts of the process had me losing sleep trying to get the principles. It was hard but also intense and full of one 'aha' after another. But, here it's kind of like 'Duh, of course, we have to act! What's up with *that*?"

"So how are you experiencing your energy as you say that?" Tom's question invited Sam to observe.

"My energy is low. It has the flavor of a 'so what?'."

"And what are you noticing about what you're saying?"

"I think I already know what there is to know about ACT."

"The three most dangerous words in the English language—'I already know.' Why do you suppose it could be said that this statement is a grounded assessment?" Marguerite asked, sounding mildly curious.

"I wouldn't be open and receptive. I'd be defended. Not curious. I'd be gathering evidence for my conclusion 'I already know what there is to know.'" Sam's response was *un*guarded. "And that could be dangerous," he added.

"Great observation. And that all-too-familiar human instinct to assume that most things are *un*interesting—that most things are *not* chock full of delicious possibilities—where does it originate?"

Sam sat up straighter. "We do seem to assume that," he thought after filtering Marguerite's statement through his experience.

"Monkey mind!" he said out loud. "Here we go again. Of course, monkey mind would have me assume I already know everything I need to know about the art and science of producing action. I have nothing more to learn about ACT. That's what makes it *un*interesting. Because if I have nothing to learn, I won't change anything. And we could just go on the way we always have. Boring but predictable. That little trickster would just love that, I suspect."

He laughed, but not wholeheartedly.

"For sure," said Marguerite. "You'd keep on doing what you've always done hoping for a different result. Can you see why change in human affairs is such a slippery slope? Big time management gurus and authors of business books are never out of work. They propose the same ideas today that they proposed thirty years ago. Packaged a little differently maybe, but mostly—not all—the same stuff. It could be said that until an idea of value is implemented, it's brand-spanking new! No wonder the gurus and the books abound."

Tom and Marguerite laughed. Sam thought it was depressing. He wanted to demonstrate change. He wanted his department's productivity stats to go through the roof.

Marguerite picked up the thread of the conversation. "Of course to any but the *un*-game players, the action conversation is old hat. The average and good managers may be in the grip of 'I already know.' I already know how to manage. I've read *The One Minute Manager*, *The Fifth Discipline*. I've been to seminars on kick-butt customer service. I know all about emotional and social intelligence. I have experience.'

"They've done all that reading and studying. They all too often think or at least hope, *un*fortunately, that those activities plus their daily actions make them great managers. It's like them going to a restaurant, eating the menu, and thinking they'd just savored the advertised meal. Not!"

Tom chimed in. "Yep, it's not the content of the book or the seminar. The content is the booby prize. So is telling. People don't learn deeply by being told. They learn deeply through engagement. And what engages people? Contact does! Contact engages their brain, mind, and heart. Management is a contact sport! Employee engagement isn't free. You have to earn the points you put on the board." The marketing manager sounded pleased with his analogy.

The three managers were silent for a while. Sam thought about the power of feeling actively engaged. It was so much more satisfying than being talked at. He recalled times when he'd felt bored. It was often when he attended a lecture. "Information is not always powerful," he concluded. But he didn't say this.

Tom pitched a question into the comfortable and fertile silence. "So in COSA, what would you be acting upon, Sam?"

Sam inhaled deeply, remembering Coach Zabar saying it would bring oxygen to his brain. "Gotta feed my rational mind," he said to himself. "Otherwise that little trickster could sneak in here and get me to go out of my mind."

In response to Tom's question he said, "The individual or the team would be acting on what they've become aware of through the rest of the COSA process. For example, if we're talking about me, I'd be acting on a new way of seeing something—something that no longer worked, if in fact it had *ever* worked. So, if I'd become aware of having the thought 'excellence is zero defects' and subsequently saw that excellence is actually impossible if we only shoot for zero defects, then that awareness would produce a completely different set of actions than if I set my strategy based on my original conclusion.

> People don't learn deeply by being told. They learn deeply through engagement. And what engages people? Contact does! Contact engages their brain, mind, and heart. Management is a contact sport! Employee engagement isn't free. You have to earn the points you put on the board.

"Without awareness of what should precede action, effective action may not be possible—and that practically guarantees *un*sustainable business practices."

"In other words, the future impact on business and other human affairs will be pretty grim if we don't step up our game?" asked Tom.

"Yes," said Sam. "I'd actually say: Given the power of the COSA process to *un*cover the thoughts, beliefs, opinions, and conclusions which are 'holding us hostage' to a way of thinking that's endangering our place at the head of the global leadership table, it's imperative to step up our game, especially the *un*-game."

This confident man hardly resembled the Sam they knew.

"What's currently impossible, which, if it *were* possible, would change everything?" asked Marguerite. It was a question Coach Zabar had asked all of them at some point in their COSA coaching.

"That's a very provocative question," Sam responded. Some people might think it strange, but he liked to get out of his comfort zone at times. He felt awake.

"We can't change much with our current way of thinking," he said. "Our current mind-set is 'Hurry up and act.'"

> Given the power of the COSA process to *un*cover the thoughts, beliefs, opinions, and conclusions which are "holding us hostage" to a way of thinking that's endangering our place at the head of the global leadership table, it's imperative to step up our game, especially the *un*-game.

All of a sudden Sam sat up straight, stared at his two mentors, and exclaimed so loudly that the occupants of the nearest tables looked up. "Oh…my…God. I just got something. It's a wake-up call. 'Wake up, Mr. and Ms. Dreamer. Wake up, CEO Dreamer. Wake up, Company and Board of Director Dreamers. Wake up! How we're doing business doesn't fit our 21st century global reality! The thinking that drives our actions isn't getting the job done!'

"What I'm noticing is that in most of our affairs, at work or anywhere else, we start at the end! Not good! We start with action. Sure, we have a company vision and mission. We may even have a set of values which we say guides our actions. We plan—strategic planning, long range planning, this quarter's targets. But we mostly enter the playing field and act as we always have."

Sam stopped as if to review something. He nodded and then continued. "Whereas in the COSA process, the action we take is the natural outcome of what we've just become aware of. It makes sense to act. When we've gone through the first three steps of the process, we can produce high quality decisions and actions."

Marguerite and Tom were listening closely. "Go on," they said almost in unison. Sam did.

"It has awesome implications for shifting not only how we act locally but also globally. Values may adorn corporate walls, but they hardly guide the creation of a path leading away from the status quo toward an *un*tried way of doing business. The status quo exerts a great pull when we have no new thinking with which to lift our mental fog. We aren't awake to who we are. How else would you account for the fact that most businesses, even in the face of mounting challenges to people and the planet, still only consider shareholder profits the true measure of a company's success? "

Sam looked around as if he'd just come out of a trance. "Did I really say that?" he wondered.

Tom and Marguerite looked at him. Noticing the same encouragement in their eyes that he'd extended to Bob in their recent conversation somehow deeply satisfied him.

"I didn't see that until just now. I'd only flirted with thoughts about the quality of the actions that COSA makes possible. Maybe that's why the ACT piece didn't have any sizzle for me. It was just the next apparent step to take. Ho hum.

"But now I see that in COSA, ninety percent of the real work precedes the action. Some people might compare it to planting a garden. The activity is largely underground. It looks like nothing's happening, when in fact there's a ton of purposeful activity going on. Without the preceding work, we'd have a meager harvest! And then the first green shoots break ground. Wow. We're going to have a bumper crop!"

Sam thought the garden analogy had to be accurate. Without the three preceding steps of the COSA process, the power of the 'A,' the action, was severely circumscribed! It boggled the mind.

Sam continued, almost *un*aware of the other two managers.

"So in answer to the question 'What's currently impossible, which, if it *were* possible, would change everything?' I'd say—what's currently not possible is the large scale commitment in action of leaders and managers to make self-observation and observation central—especially of the *un*spoken, *un*written rules that govern their organization.

> In COSA, ninety percent of the real work precedes the action. Compare it to planting a garden. The activity is largely underground. It looks like nothing is happening, when in fact there's a ton of purposeful activity going on. Without the preceding work, we'd have a meager harvest!

Committed leaders would be fierce about surfacing what no longer serves them in order to produce extraordinary results. And they'd learn to look from their hero's heart while outplaying their individual and collective monkey mind. The bottom line is: they'd actively foster a learning organization. It would be a paradigm shift of huge proportions."

"And why do you say that's currently impossible?" Tom asked.

"Because companies are *un*aware that this could *un*lock the level of thinking Albert Einstein was probably talking about when he said that we couldn't solve our problems with the same level of thinking that once created them. For *un*leashing our enormous potential we need to go beyond that level. Companies have limited power until they *do* know." Sam loved his theory.

"On-target theory, Sam," said Tom, "although we don't want to become enamored with theory at the expense of effective action. Would it be all right with you if we had a paradigm shift in which managers would just pay attention to a new way of approaching the basics? You know, like creating great relationships with internal and external customers, developing departmental goals that excite and propel, finding novel ways to increase productivity, reducing turnover—the basic stuff that management is made of?"

"Definitely," Sam said enthusiastically. "Because we think we already know the basics. And as we said earlier, that does us no good at all. I want team meetings which surface and explode old ways of thinking in an on-going manner. Ones that would make old Albert Einstein proud. We'd produce a lot of positive changes." He added with a hint of pride, "I can already see the change in myself.

"I'm routinely asking myself now 'Is there another way of looking at this?' Or 'What would someone who was being creative do right now?' or 'What if I looked at this with courage as a guide?' or 'How might I see this differently?' It certainly helped me in my conversation with my so-called difficult employee."

"Well, it's obvious you now have the spirit of the 'A' in COSA. You'd probably appreciate some tools that would help you move step by small step toward a goal you've set, is that right?"

Tom had asked that question while Marguerite leaned back, just listening and watching. They made a very good team, Sam noted. Supporting each other, not competing.

"For sure. I'm up for any tool I can get my hands on. What's become crystal clear is that my number one extremely loyal opponent on the playing field is that little trickster that wears so many distracting uniforms."

Tom chuckled. "Oh, our pal, monkey mind? The one that greets you at the line of scrimmage and says 'Turn Around, Pal?' You mean you won't tap dance away when you meet the little critter?"

"Not a chance," retorted Sam. "I'll keep my eye on the goal and get myself support from one of you! You'll help me see what our little pal has to offer me." Sam grinned as if he could hardly wait to see what monkey mind would come up with next.

"Great. So, Marguerite, shall we show Sam the distinctions on goals that he probably isn't considering right now?"

"Good idea," replied the programming manager, picking up the cue. "You know a lot about goals, I'm sure. Like S.M.A.R.T. goals."

"Specific, measurable, achievable, realistic, and time-bound." Sam's response shot out like a rocket. This was basic stuff. He knew this.

Marguerite nodded but said, "Let's make one important change. Let's let the 'R' represent 'Relevant.' What we mean by this is that the goal must be relevant to something that has real value for you, like an intention in your inner world that you long to make real in the outer world. Do I remember correctly that you have an intention to be a great manager? And another to be an effective communicator?"

"That's right," Sam confirmed. He recalled bits of related comments about goals he'd heard in conversation with Peter Black. His recall was sketchy, however. He and Peter had focused not on action, but on the third step in COSA, the SAY YES principle.

"Can you give me an example of how you actually demonstrated your intention in the outer world?" Marguerite asked, bringing Sam's attention back to the present.

"Oh, right. I communicated very well with Bob, the guy I thought I'd have to fire. And I helped him see that he'll wither unless he follows his dream to be a green economy activist. That was a demonstration of my intention to be a great manager." Sam reddened but held Marguerite's gaze.

"Yes. That's a good example for the 'R' in a S.M.A.R.T. goal. You can, of course, create goals that are larger than having a so-called tough conversation. The principle is the same. Without a relevant intention that comes from your hero's heart and not your monkey mind, a goal will not pull you. And you need the extra help of a goal pulling you. It has to have juice for you. Without it…"

"My 'I don't wanna' may be stronger than my 'I'm willing.'" Sam completed Marguerite's sentence, remembering their conversation when the distinction between wanting and being willing had first entered his awareness.

Sam experienced the distinction between the two differently now. The level of engagement with the entire COSA process had increased his competence to apply it in effective action.

"Yep, the rest of a S.M.A.R.T. goal is pretty standard—beyond a relevant intention that pulls you emotionally, goals should be specific, measurable, achievable, and time-bound. But there's one more thing worth paying attention to," Marguerite said.

"What's that?"

"How you think about goals, that is, your mind-set around goals. Without taking that mind-set through the COSA process, you're likely to do the same thing with goals that you've always done. Nothing will change. What you've just learned will become a rule monkey mind will manipulate as a concept rather than a principle that helps you design goals worth playing for on your field of dreams."

"Please take me through the process, then, so that I can *un*cover what might be in my way of achieving my goals with greater ease."

"We'd be delighted to take you through the COSA process," said Marguerite speaking for Tom and her. Tom quickly asked and they answered the questions to get them into the ontological space that was so important for producing extraordinary results in coaching.

"So what comes up for you when you think about goals, either in your life at home or at work?" asked Tom, encouraging Sam to begin to observe.

Sam furrowed his brow and said, "Well, they have a different quality about them. Sometimes my personal goals are more fun. I don't think of business goals as fun, although doing stuff to be a great manager is always fun to me. Call me weird."

"No, I think I'll just call you talented. But I digress. Say a little more about business goals not being fun."

Sam noted Tom's acknowledgment as well as the warmth around

his heart. "To me goals are immediately followed by 'They're going to be a lot of work.' I have to psych myself up for them."

"So think of a specific example."

"OK. I got one."

"Can you describe how you experience your energy as you recall the goal? What's it like?"

"Constricted."

"Not like play, huh?"

"No, not like play."

"That's an interesting conclusion," said Tom.

"What conclusion?"

"Goals are work." They were quiet until Tom broke the silence.

"Do you know how the dictionary defines 'goal'?"

"No." Sam was curious. "How?"

"A goal is an area or an object toward which play is directed. What are you noticing on hearing 'goal' defined like that?"

"Play seems to be the key word, or at least the one that stands out for me. And play has to do with fun."

"Yeah, like in a game." Tom Pierot smiled wryly.

"Hmm, the *un*-game." Sam looked pensive. "It's not just about *un*covering thoughts, beliefs, opinions, and conclusions. It's about doing it with clarity of intentions and focus. Like the quarterback whose intention it is to be a masterful leader, who then directs his focus on the receiver for the next play. He's clear. He's focused. He knows the next move. That's called doing it with ease." Sam's voice now increased in speed and volume. "He connects. Ha! Now the celebration. Way to go! And now on to the next play." He paused.

"How are you experiencing your energy as you hear yourself say that?" asked Tom.

"Great. I'm ready for the next play. I'm having fun even though this is 'pretend.'"

"Yes, the brain is funny. It doesn't even matter that this is play-like. It might as well be happening for real. We engage as if it *is* real. We're wired that way."

Marguerite chimed in. "I think you're not quite finished exploring your conclusions around goals. What is it that has your energy around goals be so heavy rather than light as in a game?"

"Well, what if you don't reach the goal? There are consequences." Sam thought about his productivity stats and his glum boss who'd be back in town in three weeks.

"So?"

Although taken aback by Marguerite's one word response, Sam replied, in effect saying "yes" to a lesson. "I guess I could look at it differently. Like the quarterback doesn't complete every pass. But he's not frozen in fear. And he doesn't focus on avoiding the consequences. He designs his next play, and so can I. How many times am I going to have to learn that?" Sam moaned.

"What are you noticing about what you just said?"

"I'm judging myself harshly."

"You are, aren't you? 'I should have learned this already' is implicit in your comment. And how well does judging yourself harshly support you in learning the lesson you said is important for you to learn, namely shifting from 'a goal not scored is bad' to 'I can design my next play on goal'?"

"It doesn't support me at all."

"So are you looking at it differently, or are you only *talking* about looking at it differently?" Marguerite's faintly mocking smile was the kind that was permitted among good friends.

Sam was quiet but his brain was hard at work. Finally he said, his voice dispassionate and clear, "I was only talking about it as a concept. My moaning about the lesson eluding me is more of the same heavy energy I experience around goals. Without my conscious knowledge I was empowering the conclusion 'A goal not scored is bad.' Of course I can't be like the quarterback if I don't empower the conclusion *he* does!"

"Outstanding, Sam. So what are you noticing about what you've just become aware of?" Marguerite asked in a calm, non-critical voice.

"I just took my eye off my next move on the goal which in this interaction with you was simply to design the next play, namely looking at goal-scoring like a quarterback instead of the way I *had* been looking at it. My moaning belonged to monkey mind who was telling me there's something wrong with me if I don't complete every pass."

"Your seeing this will serve you well. Is what monkey mind is saying the truth?"

"No. It's designed to keep me from seeing the truth."

"Which is what?"

"By seeing what I hadn't seen—namely that despite my protests I hadn't changed how I relate to goals—I can now radically alter my relationship to setting and accomplishing goals."

"You can, can't you?" said Marguerite with a satisfied smile. But there's still something more about goals for you. What is it?" she added after allowing Sam the obvious pleasure of his work well done.

"Well, there are so many smaller goals before reaching the big one, and they're often not much fun."

"Is it that some of your actions advance the ball toward goal and others make no visible difference?"

"Uh-huh, kind of like that."

"Is it kind of like that, or is it like that?"

Sam noticed that he felt mildly defensive, but as soon as he noticed it, he shifted.

He laughed. "It's like that, Marguerite, and please note I'm not saying 'I guess so'!"

Sam felt a rush catching monkey mind in its sneaky act.

"Practice makes progress," he said, satisfied he hadn't fallen into yet another trap of thinking that practice could or even should make perfect. Life was good!

Marguerite picked up the thread of the conversation. "You said there are a lot of smaller goals before you achieve the big ones. It may help to make a distinction between tasks and goals. Many people collapse those two distinctions, but they're not at all the same. Do you have a 'to do' list?"

"Every day. I like checking off the ones I've completed."

"What's the experience you have at the moment of completion?"

"Oh, I feel pretty good. A sense of accomplishment." Sam wondered what this questioning was going to reveal.

"Does it last?"

"No, I just move on to the next item on the check list," Sam sighed.

"Well, that's the nature of task completion. We experience relief. But what we experience with goal completion is different, isn't it?" Marguerite looked expectantly at Sam.

"It really is. You know the guy who scores in football always does some sort of crazy dance. It turns me off, but I love to see the winner celebrate at the end of the game. There's something gorgeous about seeing pure ecstasy."

"You put that quite strongly. So it's different from the relief of accomplishing a task."

"Totally. People experience pure *un*adulterated joy when they reach their goal!"

"Very good, Sam. Yes, that's the difference. When you reach a goal, then you can't help but be joyous. What are you noticing about how you've been relating to goals and tasks?"

"I've made no distinctions between the two, Marguerite. As a result my relationship to goals has been influenced by my experience with tasks. Tasks are burdens pretty often. When I get rid of them, all I feel is relief."

"What possibilities, if any, do you see here?"

"I can get my expectations in the right place. That's what I can do. It would be silly to expect a hamburger to be a Porterhouse steak." Sam laughed. "Task accomplishment is obviously necessary to get to the joy of scoring the goal. But tasks aren't the goal."

He stopped and scanned his thoughts.

"The second thing I see is that I often just have tasks on my list. I either have goals someone else gave me or a long list of tasks that I haven't connected to a real juicy goal that got its start as a longing in my own hero's heart, like the intention to be a great manager, an adventurer, a great team player." Sam fell silent. He noticed how comfortable he'd become talking about "hero's heart" and using words like being "joyous." It was extraordinary.

"Terrific, Sam. Anything else?" asked Marguerite.

"Yes. I now have another clue as to how I experience my energy around action. My actions often come from a driven place, not as a response to a goal I cherish like wanting to work at L-4 Germany, which comes from intentions that really matter to me—being a great manager and being well-traveled."

"Good for you for saying this out loud, Sam. What you're talking about is very common. We call it driven behavior. People are very busy. They work very hard. And they get very tired. Do you know where they are on Life's Playing Field?"

Sam remembered the graphic resembling a football field clearly. "I can relate. I'm in the 'My Outer World' side of the field, let's say at some meeting where I'm presenting. If my agenda is to impress my boss—who, me?—I'm cut off from the other side of the field, the 'My Inner World' quadrant, home of my hero's intentions, which determine my goals worth scoring. That hasn't been true for me since I started the *un*-game coaching. We're so intentional to link what we do to what's important to our hero's heart. For example, the conversation with my 'difficult' employee was linked to my intentions to be a great manager and an effective communicator."

"Excellent, Sam. It's valuable to see that. The two worlds need to be connected for you to play a champion's game. How will you put into action what you've learned in this conversation?"

"I'll certainly remember the definition of goal. That in itself is huge. And I'll recall the difference between tasks and goals as needed. I'm energized just thinking about that. Then I'm going to review the goals I inherited and see if I can own them in light of my intentions and values. All those activities will have me look at goals from a much more powerful place."

"Anything else?" asked Tom.

"Yeah. Feeling like I do, I can only imagine how my team feels. I don't know how yet, but together we're going to create goals we all own. I think we're on our way, but this will take us to a new level. 'Goals worth playing for' has a completely different ring to it, especially now, than completing the task of writing performance standards."

Both Tom and Marguerite smiled.

"I'll schedule that conversation for next Tuesday. And with what I just got, I can shift my former goal paradigm to one I like better," Sam said enthusiastically. "I could even take myself more lightly, couldn't I?" He smiled broadly. "Since a goal is an area or an object toward which play is directed, right?"

"Yes, you could," replied both managers, looking pleased with the work of their protégé.

Sam couldn't quell his enthusiasm about what had been *un*concealed in this conversation.

"I'm amazed when I see the power language has to dictate our experience. Like my 'moaning language' alerted you, Marguerite, to my disempowering conclusion around goals. I've always been sensitive to language, but never as sensitive as right now. The power of distinctions," he marveled, shaking his head.

"Well, when you think about it, the word 'distinction' is interesting in itself. Before something is distinct, what is it?" asked Tom.

"Indistinct. *Un*recognizable. Out of focus. In the fog." Sam had thought about this before.

"Exactly," said Tom. "*Un*usable. But once it's distinct, your brain has infinite capacity for designing uses for it. The sky's the limit. It literally *un*chains your brain. So yes, language dictates your experience. We'd all do well to observe how we use language. If we don't produce the desired results, we can look at our language as a clue. It may be a gold mine of information about what we're up to. And it may surprise us."

"Yeah, and that goes for inner as well as outer dialog," agreed Sam. "I can be observing my monkey mind chatter which, by the way, I've decided to call 'night language,' because that little sucker makes about as little sense as the language in my dreams."

He hesitated before continuing. "On the other hand, it could be said that the chatter makes total sense in supporting why I *shouldn't* be accomplishing my goals even as I'm motivated to achieve them. It acts as the brakes when what I really want is to step on the accelerator."

> It could be said that monkey mind chatter makes total sense in supporting why you *shouldn't* be accomplishing your goals even as you're motivated to achieve them.
>
> It acts as the brakes when what you really want is to step on the accelerator.

Sam lingered on that thought then said, "I can also be observing how I talk to you or to my team. I call that 'day language.' I have some control over what I choose to use. Because I love language, I'm going to have a helluva lot of fun with this. You guys are so the best. Have I told you lately how grateful I am for your support?" He flashed an open, generous smile.

Both Tom and Marguerite smiled back, clearly enjoying the acknowledgment.

"You're doing really good work," Tom said. "You'll be thrilled to learn, as we were, that there's still more to *un*cover in the *un*-game. You're now awake. You'll fall asleep again, but once the dreamer is awake, he or she is capable of changing the dream. Wouldn't it be great if we used what we become aware of as a springboard to designing the future we'd be proud to hand over to coming generations?"

And with that, the accidental meeting that was so transformative for Sam ended. He couldn't imagine what else there was to be learned. But awake *un*-game players would declare nothing off limits for exploration. After all, they had each other and the COSA process.

Dear Reader

1. You have now studied the four-step process, four-play to business as *un*usual, which we can use for *un*covering our most closely held thoughts, beliefs, opinions, and conclusions. In order to produce effective action, the entire process is needed. Which of these steps, if any, will you need to explore further in order to gain some competence? How do you expect to conduct your exploration? Which step is the most challenging for you? Least challenging? What's the thinking that led you to your answers?

2. How would you describe or define the *un*-game? What is its purpose? Is there more than one purpose?

Chapter 17

THE *UN*-GAME: BUSINESS AS UNUSUAL

It was a crisp, cool, sunny day in October, four years after Sam Adler had come to work at L-4. Sam, now almost thirty, was in his hotel room reviewing the agenda for the *L-4 Global Workforce; Global Development* meeting. He'd flown from Frankfurt to New York, the events of the last four years *un*folding in his mind's eye. A more mature man, he'd realized his dream of being the quality control manager for L-4's German division. The COSA process and the *un*-game it allowed him to play had made his *un*foreseen fast ascent in the L-4 world possible. Sam was as grateful as he was proud.

What else made him proud was that he was now part of the inner circle of recognized great managers, the *un*-team, as they called themselves. The *un*-team was much larger than he'd originally realized. He smiled as he recalled some of his conversations with his original *un*-team. They'd always challenged him to step out of the confines of his established mind. How expanded his world had become! It was going to be great to see them all again.

He'd be seeing Samantha Osler at the meeting too. She was now in the training division. System theory was her specialty. Given the environment of 21st century *un*certainty and its enormous implications for relationship transactions, leadership, management and team development, this specialty was a fit for her interests and talents.

Sam Osler loved her work, and as it turned out, she loved Sam Adler too. Sam had proposed marriage by the light of a full moon on one of the romantic, old-world bridges in Heidelberg, Germany. And she had said "yes." Sam remembered his thrill at her "yes" as if it were yesterday. Her luminous eyes warmed his heart then as now.

Sam had allowed for a free pre-conference day to reconnect with his mentors and to spend some time with his wife, whom he hadn't seen in five days. An eternity.

He'd call Maria Nordstern, he decided. She'd never told him what rules she broke, and she'd left him with an *un*answered question.

Sam's attention refocused on the conference. It would be his first as a bona fide *un*-team member. He couldn't wait to experience the hundreds of L-4 *un*-game players from all over the world. They shared his ambition to make the COSA process widely available. Without the skill-sets and mind-sets the COSA process offered, change was just too slow.

Change was the focus of the New York meeting. Sam had heard that L-4's CEO, Bill Gordon, wanted the capacity to produce substantive, accelerated, and lasting change in the hands, hearts, and minds of the thousands of L-4 employees world-wide.

"The shift is about to hit the fan," Sam thought, whistling softly as he considered L-4's goal: "Everyone an *un*-game player in four years."

"How democratic." Sam let his thoughts ramble. "In the age of complexity, we all need to upgrade our mind-sets and the human systems that reflect them. Collaboration, transparency, a flatter organizational structure, and an understanding of complexity and its implications for our systems will be key in the coming world."

Some things don't change—Sam could theorize with the best of them. The difference, however, was that he could laugh at himself now with a generosity of spirit that had eluded him during his early COSA coaching.

Sam picked up the phone. "Hi, Maria. Sam Adler. How are you? It's been too long since I've eye-balled you. Do you have any time today? I'm not going to let you get away without answering some questions you've always side-stepped," Sam bantered, feigning strictness, in the easy interchange between equals.

An hour later he entered the Human Resources Department.

🕴🕴🕴🕴

"OK, now that I have you cornered," Sam said after bear-hugging Maria and getting the local L-4 news plus answering her questions about life in Germany.

"I want to know what rules you've broken to gain entry into the elite *un*-team society. You never told me," Sam chided.

"That can be a short conversation," Maria laughed playfully. "I often didn't fulfill the conventional training function."

"That's strange given that's your job and you're a natural, and I might add, loud supporter of personal and professional development at every level of the company," said Sam in *un*disguised surprise.

"Well, remember that in your role as catalyst one of your jobs is to develop your people's capacity, right?"

"Right."

"And how do the managers you observe develop their people's capacity?"

"They ask you to find or develop training programs," Sam answered. If there was a training need, HR was supposed to meet it."

"Right," acknowledged Maria. "HR-sponsored training can help employees gain knowledge and skills for better job performance. And I have fun providing that. What I reject is managers who prefer to avoid the tough conversations with their people in favor of sending them to training programs—for example, in conflict management skills.

"The managers themselves need to learn the distinctions and the skill-sets necessary to have those conversations. Instead, the problems they could resolve through conversation, they handle poorly—or worse, leave altogether *un*attended. In favor of what?"

Maria harrumphed. "Training programs for others, not themselves, which could never match the results of a real-time, authentic conversation."

"I see. Not on your watch, huh?"

"No. In such cases I find ways to work with those managers to increase their capacity to develop their people themselves. I break the *un*spoken and *un*written rules by shifting the focus of the work to where it belongs, namely to them!

> Managers often prefer to avoid the tough conversations with their people in favor of sending them to training programs—such as in conflict management skills.

"I rob them of the illusion that it's a technical problem—their people aren't skilled—that needs a technical solution such as skills training. No. It's an adaptive challenge—theirs! And it needs an adaptive solution, a change in their own behavior generated by a change in their thinking."

"Oh, that's one of the ways in which she developed L-4's managers and saved the company all that money," Sam thought. The pieces of that *un*finished puzzle were falling into place.

"*Un*resolved question number two. You're responsible for some of my sleepless nights. I've never gotten to a satisfactory answer on this."

"What's the question?"

Sam had written the question written down.

"What's the conventional wisdom regarding change that stunts companies' capacity to reach their highest potential?"

Maria, knowing something Sam didn't, namely that they would have a reunion of the New York *un*-team, was not about to answer that question. She thought the whole group might want to broach it together.

"Tell you what, Sam. I promise you'll have an answer to that question before you head back home to Baden-Baden. If you don't, come and see me before you leave, OK?"

"You've done it again, Maria. Slipped through my fingers." Sam was cheerful. "I'm willing to live with the *un*certainty a while longer even though I don't want to."

His bantering was very different from the response that would have been typical for him four years ago.

"But will you answer a question on the 'personal keys to excellence' for me?" he asked. "All the tools in the COSA process have been power tools for me. I'm not sure I'm making the most of this one with the managers I'm coaching."

Sam had gotten the tool the *un*-team had discussed at their third and last review of Sam's coaching progress.

"Sure. What is it?" asked Maria.

"OK, so we *un*cover the keys to excellence for the managers-in-training by having them identify people they admire and the qualities those people possess. We take them through the additional steps in the process. The end result is those basic desirable qualities or core values within the manager that we've coined 'personal keys to excellence.' Everyone has his or her own unique set," Sam summarized.

"And your question is…?"

"It seems to me that all the qualities we choose to get into the ontological coaching space are sufficient to call on in any situation dominated by monkey mind. Why do I have to have 'personal keys to excellence? What's the added value?"

"That's a great question, Sam, and what do you see as an answer as you look at your keys?"

Sam noticed that Maria had invited him to observe. The *un*-team was highly skilled at helping a person *un*cover his or her own answers. Some things change, some don't.

Sam pulled out the three-by-five laminated card which was the blueprint of his personal power. On it was written: "I am visionary, clear, courageous, effective, authentic, empowering, supportive, truthful, compassionate, flexible, persevering, committed, loyal, and funny"—listed vertically like a shopping list.

"This," he said studying the card, "*un*like the qualities that we use to corral monkey mind, are qualities that are uniquely me. Not everyone is funny, for example. Nor do they want to be. But that's part of what makes me Sam Adler and not Sophia Zabar.

"Your question makes me realize, Maria, that being able to call on these qualities in a tight situation expands my options. I usually don't ask the question 'What would someone with my personal keys to excellence do in this situation?' I might get different answers if I looked at 'How would a person who's being 'funny' handle this?'

"That might support me in lightening up when monkey mind makes it all very significant, huh?" Sam smiled.

"Yep. And doing that would come naturally to you once you call up that quality consciously. Because it's *you*. Your keys are who you naturally are. It's natural although not normal for you." Maria studied Sam's face.

"What do you mean 'it's natural but not normal'?"

"It's natural to be who we are because it's who we are. However, the world works very hard to make us into someone else. So it's normal for us to be who we really are *not*. We yield to the pressure of a socialized mind-set."

"That's a good way of looking at it, Maria. And that's exactly what we're working to transform. The socialized mind-set obeys its own rules and doesn't question. We need to reach a higher level of thinking if we're going to change the status quo."

"Do you see anything else about being aligned with your personal keys to excellence?" asked Maria.

"Well, when I'm me it's no effort. I don't have to work at it."

That was a revelation for Sam. Ease. No effort to be oneself. That really was so simple yet so profound.

"If I use my blueprint to design my actions, it gives me a sense of integrity, a sense of feeling at home with myself. If I don't, I experience frustration, resignation, and, if *un*resolved over time, even cynicism. In other words, Maria, monkey mind has its way with me, dissipates my energy, and compromises my effectiveness."

"So having your personal keys to excellence amplifies and focuses your own personal power over and above the ontological qualities you choose when you consciously get into the ontological space. Is that how yo see it?"

"Uh-huh."

"Is there any situation that's *un*resolved for you right now that you'd like to take a look at?"

"No, believe it or not, I'm good to go. I was just curious. This is really helpful. Why do you ask?"

"Oh, I was just thinking since you brought up the personal keys to excellence, that I'd share what I've learned along the way," said Maria.

"Great. I'm up for that. Go ahead." Among the things that don't change?—Sam didn't let many learning opportunities pass.

"Here's what I ask when I notice that one of my protégés is out of alignment with his or her personal excellence keys," Maria said. "'Which one of your keys to excellence are you *not* demonstrating in this situation right here, right now?' Perhaps the person has neglected 'courageous,' and the troubling situation could benefit from his courage. Perhaps she wants to give up on something that's clearly important to her. What would she do with that challenge, if she were being 'persevering'?"

"So as always," Sam said, "it gives people a way of distancing themselves from their experience. They're no longer subjected to their experience, that is, they're no longer the subject of their experience. By seeing the situation through the eyes of someone with their own keys to excellence, they've made the situation one they could see objectively. It's endlessly fascinating to me because it gets people in touch with a great power they have—observing their monkey mind from their hero's heart. Monkey mind is no match for the hero's heart. Therefore the observation allows them to surrender to a lesson that affects the next play on goal."

Maria and Sam continued chatting for another few minutes, made plans for meeting up at the conference, hugged, and said good-bye. Sam had enjoyed their conversation. It had been a sharing of equals.

"Remember your promise, Maria," Sam warned her good-naturedly. "I'm not going back to Germany without getting your final answer." They waved at each other and went their separate ways.

✶ ✶ ✦ ✶ ✶

As Sam entered his hotel room, his phone rang. It was Bob Harley, the former employee he associated with 'difficult' conversations. The fact that it had been a while since he thought of conversations that way made Sam feel accomplished.

He was glad Bob had found him. As they'd envisioned together four years earlier, Bob, after some fits and starts, had landed a leadership position in a "for social-profit" coalition. As part of his "dream" job he would soon be in Germany studying the German clean energy model. Did Sam know that Germany employs almost as many people in clean energy as in automotive enterprises? That the European Union sees green products as their Silicon Valley? And yes, it would be fun to look his former boss up!

Sam smiled. It didn't escape him how different this Bob was from the Bob who'd worked for him.

As he hung up the phone, the door to his hotel room opened, and he was greeted by the radiant smile of the tough and tender woman he loved who came rushing toward him. His wife had arrived from Montreal. The rest of the day belonged to just them. Bob Harley, *un*answered questions, and next day's *Global Conversations; Global Workforce Development* meeting promptly lost their claim on Sam's attention.

✶✶✶✶✶

Sam was all business the next day as he joined seven others at one of the twenty-five tables set up in the meeting room L-4 had chosen near the UN Plaza. His former mentor, Peter Black, was at his table. He sat down next to Peter.

"How extraordinary to be here," Sam thought, "with two hundred COSA-trained managers and coaches, all able to speak its common language and play the *un*-game." But the contact he'd had with Peter had produced an *un*breakable bond. The way Peter's face lit up when he saw him, Sam knew his own feelings were generously reciprocated.

The first speaker before Coach Zabar was L-4's CEO, Bill Gordon. Sam had never heard him speak in person before. The room broke into thunderous applause as Bill Gordon stepped up to the podium. He acknowledged the assembled managers as the company's leading edge and thanked them. He then spoke about sustained and responsible leadership that's driven by purpose.

> It's not enough to be driven by financial goals and results. Any 21st century business must also aspire to benefit people, our global environment, and society overall.

"Yes," murmured Sam, restraining himself from not shouting it when Bill Gordon asserted that it wasn't enough to be driven by financial goals and results. Any 21st century business must also aspire to benefit its people, our global environment, and society overall.

The CEO spoke with passion about *un*leashing extraordinary energy in people. "It's imperative that we have their energy," he asserted. "We must live our core promise to benefit and empower everyone who's touched by our business."

Sam knew that those weren't empty words. He nodded as Bill Gordon then asserted "The core promise only works when we operate from four enduring values."

Four enduring values. Sam reflected the number four was rather significant in his life. L-4, the four-step COSA process, four incredible mentors, "Everyone an *un*-game player in four years."

"An observer must see our values in action every day, in every activity," Bill Gordon continued. "Furthermore, we deliver on our core promise by benefitting the marketplace, which means we invest in local economies and drive marketplace innovation by strengthening the community. And we support the development of local partnerships with leaders and organizations through resources, expertise, and time. We also support these partnerships by enriching the workplace, which is all about how L-4 employees at all levels treat each other with respect and fairness. Finally, we support these relationships by conducting business in ways that protect and preserve the natural environment." Protecting the environment. Sam knew there were a lot of companies who were "green washing" these days. But not L-4.

The CEO then said something that people knew was coming but nevertheless caused a wave of murmurs in the room: "L-4 has incredible power. Not by our position in the market place, which is considerable, but by the power of the thousands who work with us. We've done well to *un*leash more human potential than many think possible. You are the evidence. But you are too few, and we've developed you too slowly. We need to increase our collective capacity quickly in order to achieve our 2020 goals. So here's your mandate. You're hearing it from the horse's mouth."

Bill Gordon knew how to get and keep attention—not only by his position but by his ability to engage an audience. "What I want to see, and what you'll make real is 'Everyone at L-4 an *un*-game player in four years.'" He ended his talk by suggesting that attendees consider the same four questions he'd given his top leadership team.

- How will you, personally, define your purpose as a professional now? How will we frame our aspirations in terms of the social and environmental returns we wish to deliver in the next year?

- How will we foster the kinds of relationships and partnerships that enable L-4 to be productive, healthy, and resilient?

- What will we do to inspire innovation, diversity, and learning as a natural part of doing business?

- What do you stand for? What are the *un*shakeable promises you will make to our customers, your colleagues, L-4, and your world?

Sam elbowed Peter Black conspiratorially. If you looked back on standard business practice as few as thirty years ago and compared them to what L-4's CEO described in his opening remarks, it was evident that Bill Gordon proposed a world of corporate responsibility which in no way resembled the past. It was an acknowledgment of an inter-related global community in which no players can exist in isolation and thrive. Peter got the meaning of Sam's nudge.

When the L-4 CEO left the stage, the room was abuzz, but the din diminished when the next speaker was introduced. A hushed silence came over the crowd as Coach Zabar, who—four years after he'd met her—was no longer old in Sam's eyes, climbed the platform to the podium. People settled back in their chairs.

The master coach began her talk with a warm welcome and the names of all the countries that were represented. Then she spoke about the privilege it was for her to be in the room with all the co-creators of the new reality that was emerging in L-4 because of their dedication and their skills. She expressed her profound gratitude for L-4's CEO and top leadership who made this meeting possible. She thanked those assembled for their partnership and reiterated what Sam had heard many times in the last four years—

that the world of business needed them to accelerate the revolution of the heart and the mind that was currently underway world-wide.

"You and I are up to the challenge," Sam's master coach said. "And that's why we're here at *Global Conversations; Global Workforce Development*. What I'm going to speak with you about is not just what the *un*-game is now. I'll also set up our inquiry as to how we might move the *un*-game to the next level.

"Ladies and gentlemen, you and I both know that the *un*-game is a big game which L-4 is supporting at the highest level. But it goes beyond L-4. Humanity is at a crossroads without precedent. We are in the midst of a gigantic paradigm shift in all areas—economic, social, cultural, psychological, and spiritual. New world views are emerging, and as a result we're redesigning human systems that we wouldn't have dreamed of even ten years ago. We're living in a new norm of guaranteed *un*certainty, and truth be told, most of the now seven billion of us understandably fear a negative future instead of imagining a positive one.

"It could be said that the second biggest crisis accompanying this enormous global paradigm shift is the crisis of imagination. Imagination suffers in the face of *un*resolved fear, doubt, worry, and *un*certainty. And you, dear colleagues, are a large part of the antidote. You heard your CEO, and I agree. *You* are the ones who can cause the shift that's now more than ever needed in the world."

The silence in the room was palpable. Even the discreet wait-staff that arranged the coffee and snack tables stopped moving.

"So what is the first crisis?" Coach Zabar asked.

"The first crisis we're facing is that as individuals as well as nations we are adrift. We have no container in which to hold what's happening. For Americans who have always been more outer-directed, more action-oriented, this is an especially tough challenge, but we all share in the challenge. No country is immune. None of us is certain in the midst of *un*certainty how to answer the question '*Who are we?*'

"We're facing a world that's challenging many of the assumptions we've labeled as incontrovertible truths—assumptions like 'America will always be the *un*assailable leader of the free world,' 'Warfare and our role in warfare as the global community knows it will prevail indefinitely,' 'Earth can sustain any assault that we perpetrate on it,' 'Economic systems of the West are stable and can weather any storm,' 'Technology will save us from ourselves.' And the list goes on."

Coach Zabar paused before asserting softly, "And…we are shaken to the core.

"You and I have a great deal of compassion for the turmoil most of the people we work with are engaged in. And we can help, because thanks to the inspired leadership of L-4 and for what you and I have been able to learn together, you and I *do* have a container in which to hold what's happening and not happening. Because we have such a container, it's possible for us to play the *un*-game. In a moment I'll make the container you and I share visible, but first, let me define what I think the *un*-game is.

> The *un*-game is a game people are able to play once they see their opponent—namely their commonly-shared immunity to change—learn the process for confronting it, and then develop the practices that support them in winning the match.

"The *un*-game is a game people are able to play once they see their opponent—namely their commonly-shared immunity to change—learn the process for confronting it, and then develop the practices that support them in winning the match.

"The well-played *un*-game depends on people not only understanding at a deeper than conceptual level their change-prevention system—which is very robust, especially in times of enormous flux like now—but also on redefining what's possible for them and their organizations and devising systems that can deliver the change. It's more than a tall order.

"The challenge is made even taller, because the immunity to change exists in all of us, not just in individuals but in organizations like L-4, in communities large and small, and of course in nations. As such, we must remember that the purpose of the *un*-game is nothing less than to shift our immunity to change such that the mental gridlock locking us into paradigms that no longer work can give way to paradigms that allow us to develop resilient and creative people. We must surface and shine a light on our prevailing world view: our most closely held thoughts, beliefs, opinions, and conclusions. And we must do this because of and in spite of the global diversity that now is just a key stroke, not a world away.

"This enormous challenge, as you know from having gone through the process yourself—empowering L-4's great-managers-in-training—is further complicated because we rarely recognize our real world view without help. It's invisible to us. It could be said 'Our world view lives us' rather than 'We live our world view consciously.'"

There were nods in the room. All the great managers and coaches knew intimately that perfect hiding place of monkey mind inside our world views. They knew but appreciated the reminder.

"Are we having fun yet?" Coach Zabar asked with a playful smirk, aware of the weighty energy in the room. "Just because this is a serious subject, we don't have to take ourselves so seriously. Let me give you some *un*solicited advice—Jest for the health of it!"

What? Advice? Chuckles of delighted recognition flitted around the room when the *un*-team managers caught the coach's rare pun, and the somber mood lifted.

"The good news, as you all know, is that you and I have a container which is big enough to hold what's happening, and we've been given that container in part through our exposure to

and our mastery of the COSA process. We're supported by some
of the world view changes that have occurred for us through our
engagement with this process.

"We comprehend some of the global trends L-4 must pay
attention to, not only as a world business leader, but as part
of a cadre of global leaders who accept our responsibility for
shifting the global mindscape. You and I know that this will occur
with one conversation at a time. Our global challenges call for
producing extraordinary results. Nothing less than transforming
our narrative—our story as to who we at L-4 are and who we are
willing to be—will do.

"Bill Gordon knows this," she continued in a solemn voice,
"and he's leading the way, showing us the direction and giving us
the tools. As great managers, your job is implementation. *You* are
invaluable. *You* are our leading edge.

"Let me remind you that you and I know who we are and who we
are *not*. And I'm talking about us personally, even more than about
us as a corporate identity. We are *not* our public personas. We *have*
a public persona. We are *not* who we're afraid we are, that is, we are
not our psychology. We *have* a psychology that demonstrates itself
through our doubts and worries, our thoughts, feelings, and body
sensations, but we *aren't* those. We *have* them."

Everyone in the room heard the passion and absolute certainty in
the coach's voice when she said, "No, we are more than that."

Softening, she added, "I'm reminded of an interchange between
a Zen master and his student. The student said to him, 'I think,
therefore I am.' The master asked, 'And who are you when you are
not thinking?'"

The audience laughed. They recognized where the coach was
going. Since they shared the language and experience of the COSA
process, her words reminded them to take themselves lightly
and not to divorce organizational development from personal
development.

"Well said. We don't park our personal selves at the door of our office," Sam thought.

The coach continued. "We know who we *really* are, who every single one of us is, including the people who used to drive us crazy, or still do because we, too, are a work in progress."

The room filled with chuckles of recognition once again. Coach Zabar smiled affectionately.

"We are heroes with a hero's heart and alas, a monkey's mind." The coach shrugged her shoulders in mock regret.

"Within our little trickster's mind resides our immunity to change and all the current mischief we see around us. Why? Because collectively the world is clueless as to how to move to the next level that's now required of humanity. Heroes are the ones who are able to observe their public persona and who they're afraid they are. The hero has the vantage point, and you and I have been teaching heroes all over the L-4 world how to be observers with the help of the COSA process. Our mandate is to find the ways to bring COSA to more people more quickly. And we will. Have no doubt about it.

"There's an African proverb—its country of origin is disputed—which I want to share with you," the coach said. "You may have heard former American Vice President Al Gore say it to the global community regarding our role in slowing global warming for future generations. 'If you want to go fast, go alone. If you want to go far, go together. We must go far fast.' And we're the people who can do it. We're the people we've been waiting for!"

Two hundred people rose in the midst of thunderous applause. Sam had been entranced at times with his coach and her presence, wisdom, skills, and grace, but he'd never imagined her as a transformational speaker who could so effortlessly engage large audiences.

"So knowing who we really are," Coach Zabar said gently, "is the container that allows us to hold the world's grief and fear. Not to worry. All is well. Fear and grief are essential partners to transformation, and that is what's now called for in personal, business domains, and in the rest of public life. Knowing who we are also allows us to see that some of the global trends we're witnessing currently may well be part of our collective immune system asserting itself."

Coach Zabar paused and looked around the room, making sure her audience was with her. She needn't have been concerned.

"We might see these positive trends as an expression of our collective hero's heart," she said. "They are the antithesis of the immunity to change which is alerting us to the dangers of straying from the status quo. The two in tandem often work at odds with one another. It's as if we're driving our car with one foot on the accelerator and one on the brake. The penultimate challenge is to take our foot off the brake when necessary, in order to arrive at desired destinations while protecting our capacity to brake when braking is called for.

> Knowing who we really are is the container that allows us to hold the world's grief and fear. Not to worry. All is well. Fear and grief are essential partners to transformation.

"We can and we must do that. The mandate and the questions Bill is asking us to consider should cause us to look at the current global trends we must support and accelerate. How do we know we're supporting those trends in L-4 and the business world at large? What's our role, and what's available to us to be significant players in the transformation that's needed now? Those are the questions our design team, with Bill's and your input, has created for your inquiry."

Coach Zabar approached her close. "Here are some global trends we see that may be arising from our collective immune system," she proposed. She flashed a PowerPoint slide on the screen above the speaker's podium.

Global Trends

- We're seeing a culture of cooperation, collaboration, and participation emerging in the world.
- There is a move toward transparency in business and other institutions.
- People are clamoring for a better world.
- Cultural capital is an emerging phenomenon.
- Increasingly smart technology is used creatively to solve entrenched problems.
- Holistic well-being, or life in the slow lane, is gaining traction.
- There exists what could be called "significant happiness hunting."

"If we embark on our journey without a trends atlas," Coach Zabar said, "it could be like going on a trip without a GPS. So here's your GPS. Remember what the purpose of the *un*-game is: to shift our immunity to change such that the mental gridlock can give way to paradigms which allow organizations to grow a resilient and creative workforce and to become as nimble as a greyhound.

"No, I didn't say a Greyhound bus!" she chided in response to some giggles.

A second slide appeared on the screen with the questions the assembled group of global great L-4 managers and coaches would consider. They were:

Shaping a New Future

- What are the ramifications of the global trends given the purpose of the *un*-game?
- What have we learned as it relates to our capacity to change our immunity to change through the COSA process, brain research, and adult learning and development theory?

- What's possible now with managers and coaches trained in the masterful delivery of the COSA process that wasn't possible before?

- What's our role, namely those who can lead the COSA process, in shaping a new future for L-4 and the wider community, especially given Bill Gordon's mandate and the questions which we must consider?

- What's one thing you'll take on immediately when you return home that will make the four-step COSA process more quickly available to more L-4 employees?

Coach Zabar ended by saying, "There's enough knowledge, skill, and wisdom in this room to change the world. But more importantly," the coach paused and looked lovingly at every table, "there's enough love in this room to *transform* the world. Thank you."

The crowd stood, whistled, and yelled "Merci. Gracias. Thank you. Danke schön. Dhanyawad. Arigato. You're the best, Sophia! We love you too!"

The coach smiled and waved them away. "Go on your break," she said.

Still processing her speech, Sam mused that Sophia was the Greek word for "wisdom." "How fitting for Coach Z," he thought. "She most certainly has lived up to her name. What a legacy!"

He glanced back at the screen, and noticed two quotes below the last question. He recognized the first, "Give me a lever long enough and a fulcrum on which to place it, and I shall move the world." as belonging to Greek mathematician, physicist, and inventor, Archimedes. The second quote made him laugh out loud. How typical for *un*-game players. It was a quote of *un*known authorship. "Anyone who thinks they're too small to make a difference has never been in bed with a mosquito!"

Sam was certain that he had a place to stand and a big enough lever to make a difference that would be a reflection of his personal keys to excellence—a difference he could and would be proud of. He left the room and joined a group in lively conversation.

After the break the *un*-team managers worked until they finally ended the session at 5:00PM. The future held great promise. A framework for achieving their new mandate had emerged. COSA-trained managers never lost sight of the 'A' – ACT in COSA. It's what gave them the reputation of having laser focus. No wonder. Laser focus derives from clarity.

What they proposed as a first pass was a development model that would enroll all L-4 employees in a four-day "Mastering the Four-Step COSA Process" training course followed by coaching support as appropriate. Managers would go to the next level. "Empowering the Four-Step COSA Process" would be another four-day event, which would train them to keep themselves and their reports on the COSA track to manage their work life.

> Anyone who thinks they're too small to make a difference has never been in bed with a mosquito.

"Advanced COSA Coach Training" would be for the talented managers who'd join a designated cadre of COSA process trainers. That cadre would help meet the requirement to "go far fast." There'd be a bi-annual learning event to refresh people's capacity to deal effectively with their tendency to slip into *un*consciousness, that is, business as usual. The event would be a useful reminder of the fact that to be human—age and wisdom notwithstanding—means to be alternately awake and asleep.

Both Sams gave the meeting high marks as they walked back to their hotel holding hands. They felt connected to a community they loved and whose opportunities they would embrace. L-4 played for high stakes. What could be better when you're young, full of concern, hope, and the desire to make a difference?

Inside their room Sam hugged and kissed his wife. "It doesn't get any better than this," Sam said. He was glad to be alive. Besides, he was pretty sure he would not be spending this night in bed with a mosquito.

The next day they'd fly back to Germany together, but this evening they were meeting Maria for dinner at 7:30 and to discuss Sam's burning question: *"What's the conventional wisdom regarding change that stunts companies' capacity to reach their highest potential?"*

✝✝✝✝

The handsome couple walked into Giovanni's, the little Italian restaurant where they'd had their first meeting. They were ushered into a small side room where a chorus yelling "Surprise!" greeted them. Assembled were none other than Sophia Zabar, Maria Nordstern, Peter Black, Marguerite Chan, and Tom Pierot. Now there were seven people who at this moment in time wanted to be nowhere else in the world other than at Giovanni's.

"This is to celebrate your first Global L-4 *Un*-Team Convention," announced Sophia.

"Besides, we like you guys," said Marguerite with a wink.

"We wanted to be sure we got to spend a little time with you before you headed back to Germany," added Tom.

"Plus we like to celebrate," said Peter. "It's required after the good work we've done together."

Maria just smiled.

Everyone engaged in good-natured teasing, had a few chuckles, agreed on several good wines, and studied the menu. With good wine, good food, good friends, and good conversation, the group settled into an evening they'd always remember. Sam's burning question was forgotten by all but Sam himself, who tried discreetly to steer the conversation to his question, but to no avail. People paid no attention to his cues. Finally Maria said, "Sam, you seem to want to say something, but you're going 'round and round.' Why don't you land that plane?!"

Everybody burst into laughter. Sam could be rather indirect at times. Mostly he didn't mind being called on it.

"OK you guys. Help me out here," he retorted. "You've been dangling this question in front of me for four years. How about *you* guys landing the plane?"

"So what's the question?" Sophia looked genuinely curious.

"What's the conventional wisdom regarding change that stunts companies' capacity to reach their highest potential?" answered Maria.

"Oh, *that* one. And you've never arrived at an answer that satisfies you?" she inquired of Sam.

"No," responded Sam simply.

"Who here has worked in companies other than L-4?" Sophia asked.

All hands went up.

"Can you characterize the differences between those companies and L-4?"

An animated discussion ensued. His burning question would finally have an answer—but suddenly the answer to the riddle dawned on him. The music of *Chariots of Fire* once more in his ears, Sam blurted out, "It's one of those invisible, *un*examined assumptions that only the great and *un*common companies, leaders and managers do *not* subscribe to," he said, squaring his shoulders in that subtle way that announced, "I know."

The group turned to Sam, giving him their *un*divided attention.

"Conventional wisdom regarding change, articulated or not, maintains that people don't change much—implying they can't change." Fueled by his passion and the courage of his conviction, Sam fleshed out what he was seeing.

"Even though companies spend a lot of money on non-technical training, their expectation for change in the emotional and social intelligence skills of their employees is low. But they just don't know what to do other than conventional training to try and get the desired changes. They seek no better alternatives. They're gathering evidence for their conclusion 'People don't change much.'"

Sam looked around for affirmation and found only attentive listening.

"Of course, that conclusion holds companies, their leaders, and their managers back from reaching their highest potential. Belief, after all, creates the fact," he concluded.

"I see you're still talented in connecting the dots," smiled Sophia.

"But what if the conventional wisdom is even more damaging to reaching our highest potential than that conclusion?" she asked.

"That would interest me," said Sam.

"Me too. Tell us, Sophia," said some of the others.

"This is invisible for the most part," began Sophia, "which as you know makes it so damaging. The conventional *un*examined assumption is in fact three assumptions: 'People don't change much.' 'They must change.' 'And we don't know how to make it happen.' So we try this and that in the *un*likely event that something will be the magic bullet that hits the mark.

"You can see why *un*bridled, passionate enthusiasm for change initiatives and training, other than technical training, is in short supply. Resignation and resistance would only be natural when we consciously or *un*consciously empower that three-pronged conclusion."

All seven people at the table were silent. Sam broke the silence first. He hadn't seen the impossible bind, "People don't change." "They have to." "We don't know how." It was a bind a rapidly changing world would have to *un*tie. "*Un*chain the brain," he thought. To Sophia he said, "Well, this is just like old times, Coach. That three-pronged sucker puts us in quite a bind. What's the way out?"

"Well, let's look, everybody. "Do people *really* have to change?"

"No," said Sam Osler. "They have to learn something, the learning of which changes what they see as possible options for action." Sam Osler knew, not only from having been coached in COSA, but also because she put what she'd learned into action in the training programs she now designed and executed all over the L-4 world.

"Yes," Tom Pierot chimed in. "Actions that they can then try out, keep, or modify as they learn from them."

"This conversation around people-changing has always been murky, Sophia. The three-pronged conclusion you brought to light makes the reasons for the murkiness apparent," said Maria. "Companies and their leaders are *un*aware of it and the proverbial strait-jacket it puts them in. They'd do well to recognize it and shift away from engineering scattershot change initiatives they don't really believe in, to creating a learning environment in which employees have the freedom to try and the courage to fail."

It seemed as if everyone at the table breathed a sigh of relief.

> Company managers would do well to shift away from engineering change they don't really believe in, to creating a learning environment in which employees have the freedom to try and the courage to fail.

"Kind of what happens as a result of COSA and the *un*-game, huh?" Sophia asked rhetorically before adding, "People courageous enough to play the *un*-game can experiment with small, safe steps, testing out whether the assumptions that hold them back from changing their status quo really have the benefits their monkey mind is advertising."

"So let me see if I get what you're saying, Sophia," said Marguerite. "Our company leaders' lament that people don't or can't change is an entirely *un*conscious use of the precious equipment we have on the playing field. We're using money, time, creativity, enjoyment, physical vitality, and relationship *un*consciously—chasing evidence for a conclusion that doesn't serve us at all."

"That's a unique, creative, and accurate description, Marguerite.

No cheese at the end of *that* tunnel. Thank you, Marguerite."

"Yeah. Thanks, Marguerite," shouted several delighted *un*-team managers.

Peter said, "So in a real sense, once people see the restrictive conclusions they're empowering, they can create the learning environment in which our immunity to change can safely be examined and utilized to allow, not force—some change of mind that would result in probable, organic, and sustainable change in the outer world."

"Which says to me," said Sam, "that the elusive prize— sustainable change—is a natural outcome of learning to play the *un*-game well."

"Right on," nodded Tom.

"So, from my perspective," offered Sam Osler, "in non-technical training, we would design programs that redirect the focus of change from the perceived impediments to goals, to illuminating the thinking that created those so-called impediments in the first place. As we know, what we make the impediments in our adaptive challenges mean only exists in language."

> It could be said that the elusive prize— sustainable change— is a natural outcome of learning to play the *un*-game well.

"My wife is brilliant," Sam thought before recalling the hardest adaptive challenge he'd faced in his COSA training: his struggle to understand that "difficult" people per se didn't exist. They only exist in the internal conversation of the person making that assessment. Both Bob Harley and he had been the beneficiaries of the good work he and Peter had done on that immense challenge.

"And we know that redirecting the focus will ultimately change how we perceive the impediments to our goals and will produce sustainable rather than short-term results," said Sam O. " We've all experienced it and are now supporting our other managers to do the same thing."

There were nods and "uh-huhs" around the table. Sam Adler wore a proud smile. His wife was not only gorgeous; she was fabulously perceptive and great with relationships. He knew that first hand. So what if he was over-the-top enthusiastic!

"You're right, Samantha," said Maria. "It will be high quality change because it will emerge naturally out of what participants become aware of in real time. It won't be forced change. Forced change is simply not sustainable.

"It's like erroneously assuming a challenge is technical—for example, losing weight or being organized—for which there's a technical solution. No! Challenges that require behavioral changes are adaptive challenges and need adaptive solutions to be sustainable. We in business will make a quantum leap in effectiveness when that distinction becomes clear to us."

> Challenges that require behavioral changes are adaptive challenges and need adaptive solutions to be sustainable. Business will make a quantum leap in effectiveness when that distinction becomes clear.

"Thanks for that clarity," Sam A said. "Right now, what company leaders don't know they don't know is hurting them. In all areas they care about no less. Innovation, profits, productivity, customer satisfaction, turnover. Everything! That kind of training would make the tired old assertion 'People are our greatest asset' a grounded assessment rather than an *un*fulfilled wish."

"Yeah," said Peter. "Mark the day when people know how to defeat their immunity to change as the day sustainable change triumphs. We will give people not a fish, but the capacity to fish for the rest of their lives."

"Great. But for now let's eat," suggested Tom, as the entree was arriving. "I think all of us at this bounteous table are doing a great job of gathering evidence for the conclusion 'We're able to *un*leash our power to produce extraordinary results in the goals we're playing for.'"

"Well said, Tom," proclaimed Sophia. "Let's hear it, everybody." Sophia raised her glass and proposed, "Let's drink to COSA and the *un*-game, in whatever form and with whatever tools the *un*-game will be played. And to all the great managers and coaches who are making this exercise in applied hope for a yet *un*imagined, bright future possible. Let's drink to business as *un*usual in all our affairs."

As one, the small group of great heroes, affectionately self-described as the *un*-team, smiled at one another and clinked their wine glasses with that of their beloved coach. "To business as *un*usual."

And Sam, who had assumed earlier that "it couldn't get any better than this," was certain, at least at this very moment, that he really didn't know just how good it could get.

Dear Reader

Congratulations. If you're reading this you've taken a courageous inner journey. How? Well, look at it this way. Things are not always as they appear. The characters of "The *Un*-Game"—Sam Adler, the coach, the great managers, and Sam Osler—are more than casual characters in a story. They are you and I on our hero's journey, willing and increasingly able to meet the seemingly frightful challenges our irrational mind hands us. They are, I suspect, where we've been and where we might be if the *un*-game interests us more than our illusion "I already know." As you've read, "I already know" may well be the three most dangerous words in the English language.

1. The *un*-team often makes the *un*conventional normal. For example, they want to establish a norm where managers no longer see mistakes as punishable offenses but as genuine learning opportunities. How satisfied are you that you're creating a work environment where employees experience the freedom to try and the courage to fail? How, if at all, do you see this applying in your personal life?

2. Sophia Zabar says "The *un*-game is a game people are able to play once they see their opponent—namely their commonly-shared immunity to change—learn the process for confronting it, and then develop the practices that support them in winning the match." You may already have some practices to go beyond your very own immunity to change. How well are they working for you? What would have to happen for you to seek additional practices or start some if you don't have any?

3. The purpose of the *un*-game is nothing less than to change our immunity to change such that the mental gridlock locking us into paradigms that no longer work can give way to paradigms that allow us to grow a resilient and creative workforce. What mental gridlock, if any, would you change at work? What's the

change you would see? How would your workplace be more resilient with the change you propose? What will your part in the change be, if you decide to take your vision to action in the outer world of your "playing field"?

4. Coach Zabar and the *un*-team have essentially created an environment in which deep, authentic learning that makes sustainable change possible can take place. If resources to create such an environment interest you, contact the author at www.theungamebook.com

Afterword

Included here are the results of a large, twenty year long, world-wide research project designed and implemented by the well-respected Gallup Organization. What the Gallup Organization decided to identify are the core characteristics of great managers and great workplaces. They interviewed more than a million employees and eighty thousand managers from numerous countries across many industries, from companies large and small. They asked them hundreds of questions about every imaginable aspect of the workplace.

Gallup came up with just twelve questions employees must be able to answer with an enthusiastic "yes" to have a great company. They caution CEOs and managers *not* to answer the questions. Only their employees are to answer them.

You'll see some information that probably won't surprise you. What *may* surprise you is that despite the fact that most agree that it makes sense, most workplaces aren't like this. And this is so even after having this knowledge for over thirty years! Having read this book, you are now clear why despite the fact that intelligence and the resources to create such workplaces exist, we are creating them only sporadically.

Anyone can learn the four-step COSA process that enables you to *un*leash your power to produce *un*common results with your employees—and by extension, your business. "The *Un*-Game" asserts you can close the gap between what you want very much—a company that can answer those twelve questions with a resounding "yes"—and your ability to bring such a company into physical reality.

I hope you find the twelve questions useful in designing a vibrant high-performance workplace. Remember, however, that this is an adaptive, not a technical challenge.

Ingrid Martine

The Gallup Organization Measuring Stick for Comparing the Strength of One Workplace to Another

Below are the twelve questions which employees must answer with a high degree of satisfaction (use a scale of 1-5, 5 being extremely satisfied) in order to consistently produce quality work and designate you a quality employer. Please note if the first six aren't answered affirmatively, seven through twelve become irrelevant. In other words, the concerns these questions reflect must be addressed in sequence. Contrary to some opinions, it's abundantly clear from the data that the managers of our companies are our leading edge, and that we'd do well to develop their capacity in order to help us create organizations that can meet the unprecedented challenges that face us in the dawn of the 21st century.

A great manager's reach is limited without his or her company's genuine support. The great manager is someone who challenges conventional wisdom, and he or she needs a company who will challenge it too, in its policies, practices, and in its language. Company leaders and managers must be willing to challenge their conventions around all their sacrosanct systems, including selection, training, performance management, and compensation systems. It's a courageous act, and it's important and urgent for us to be willing to be courageous, even when we are reluctant.

The Twelve Questions Employees Need to Answer with "YES!"*

1. Do I know what's expected of me at work?

2. Do I have the materials and equipment I need to do my work right?

3. At work, do I have the opportunity to do what I do best every day?

4. In the last seven days, have I received recognition or praise for doing good work?

5. Does my supervisor, or someone at work, seem to care about me as a person?

6. Is there someone at work who encourages my development?

Stop here if you get any "nos" for questions 1 through 6. Questions 7 through 12 would then be irrelevant.

7. At work, do my opinions count?

8. Does the mission/purpose of my company make me feel my job is important?

9. Are my co-workers committed to doing quality work?

10. Do I have a best friend at work?

11. During the last six months, has someone at work talked to me about my progress?

12. This last year, have I had opportunities at work to learn and grow?

*Buckingham, Marcus, and Curt Coffman. *First, Break All the Rules.* New York: Simon and Schuster, 1999. Print.

Glossary

Adaptive challenge – a challenge which requires a change in behavior from the person experiencing it. The mistake that's often made is to treat the challenge as a technical problem to which there's a technical solution. For example, for most people being organized is an adaptive challenge, not a technical one. The author asserts that business will take a quantum leap in effectiveness when the distinction between an adaptive and a technical challenge becomes clear to us at more than the conceptual level.

Adaptive solution – a solution directed at an adaptive challenge. It's sustainable because it's a match for the challenge at which it is aimed.

Authentic action – an action that makes sense in relation to what one has just become aware of. For example, if you've just become aware of a persistent toothache, an authentic action is to call the dentist to make an appointment.

Being willing – a quality of being which we locate (not physically, but in language) in the ontological domain, the domain of "being." It's distinguished from "wanting." One can be willing even though one may not want to do something. In "The *Un*-Game," the protagonist learns that distinction. It allows him to push past doubts, worries, and fears. To express being willing in action is a powerful and courageous act. It comes straight from the hero's heart.

Blueprint of one's personal power – also referred to as personal keys to excellence. A list of generally admirable qualities whose expression in action is natural for the person. They are his or her standards of integrity. When one aligns one's actions with those qualities, one experiences a sense of well-being. When one acts contrary to those qualities, one experiences a sense of dissonance. For example, a person who has the quality "persevering" on his or her blueprint experiences discomfort when not persevering.

Chaos Theory – various branches of thought developing from the mathematical study of the behavior of physical systems which are governed by deterministic laws—but which contain behavior perceived by the human mind as random and unpredictable because of the system's extreme sensitivity to initial conditions and variables. For example, the study of the behavior of the flow of water. In the context of "The *Un*-Game" it's understood that physical reality is unpredictable—although if its mysteries were understood, we might not say that. The reference to both complexity and chaos theory in the book is simply an invitation to the reader to adopt the very useful mindset "I don't already know" so that we can choose to counteract our tendency to assume that "how we think things are" is immutable fact, rather than an assessment based on incomplete data.

Coachable – People are considered coachable when they're willing to dismantle their mental paradigms, that is, to shine a conscious light on their thinking—and are willing to regain the quality of "being willing" when they momentarily lose it. They're coachable when the desire to be conscious and awake surpasses their desire for the comfort of that which is known but which may inhibit progress toward a goal.

Collective immune system – In the context of "The *Un*-Game" it is the polar opposite of the immunity to change (the immunity to change being that which alerts us to the dangers of straying from the status quo even when the status quo is dangerous and *un*sustainable). The positive trends that Coach Zabar highlights in her speech to the global *un*-team are expressions of our collective immune system defending us against some of the trends that are said to be negative and the cause of global woes. When the two are experienced in tandem—"immunity to change" and "collective immune system"—it is as if we, the global community, are conducting our affairs with one foot on the accelerator and one on the brake. The collective immune system is considered the accelerator, the immunity to change the brake.

Complexity Theory – various branches of thought developing from the scientific study of large scale real world systems which contain behavior perceived by the human mind as random and *un*predictable because of the multiplicity of elements contained in and/or influencing the system. For example, the study of the behavior of the stock market. In the context of "The *Un*-Game" it's understood that complex systems are *un*predictable and that just because our capacity for comprehending all the elements influencing a system is limited, it doesn't mean we should accept as immutable fact our usual and customary assessments about "how things are." The reference to both complexity and chaos theory is an invitation to the reader to adopt the very useful mindset "I *don't* already know."

Conclusion – a mental paradigm we consciously or *un*consciously hold to be true. We think that we always arrive at conclusions based on evidence. In "The *Un*-Game" the author asserts that this isn't accurate.

Conscious – as opposed to *un*conscious. Conscious use of what's available to move one's agenda forward means the person is awake and aware of using the "equipment" on life's playing field to make a play on goal. For example, a conscious use of "relationship" is to have a direct, non-manipulative conversation.

COSA – the four-step process that gives people the skill-set to become effective *un*-game players. The 'C' stands for CHOOSE; the 'O' for OBSERVE; the 'S' for SAY YES; and the 'A' for ACT. The steps must be taken in sequence in order to produce *un*common results. No short cut exists. The COSA steps are taken by the best and highest part of the person, the "hero" within each human being. "Hero" is used without the feminine version "heroine" because the hero archetype encompasses both the masculine and the feminine.

To CHOOSE is to choose who you're willing to be, moment by moment by moment as you move through life. Like now. And now. And this evening at home when it becomes the now. This has everything to do with the distinction of "wanting" versus "being willing." In "The *Un*-Game" the protagonist learns how to choose consciously rather than *un*consciously. It's Step One of COSA.

To OBSERVE is to self-observe—usually with the help of a coach—something that you've said you're willing to look at, something that interests you about your thinking, your emotions, and/or physical sensations. This type of rigorous and systematic observation challenges your world view. As with the other COSA steps, this step can only be taken by the hero. For example, conventional wisdom may advise "Don't just sit there. Do something." A coach might tell you: "Don't just do something. Sit there." What would be useful to observe are your thoughts, beliefs, opinions, conclusions, and physical reactions to that statement. Observation would reveal your thinking which is a valuable clue to your actions. In "The *Un*-Game" it leads the young manager to become a much better manager. It's Step Two of COSA.

To SAY YES is to surrender to your lessons, whatever they may be. It doesn't mean to give up or to capitulate. It's to be willing to embrace the lesson that you've learned through the rigorous, systematic observation that you and a coach have done together. Saying "yes" to your lessons is the ultimate challenge. There's nothing more powerful than taking a stand for saying "yes" to the lessons that are yours to learn as you travel on your hero's journey. It's a most courageous act. Saying "yes" in this step of COSA determines the quality of the actions you eventually take. Actions taken as a result of this step are high quality actions. It's Step Three of COSA.

To ACT is to perform the action that is the natural outcome of what you've just become aware of in the observation step of COSA. It's authentic action. The lesson learned is articulated in the "say yes" step of COSA. Now it makes sense to act. When you've gone through the first three steps of the process, you can produce high quality decisions and actions. For example, if you learn that it's actually impossible to achieve excellence while subscribing to the conclusion "Excellence is zero defects," then that awareness would produce a completely different set of actions than if you set your strategy based on the original conclusion. Ninety percent of the real work precedes the action. It's like planting a garden. It's all underground. It looks like nothing is happening, when in fact there is much purposeful activity going on. Without the three preceding steps of the COSA process, the power of the action is severely compromised. COSA-trained managers never lose sight of the 'A' – ACT. In "The *Un*-Game" it's what gives them the reputation of having laser focus. Laser focus derives from clarity gained through steps one through three. ACT is Step Four of COSA.

Day Language – as opposed to night language. It's the conscious thinking the protagonist refers to that makes rational sense to the thinker—the rational thinking one would express to others without reservation or self-censoring.

Equipment on the playing field – a metaphor for what we perceive is available to us for accomplishing our conscious and *un*conscious goals. It refers to money, time, relationships, creativity, physical vitality, and enjoyment. We can either use that equipment deliberately or *un*consciously. The former allows us to play the game of life well.

Evidence – what we traditionally think leads us to formulate a conclusion. In the context of "The *Un*-Game" this is inaccurate.

Goal – an object or an area toward which *play* is directed. In "The *Un*-Game" the author suggests that a goal is the demonstration or expression of some important value or intention. "Goal" is distinguished from "task" in that its achievement provides the experience of joy and celebration as opposed to only relief (which is the experience one has upon task completion).

Hero archetype – In mythology a hero is one who ventures forth from everyday reality into a region of supernatural wonder to meet challenges. Power which is used to make the world better is bestowed upon him or her. The archetype represents both males and females. In "The *Un*-Game," the protagonist leaves his world of conventional management and enters a coaching adventure with a master coach and four great managers. He brings back the *un*conventional wisdom he gains to improve his department and the larger world.

Hero's journey – Joseph Campbell, renowned expert in world mythologies, has found that all cultures have a version of the hero archetype. The hero's journey begins with the hero's response to a call to adventure. The hero is guaranteed to face tasks and trials on a path unique to him or her, which the hero may survive alone or with help. If the hero survives, it results in the discovery of important self-knowledge which the hero uses to improve the world. In "The *Un*-Game," the hero, Sam Adler, accepts the call to become a great manager. He faces challenges to his established world view. The four-step COSA process, as facilitated by his master coach and four great managers, supports him on his hero's journey.

Immunity to Change – a dynamic which actively prevents us from making changes (often despite wishing to do so) because of its devotion to our existing way of making meaning. In "The *Un*-Game" the author uses it to be synonymous with the metaphor monkey mind although it can be otherwise described as a complete system which is not the focus of this book. Refer to *The Immunity to Change* (Kegan and Lahey), for insights into the immunity to change as a complete system. Another fine resource is *Beyond the Walls of Resistance* (Maurer).

Inner world – as opposed to outer world, inner world is the reference to metaphysical reality—the reality of our thoughts and emotions through which we create our vision for the future.

In "The *Un*-Game," the hero's journey of the protagonist, Sam Adler, consists of moving something challenging from vision in his inner world to action in his outer world.

Language in the psychological versus the ontological domain – has different meaning in each of the two domains. For example, "surrender" for monkey mind (in the psychological domain) is inspired by fear. "Surrender" for the hero (in the ontological domain) is inspired by courage. This is true for the word "vulnerable." "Vulnerable" is the experience of feeling weak or fragile in the psychological domain. But "vulnerable" for the hero just means one is willing to "take life as it is." One is willing to be open, receptive, *un*defended. This is important because language is extremely powerful. It dictates the belief, then the feeling, then the experience.

Learning environment – a safe but challenging environment in which people have the freedom to try and the courage to fail. It's an environment which engages the brain, mind, and heart in order to produce meaningful change. It's an environment in which people recognize that cognition isn't enough to produce a meaningful behavioral change. People have to learn more deeply than at the conceptual level in order to give up even one of their established ways of organizing their world.

In such an environment you, who are courageous enough to play the *un*-game, can experiment with small, safe steps, testing out whether the assumptions that hold you back from changing your status quo really have the benefits your "monkey mind" is advertising. Once you see the restrictive conclusions you're empowering, you can safely examine your immunity to change and utilize what you learn to allow, not force—some change of mind that would result in probable, organic, and sustainable change in the outer world. Forced change is simply not sustainable and is not part of a learning environment.

In short, a learning environment is the fertile ground in which "the thinking" that created the problems which "the thinking" is trying to solve can transform itself into the new thinking that actually *does* solve the problem. In "The *Un*-Game" it's the environment in which the master coach and the four great managers help the protagonist learn and master the four-step COSA process.

Monkey Mind – the Buddhist metaphor for the self-limiting chatter that everyone experiences. Monkey mind is there to remind us that we're considering some change. Its job is to keep us in the familiar rut of the status quo, because to change something means danger to monkey mind. Monkey mind doesn't want us to learn anything new, because it doesn't want us to change or even contemplate change. It hates change, and that might look to the outside world as if we're getting defensive. The conversation gets too hot. It's as if our brain is overloaded and trips a circuit breaker. It could be said we're literally out of your mind—our cool, rational mind, that is.

Everyone has monkey mind, even those who are cool, calm, collected and hide the effects of the chatter well. Keeping us out of trouble is another job monkey mind has. Never expect monkey mind to be reasonable. That's not its job. Its job is to test itself against the hero's heart, ours, and hopefully get its way!

To recognize a monkey mind fit coming on, look for heightened emotions generally labeled negative: anger, frustration, fear, resignation. Add feeling victimized and impulsive. There are other symptoms like rationalizing and justifying. And we're not finished yet!

Monkey mind gets a bad rep, and people want to get rid of it. Trying that is a huge opportunity lost. Skillful monkey mind identification is useful for surfacing hidden commitments all of us have—for example "insisting on playing it safe" or "looking good" or "being right." To be all we can be, it's important that we become aware of our hidden commitments and learn from them. The four-step COSA process is one simple, elegant (although not easy) way to do that.

Since everyone has monkey mind, everyone also has a "monkey mind show-stopper"—that is, a particular, unique-to-us, self-limiting internal conversation that takes us "out of our game." As stated, it's different for everyone but its effect is the same—chaos. It makes us dysfunctional until we see it. Monkey mind takes itself extremely seriously. It loves to be right and in control. Monkey mind is known by many names: self-limiting talk, trickster, the immunity to change, and more. Humor and laughter may be great monkey mind tamers. It's possible to identify one's unique personal show-stopper monkey mind conversation.

Night language – The protagonist of "The *Un*-Game" refers to the thoughts he thinks but which he wouldn't say out loud as "night language." He also identifies the self-limiting chatter that's called monkey mind in the book as making as much sense as "night language." In other words, we shouldn't believe our self-limiting chatter. The challenge we experience, however, is that "night language" can be tricky. It can easily deceive us into accepting that what it's proclaiming is the truth rather than cleverly disguised monkey mind.

Observe – Sometimes when a coach asks a person to observe, he or she doesn't. Rather, people analyze—that is—they make assessments. Observing is simply seeing, not making interpretations about what you see. Interpretations are often *un*helpful because monkey mind is directing the interpretations to preserve the status quo. It's important to practice the distinction between observing and analyzing in action. As a concept people understand it. Understanding, in this instance, however, is the booby prize! It does little good in translating itself into effective action.

Ontological self – who you really are in your hero's heart. In this domain you, the hero, *are* (not *make*) a contribution. The ontological self is the you who is able to choose who you're willing to be. Who you really are is *un*affected by circumstances.

It's forever. It's *un*changing and *un*changeable. Nothing and nobody can take "who we really are" away from us. All of us have that core even if for some of us it seems inaccessible. Nevertheless, at our *un*assailable core we are as solid and deep as Earth itself.

The ontological self is in the domain of being. It's you/me at choice. You/me, the dispassionate, wise observer. Our ontological self is separate from our psychological self which can be mired in our emotions, body sensations, thoughts, beliefs, opinions, and conclusions. We need both our ontological and our psychological self. It's extremely powerful to be able to make and live the distinction between the two.

Ontology – the study of being. It has much to teach us. It's separate from our psychology.

Opponent on the playing field of life – a metaphor for the greatest opponent the modern hero meets on his or her hero's journey— the self-limiting chatter which is called monkey mind in "The *Un*-Game."

Outer world – as opposed to inner world. It's the physical reality in which action occurs. Intentions, goals and dreams we have in our inner world must be brought forth in the outer world. In "The *Un*-Game," taking a challenge from vision to action is our hero's journey. The trial we experience occurs on the border between our inner and outer world. This is where we meet our self-limiting chatter, also known as monkey mind, which advises us to turn back. "The *Un*-Game" uses the acronym SAP (Stop Advancing, Pal) to indicate the challenge our doubts and worries cast upon us heroes trying to do something new and "dangerous" (as perceived by our monkey mind).

Personal keys to excellence – also referred to as our blueprint of personal power. See definition of blueprint of our personal power.

Playing field – a metaphor, as in "the playing field of life."

Psychological self – We have a psychology. No matter how convinced we are to the contrary, we *aren't* our psychology. That is, we aren't our thoughts, beliefs, opinions, conclusions, and physical sensations that have such sway over our emotions. Monkey mind lives in our psychology. We need our psychology as well as our ontology. The important thing is to make the distinction between the two and be able to choose which one we put in charge at any given moment.

Purpose of the **un-*game*** – The purpose is to shift the immunity to change of the players such that mental gridlock in their organization can give way to mental paradigms or models which allow the organization to become nimble and grow a resilient and creative workforce. The *un*-game can be played on all playing fields of life, not just in organizations.

SAP – acronym for Stop Advancing, Pal. It stands for the caution we experience when we take a step toward moving something from vision to action. It occurs often. Successful people are aware of the caution put out by their monkey mind opponent. They outplay the opponent. They "thank it for sharing its words of caution" and move on anyway, because they keep their focus on the goal or the next play on goal.

Shadow side of innocence – The shadow side of innocence is when people have a vested interest in staying asleep—as in staying *un*conscious—because being awake or conscious would be too painful, too inconvenient, or too perturbing.

S.M.A.R.T. goals – an acronym for specific, measurable, achievable, relevant to one's value-generated intentions, and time-bound goals.

System thinking – the process of understanding how things influence one another within a whole. In organizations, systems consist of people, structures, and processes that work together to make an organization healthy or *un*healthy. System thinking is a set of habits and practices within a framework that's based

on the belief that the component parts of a system can best
be understood in the context of relationships with each other
and other systems. "The *Un*-Game" favors system thinking
and suggests that our capacity for system thinking needs to be
reawakened.

Talented managers – have skills and knowledge. Talent, however,
is an ability that can't be taught; one either has it, or one doesn't.
Talent respects rules but isn't afraid to challenge them. Talent
can take risks and see possibilities where others don't. Talented
managers facilitate the use of their people's talents and offer them
support for their shortcomings.

As a talented manager you may not even be aware of your
talent. But you think about people a lot, in the shower, for
example, and before you go to sleep. Or outside of work. You're
curious and always want to learn. Besides finding ways to talk
about what you've learned, you also look for how you can
productively apply it.

Tasks – as distinct from goals. In "The *Un*-Game" tasks
are distinguished from goals because in many a mind the
distinction is collapsed. This is to people's detriment because
the accomplishment of a task merely provides relief, whereas
the accomplishment of a goal generates joy and celebration.
The author suggests that this distinction can make a world of
difference in people's relationship to goals. A definition of "goal,"
as found in some dictionaries, is after all an object or an area
toward which play is directed!

Technical challenge – a challenge or problem that has a technical
solution. Do steps 1, 2, and 3. Voilà! A technical challenge, unlike
an adaptive challenge, does not require changes in behavior.
People generally find their technical challenges easier to deal with
than their adaptive ones.

Technical solution – a solution that's a match for a technical challenge or problem. A technical solution is never a match for an adaptive challenge.

Transformative conversations – are open, honest, non-manipulative, *un*guarded. Game playing is absent. They are confrontational in the sense that they confront one's world view. Transformative conversations interrogate our current reality. It could be said that they assault our world view. Yet they occur in an atmosphere of safety. In such an atmosphere it eventually sinks in that we didn't have a corner on the truth—despite the fact that we'd been absolutely certain. If we stay with it, then the new reality seems to become spacious and full of promise.

Transformative conversations could also be described as passionate, *un*bridled, authentic, and clear. They don't assume things are as they seem to be. Willing participants in transformative conversations check out assumptions and even assume that their assumptions, concealed or not, are indeed assumptions and not necessarily the truth, and that can be tough. We can't have transformative conversations without learning something we need to know. Monkey mind doesn't want us to learn anything new.

Transformative conversations tackle tough challenges. What's tough varies from individual to individual. However, each of us has challenges. Therefore transformative conversations must provoke learning, or they wouldn't be able to transform. They couldn't change the world.

Truth – In the *un*-game truth is defined as "facts." What we make the facts mean is interpretation, not truth/fact. So when someone says "to tell you the truth," it's likely not the truth but rather an opinion.

Unconscious – as opposed to conscious. In "The *Un*-Game" the author uses the term to indicate using the "equipment" on life's playing field—for example, "time"—without awareness (or even with manipulative intent). For example, a person uses "time" *un*consciously when she says, "I don't have time," but spends time on *un*related-to task/goal activities. Or "money" when he says, "We don't have the money," when tools purchased for the department remain *un*used. Conscious use of what's available to move our agenda forward means we're awake and aware of using the "equipment" to make a play on goal.

Uncover – as opposed to discover. In "The *Un*-Game" the word is used to alert the reader to the fact that people have answers already within them which they're often *un*aware of. Competent questioning by a trained coach can lead a person to find his or her own answers.

Unexamined assumptions – mental constructs or models which are so invisible to the construct-holder that it's impossible to bring them up for observation and examination without help of some kind. An *un*examined assumption is assumed to be truth/fact. Therefore one would not question it. Help for examining may be in the form of a coach but could also be in the situation. For example, the assumption "Bigger is better" in terms of making cars was assumed to be true in the United States in the 1950s through the 1970s. This assumption was challenged for the American traveler in Europe even then but certainly in the US when it became apparent that fossil fuels were not *un*limited.

Un-game – the process of *un*covering rules great managers ignore or break; challenging conventional wisdom.

Un-game – the process of identifying our most closely held thoughts, beliefs, opinions, and conclusions, and examining them to determine if they still serve us on our quest to produce *un*common results. Sometimes referred to as the *un*raveling of lies parading as truths. One doesn't have to be a manager to play. Anyone can play the *un*-game at any time anywhere.

Un-game – a systematic challenging of *un*examined assumptions that get in the way of reaching goals for producing change in a complex world. It promotes an organization-wide capacity for self-observation and reflection.

Un-game – is a game people are able to play once they understand their commonly-shared immunity to change at a deeper than conceptual level and the process for going beyond it. Organizations whose people can play the *un*-game well can devise strategies to shift their immunity to change such that the mental gridlock locking them into paradigms that no longer work can give way to paradigms and systems that allow them to develop resilient and creative people. The possibility of quantum mind-set shifts becomes available to practiced *un*-game players since awake *un*-game players would declare nothing off limits for exploration. The author of "The *Un*-Game" asserts that *un*learning is a large part of learning to play the *un*-game.

The elusive prize—sustainable change—is a natural outcome of learning to play the *un*-game well.

Un-game players – people who are at home with challenging existing rules and structures and creating better ones in the areas of their concern.

Un-team – the group of managers and coaches in "The *Un*-Game" who create the learning environment of the four-step COSA process for the development of the great-managers-in-training like Sam Adler and Sam Osler.

Acknowledgments

In reflecting on the actual creation of "The *Un*-Game," I could acknowledge the various life-changing events that made me who I am, among them my journey from Germany to the United States as an impressionable and opinionated almost-twelve year old. However, when all is said and done, it's our relationships that make the difference, and therefore I want to acknowledge them.

But for my adventurous parents, Paul and Waltraud Martin, who came to the United States to start over, this book would not have been written. Ditto for the pioneer spirit with which they gifted me. My son Jason taught me the importance of playing the *un*-game well; a parent raising an enigmatic child benefits from clarity.

There are too many great coaches to mention, but in hindsight, even those I once thought were bad, like my tenth grade French teacher and a Psychology professor in college, taught me valuable lessons I needed. But I delight in sharing the names of coaches who warm my heart and nourish my spirit beginning with Marguerite Chandler, former boss, long-time friend, colleague, and inspirer par excellence who many years ago saw the hero in me and never let me forget it. She brought me to most of the learning opportunities that have made a significant difference in my life, including the coach training program at the Academy for Coaching Excellence which inspired "The *Un*-Game." When she says, "Ingrid…" I just say, "OK, Marguerite. What? Where? and When?" And she hung with me by reading and critiquing the very first rough "The *Un*-Game" draft—and all subsequent drafts—bless her heart. I'm grateful to Richmond Shreve and Liza Ely for their partial review and all their editing suggestions. And to Beth Ann Suggs and Wayne Manning who coached me brilliantly through the coach training program that was so seminal for "The *Un*-Game." Susan Koenig, author, coach, and entrepreneur, has been my cheerleader for years. Fernando Flores and his work in ontological design influenced

me long ago. As did the controversial EST training with Werner
Ehrhard. Speaking of training, my work in the training programs
in applied behavioral science was fabulous. The programs gave my
love for empowerment of self and others the vehicle to express itself
in effective action. Robert Kegan's and Lisa Lahey's work, and their
Immunity to Change moved my understanding of mind-complexity
to a new level. Rick Maurer, old friend and colleague, resurfaced in
my life just in time for the writing of "The *Un*-Game." His shared
passion for understanding the immunity to change, his advice about
the publishing process, plus his generous feedback on the ideas
for the manuscript boosted my confidence and my energy for the
project. It doesn't only take a village to raise a child. It also takes a
village to create a book.

   I'd be remiss if I didn't acknowledge David Hutchens, author of
powerful learning stories and the questions which Bill Gordon gives
in his speech in the final chapter of "The *Un*-Game."

   If it weren't for my coaching clients and my coaching colleagues,
I'd have nothing to write about. They tested everything I ever
learned. And the organizations who asked me to do training or
consulting for them over the years gave me a training ground too.
I thank them whole-heartedly. Without my book coach, Jan King,
I wouldn't have had the courage of my convictions nor the great
people to whom she led me. Great people like Cathy and Jack Davis
of Davis Creative who are responsible for the original cover and
the ease of reading; Kim Pearson, my editor who pulled no punches
and made invaluable suggestions, most of which I eventually
implemented; and Janica Smith, who as my administrative assistant
held my hand when I wanted to insist "I can't." Rachel Crawford,
Baylor University instructor and editor extraordinaire always gently
held her ground until I fixed something that needed fixing. Her
*un*usual love for grammar, punctuation, and language in general
assured me in the final round that we would have fewer than
average errors in a book that's over fifty percent dialog. Rachel
was a surprise gift I intend to keep. It's no exaggeration to say that

through her editing skills, but even more through her *un*flagging commitment to keep her promises, she took "The *Un*-Game" to a level I never would have been able to. Thank you, Rachel.

Finally, if it hadn't been for my husband, Joe Ahlers, nobody would be reading these words. Joe, thank you for believing in me, for encouraging me when I wasn't sure I should pursue this, for doing without me when you really didn't want to, and for listening to me over morning coffee about what the writing of "The *Un*-Game" was teaching me. If loyalty and love had a name, it would be yours.

Ingrid Martine, M.A., PCC

Before immigrating to the United States at age eleven, Ingrid Martine lived in Germany. Her fascination with human behavior began as an eight year old who read—under bed covers by flashlight and against strict maternal instructions— mythological stories and Tolstoy's *Anna Karenina*. They fired her imagination and a hunger to understand people. Wanting to solve the puzzle of people losing their early enthusiasm for learning, she became an educator. Starting in academia—she has a Master's degree in French Literature and speaks three languages fluently—and then moving into the world of business—first as a consultant, then as an internationally certified executive and team coach with clients in North America, Europe, and Australia—she became interested in *un*conventional models of learning. While working as a teacher with inner-city at-risk youth who seemed to hate to learn, she began experimenting with and developing innovative educational models. Certain that a disdain for learning is *un*natural, Martine asserts that learning environments must help people—adults in corporate America included—get out of their own way. Her ability to create rich learning environments was facilitated not only by graduate work in psychology and experiential education design, but also by non-traditional learning experiences such as a waitressing and horse training, both of which required her to be "client-centered." "The *Un*-Game" is a novel whose characters work in such a rich learning environment. Martine's intention is to engage the reader in a learning process that supports exceptional effectiveness at work and transfers to life beyond work. Ingrid Martine lives with her husband, three horses, and two dogs near Austin, Texas.

You can contact the author at **www.theungamebook.com**

Would It Benefit You to Have an
Un-Game Speaker at Your Next Event?

The assertion of "The *Un*-Game" is that we need a higher complexity of mind to meet the challenges of the 21st century workplace. Technology, fast pace, global inter-connectedness require it of all of us at all levels in the workplace. The old is simply not good enough anymore.

Contact us at **www.theungamebook.com** to request a speaker, the FREE six dimensions that can make the *un*-game flourish in *your* organization, and to inquire about these and other topics:

"The *Un*-Game" for Leaders and Managers
"The *Un*-Game" for Teachers and Principals
"The *Un*-Game" for Parents and Kids
Mind-Zengineering Meets Mind-Complexity
Mind-Zengineering: Upping Our Game

Resources:

www.academyforcoachingexcellence.com and the various training programs, especially the Mastering Life's Energies course

www.mindsatwork.com and the books of Robert Kegan and Lisa Lahey, especially *"The Immunity to Change"*

www.rickmaurer.com and the work of Rick Maurer, especially *"Beyond the Wall of Resistance"*

www.davidhutchens.com and *www.pegasuscommunications.com* and the learning fables of organizational storyteller, David Hutchens

CPSIA information can be obtained at www.ICGtesting.com
Printed in the USA
LVOW031232291211

261536LV00001B/4/P